The late Tony Tanner was one of the most distinctive and distinguished critical voices on American literature. His work is familiar to generations of students and scholars, and has helped shape our understanding of the major nineteenth- and twentieth-century American writers. This book, which brings together his essays on a wide range of American authors, is written with Tanner's characteristic style and verve. Exploring writers as diverse as Melville, Emerson, Henry James, DeLillo and Pynchon, it offers an introduction to the major figures and themes in nineteenth- and twentieth-century American literature.

This volume of essays was planned by Tony Tanner before his death. An introduction by Ian Bell assesses his contribution to the development of American literary criticism, and places his work in the larger context of critical approaches to American literature and culture in recent years. This book should interest all students and scholars of American literature and culture of the period.

Tony Tanner was Professor of American Literature at King's College Cambridge until his death in 1998. His books include *Conrad: 'Lord Jim'* (1963), *The Reign of Wonder: Naivety and Reality in American Literature and Culture* (1965), *City of Words: American Fiction 1950–1970* (1970), *Adultery in the Novel: Contract and Transgression* (1979), *Henry James: The Writer and his Work* (1985), *Scenes of Nature, Signs of Men: Essays on Nineteenth and Twentieth Century American Literature* (1987), *Henry James and the Art of Nonfiction* (1995).

This book has been prepared for publication with the assistance of Dr Andrew Taylor, Research Fellow in American Studies, Selwyn College, Cambridge.

THE AMERICAN MYSTERY

American Literature from Emerson to DeLillo

TONY TANNER

Foreword by Edward Said

Introduction by Ian F. A. Bell

CAMBRIDGE
UNIVERSITY PRESS

PUBLISHED BY THE PRESS SYNDICATE OF THE UNIVERSITY OF CAMBRIDGE
The Pitt Building, Trumpington Street, Cambridge, United Kingdom

CAMBRIDGE UNIVERSITY PRESS
The Edinburgh Building, Cambridge CB2 2RU, UK   http://www.cup.cam.ac.uk
40 West 20th Street, New York, NY 10011–4211, USA   http://www.cup.org
10 Stamford Road, Oakleigh, Melbourne 3166, Australia
Ruiz de Alarcón 13, 28014 Madrid, Spain

First published 2000

Printed in the United Kingdom at the University Press, Cambridge

Typeset in 11/12$\frac{1}{2}$pt Baskerville No. 2 [GT]

A catalogue record for this book is available from the British Library

Library of Congress Cataloguing in Publication data
Tanner, Tony.
The American mystery: American literature from Emerson to DeLillo/
Tony Tanner; foreword by Edward Said; introduction by Ian F. A. Bell.
p.   cm.
ISBN 0 521 78003 9 – ISBN 0 521 78374 7 (pbk.)
1. American literature–History and criticism.   I. Title.
PS121.T36   2000
8 2110.9–dc9   99-043661

ISBN 0 521 78003 9 hardback
ISBN 0 521 78374 7 paperback

For Jean and Richard Gooder

Contents

Foreword

Edward W. Said

I first encountered Tony Tanner more than thirty years ago because
of and through Joseph Conrad. Tony had very generously reviewed
my first book which was on the autobiographical element in Conrad's
fiction and I of course had read his little study of *Lord Jim* with
admiration and profit. I can't recall our actual first meeting but I do
recall our first extended period together – it was at the University of
Zurich in January 1968 where we had been invited as certainly the
youngest and most obscure of the renowned participants to a four-day
seminar convened by Paul de Man. Emil Staiger, Hans-Georg
Gadamer, Jean-Pierre Vernant, Jean Starobinski, Jacques Derrida, Jean-
Pierre Richard, Georges Poulet were the main features: Tony and I sat
there as decidedly second-rank soldiers, and were unclear as to why we
had been invited, but we were both dazzled and repelled by the overwhelming displays of learning, profundity, and polyglot disputatiousness
of these redoubtable figures in European thought and interpretation.
It was then that I experienced Tony's amazing gift for genuinely intellectual catholicity and curiosity on the one hand combined with a
bottomless capacity for irreverence and wit on the other. We became
fast friends during those several snowy, serious days, and remained
continuously in touch ever since.

He was always the kindest and most generous of companions. I
think I saw him during all the main periods of his professional life,
starting and ending of course at King's College particularly when, in
the spring of 1997, he was my unfailingly attentive and caring host for
three weeks, but also in California, Baltimore, and then when he and
Nadia occupied the Alpha Road house in Cambridge during the late
1970s. I recall in particular that during the summer of 1978 my wife,

two small children and I stayed with Nadia and Tony while we were marooned and unable to leave Europe at a particularly bad moment in the Lebanese Civil War, and how happy and surprised I was at his hospitable patience with us all, children especially.

Being myself of a rather itinerant and unsettled colonial character I used to kid Tony about his Englishness and his steadily routine habits, his well-known chair in the combination room, his regular appearances at the various meals, his long residence as a student, fellow, and professor at King's College, his years and years of devotion to reading, writing about, and teaching literature. But he was also a Conradian character who had somehow jumped and who had a keen sense of having betrayed something of himself in so doing. I always felt that about him, a darker side to his genial, extraordinarily reliable and dependable aspects, and to which he intermittently referred. That made him more attractive to me and I think made our relationship stronger. His death left me with a terrible sense of loss and disorientation, a dear friend exactly my age, stolen away in all his great powers, his superb work still pouring forth, his intellectual energies and unrelenting wit at their highest.

Tony's achievements as a great critic and teacher strike me as altogether unique in many different ways that deserve specific enumeration here. First of course was his exceptional grounding in all periods of English literature, from as early as Chaucer and Shakespeare, until the present. This may now seem like a conservative or curatorial achievement, but in fact it was extraordinarily lived, dwelt upon, returned to, and enriched by his own conversation, teaching, writing, and everyday activity. Second was his pioneering work as *the* British scholar of American literature: more than anyone else he made it part of the literary agenda in England. Third was his unerring sense of judgement and discrimination in dealing with fastidiously precise writers like Jane Austen and Henry James. Fourth, and to me most impressive, was his capacity to make intellectual and moral sense of the most disturbing, intimate, and unsettling of human experiences. Obviously his understanding of Conrad speaks to that capacity, but so in particular does his monumental book on adultery in the novel, for me his most powerful, most dislocating, and yet most paradoxically Apollonian work. In his pages on Ruskin, Proust, and Mann in *Venice Desired* there is a similar depth to his analyses of the city's chthonic powers on writers whose own disposition was torn so operatically between the Apollonian and the Dionysian.

To say finally of Tony Tanner that he represented the best that the profession of letters has given us at the end of this century of extremes is to say very modestly what is true of him as a man, a friend, an abiding presence, a mind, and an example. For those of us whose lives he touched and changed so unalterably through his work and his friendship, the loss is immense, but compensated for somewhat by his rich legacy of scholarship and criticism.

Sources

The essays in this volume were originally published in the following form:

1. 'Lustres and condiments: Ralph Waldo Emerson in his *Essays*' as 'Introduction' to Ralph Waldo Emerson, *Essays and Poems* (Everyman, 1992). Reproduced by permission.
2. '"A summer in the country": Nathaniel Hawthorne's *The Blithedale Romance*' as 'Introduction' to Nathaniel Hawthorne, *The Blithedale Romance* (World's Classics, Oxford University Press, 1991). Reproduced by permission.
3. '"Nothing but cakes and ale": Herman Melville's *White-Jacket*' as 'Introduction' to Herman Melville's *White-Jacket* (World's Classics, Oxford University Press, 1990). Reproduced by permission.
4. '"All interweavingly working together": Herman Melville's *Moby-Dick*' as 'Introduction' to Herman Melville's *Moby Dick* (World's Classics, Oxford University Press, 1988). Reproduced by permission.
5. 'Melville's counterfeit detector: *The Confidence-Man*' as 'Introduction' to Herman Melville, *The Confidence-Man* (World's Classics, Oxford University Press, 1988). Reproduced by permission.
6. 'Henry James: "The Story In It" – and the story without it' as 'The Story in it – and the Story without it' in *Pretexts*, 1997. Carfax Publishing Limited, Abingdon, Oxfordshire. Reproduced by permission. Also published as 'Sex and Narrative' in *Symbiosis: A Journal of Anglo-American Literary Relations*, 1.2 (1997). Reprinted with permission of the editors.
7. 'Henry James's "saddest story": *The Other House*' as 'Introduction' to Henry James, *The Other House* (Everyman, 1996). Reproduced by permission.
8. 'Henry James and Shakespeare' in *Henry James: The Shorter Fiction*, ed. N. H. Reeve (Macmillan Publishers, 1988). Reproduced by permission.

Introduction

Tony Tanner on American means of writing and means of writing America

Ian F. A. Bell

John Locke began Book III of *An Essay Concerning Human Understanding* in anticipation of the peculiarly American concern with empirical philology by stressing 'how great a dependence our words have on common sensible ideas', to claim 'I doubt not but, if we could trace them to their sources, we should find, in all languages, the names which stand for things that fall not under our senses to have had their first rise from sensible ideas.' Subsequently, we find Emerson's essay on 'Nature' arguing that 'Every word which is used to express a novel or intellectual fact, if traced to its root, is found to be formed from some material appearance', and Whitman's 'Slang in America' recasts the principle in more populist mode to urge that the 'final decisions' of language 'are made by the masses, people nearest the concrete, having most to do with actual land and sea'. And for all three, words, to be expressive, had to be figurative, capable of yielding a picture, of being literally 'picturesque' (Emerson's term) at the point where they went into action through their engagement with truth and newness (the line continues down into the twentieth century *via* one of Emerson's disciples, the sinologist Ernest Fenollosa, whose calligraphic celebration of the Chinese ideogram was, with the aid of Ezra Pound, powerfully appropriated for modernist poetics). Instead of Locke, we could turn to Jonathan Edwards and the lengthy Puritan heritage of America's abiding concern with hermeneutics and the anxieties of trusting or mistrusting signs, but the thrust remains similar – that America, not exclusively by any means, but certainly most acutely, has, from virtually its first settling, been closely attentive to the material and constructive nature of language. American culture exhibits the great debates about language, representation, and interpretation to a much larger, and more expressive, extent than any other – Washington Irving was right, surely, to coin 'logocracy' on its behalf, and as Ralph Ellison observed closer to our own time, 'In the beginning of America, was not only the word but the contradiction of the word.' In America, distinctively, words build (as they do so literally in Thoreau); and this has not been a matter of solely literary endeavour: for John Adams 'It is not to be disputed that the form of government has an influence upon language, and language in its turn influences not only the form of government, but the temper, the sentiments, and manners of the people', while Thomas Paine found himself tempted by a particularly pertinent metaphor where 'the American Constitutions were to liberty, what a grammar is to language: they define its parts of speech, and practically construct them into syntax'.

The central political questions of the eighteenth and nineteenth centuries so frequently became issues of interpretation (at its broadest, of reading the words of the Declaration of Independence or the Constitution), and a recent book by Thomas Gustafson (*Representative Words: Politics, Literature, and the American Language, 1776–1865*) has identified the principal conflict at the heart of such issues – the conflict between the need to settle the meanings of words (to maintain order, community, and communication) and the need to unsettle them (to pursue liberty, independence, and self-expression); the conflict located within what Gustafson calls the 'contradictory imperatives' of constitutional and revolutionary thought. From this, we can negotiate the extent to which, in both civic and literary senses, words in America carry a double burden of representation and misrepresentation, of determinacy and indeterminacy, of acceptance and questioning, of bondage and freedom. It is a burden succinctly caught by Melville in *The Confidence-Man* where we find 'Distrust is a stage to confidence. I have confidence in distrust.'

Melville's oxymoronic stance here, I would venture, indexes the political and linguistic complex we confront in the American literary endeavour of the nineteenth and twentieth centuries, and ever since *The Reign of Wonder* through *City of Words* and *Scenes of Nature, Signs of Men* to the present collection, Tony Tanner has displayed himself as its most subtle and supple critic. The trajectory he charts is from the adventure of nineteenth-century Romance forms to the awkwardnesses of late twentieth-century postmodernity – the essay on Don DeLillo quotes from the 'Author's Note' to *Libra*:

Because this book makes no claim to literal truth, because it is only itself, apart and complete, readers may find refuge here – a way of thinking about assassination without being constrained by half-facts or overwhelmed by possibilities, by the tide of speculation that widens with the years.

That is, DeLillo inherits the permissions granted by the 'latitude' within the 'highway a little removed from ordinary travel' of Hawthorne's Prefaces. And as Tanner begins with the Emerson of philosophical flux and flow, matched by a prose that is 'vehicular as opposed to stationary; more a conveyance than a homestead; practising interminability in preference to giving a feeling of arrival; an ocean rather than a wall', so he ends with that 'darker' Emersonian, Thomas Pynchon, and the attempts to map the other forms of flow within transitional America (America is probably always transitional) by Mason & Dixon. Throughout, Tanner's trajectory is informed by the textuality of America, its special cognisance of the material manufacture of words (he has already, in *Scenes of Nature, Signs of Men*, described the Lewis and Clark expedition as 'an exercise of territorial annexation by nomination', America itself as 'a linguistic construct', and the monolithic hermeneutics of Hawthorne's Puritan communities has received no better analysis than 'an atmosphere of sadistic semiology'). No other critic has been so alert to what America writes and writes out, appropriates and disenfranchises.

If words and works can offer 'not definitive verdicts but alternative versions' (*City of Words*), then they are liable to the schism of overdetermined meaning and meaninglessness (or paranoia and antiparanoia which, for Pynchon, provides the definition and critique of such binary thinking) and to the hermeneutical anxieties which persist throughout American literature, the inquiries into whether name can ever be related to thing and the attendant worries about the prescriptive nature of such a relation. Within a culture that experiences itself as always new, the issue is felt with special urgency, and the play with the tenuousness, arbitrariness, illusoriness of words becomes a deeply serious matter – William James's vision of 'a universe unfinished, with doors and windows open to possibilities uncontrolled in advance' is both liberating and frightening. If America, following Tocqueville, was 'spoken into existence' (or written), the breath of utterance is generatively unfettered and alarmingly evanescent simultaneously. Tanner is very good on these matters; and in large part it is perhaps because his intellectual furniture has its own American colour in being open to a particular (and far from uncritical) sympathy – the Proustian 'only true voyage of discovery' ('not to visit strange lands but to possess other eyes, to behold the universe through the eyes of another') glossed by Tanner early on (in *The Reign of Wonder*) as the suspension of fixed positions and prejudices in order to achieve 'not a new philosophy but simply a new breadth of mind and a widened range of sympathy'. More immediate is Hawthorne's notion of sympathy as a key element in a writer's sense of the past and Emerson's commitment to flow and direction against any form of repose. And when (in his most recent book, *Henry James and the Art of Nonfiction*) Tanner identified James's 'central preferences' in resisting direct relations between language and the world as 'Absence rather than presence; shadow rather than substance, broken eloquence esteemed more than confidently replete utterance', he identified preferences that are shared. Richard Poirier reviewed the book (in *The London Review of Books*, 14 December 1995 – it is the best assessment of Tanner and James we have) and used the occasion to bring the other James, William, into the arena of ideas I've been adumbrating. Poirier draws from *The Principles of Psychology* to highlight the 'ghostly elements' that inhabit syntax – those parts of speech that are 'impalpable to direct examination', that are 'nothing but *signs of direction*', not to be glimpsed 'except in flight', and warning 'if we try to hold fast the feeling of direction, the full presence comes and the feeling of direction is lost'.

Full presence as much as replete utterance is antithetical to the feeling of direction sought after by this Emersonian aspect of the brothers James. And so it is with Tony Tanner's appreciation of America's literary language. If, in many ways, that language is all about 'the feeling of direction' (the list is potentially endless: we might add Cooper's anxieties about the linguistic imperialism which threatens Lake Glimmerglass, Pound's admiration for Whistler's 'keys', or the refashioned Romances of Pynchon and DeLillo), Tanner is its most eloquent articulator. Direction, not arrival; provisional and provisory structures; transitional and transitory mores – these are seats of anxiety, as are their antitheses, the civic and political institutions which threaten the enclosure of repose and finality: and they all compete within the ambitions to the new and the singular that define the culture's sense of its independence and identity. These contradictory impulses are nowhere better captured than in that brief and extraordinary phrase of Scott Fitzgerald's describing the youthful reveries of Jay Gatsby: 'they were a satisfactory hint of the unreality of reality, a promise that the rock of the world was founded on a fairy's wing'. Dreaming for Gatsby is about the invention and construction of himself, without biological parentage yet needing a fatherly origin of some sort (his choice is Benjamin Franklin, a great *maker* of things), and so he finds a satisfactoriness (a carefully non-adventurous yet consoling term) in the 'unreality' of 'reality'. This is understandable as a version of reality's infections (although characteristically suppressing the material base which such versions usually find necessary), but the figurative gloss does not allow us to remain comfortable with such a familiar idea: the consolation (and self-delusion) of the first part of the description is quite violently disturbed by the literal impossibility (as a picture) of the second. Words fail here, do not build; deliberately, they create no picture – and their failure indicates the struggle of the American writer to deal with the contradictions I have been outlining.

Tanner takes up the task of narrating this struggle. Gatsby's 'fairy's wing' is not to be dismissed merely as an 'ineffable gaudiness' designed to resist the irreversible ticking of the clock which accompanies his 'fantastic conceits' (although there is more than an element of truth in that), but is a later image of a permanent historical condition. Tanner notices a prevailing tendency to fade, the frequency of words like 'melt' in *The Blithedale Romance*, and asks us to see how 'dematerialisation, attenuation, liquidation, vaporisation and other words of desubstantiation seem variously to dominate the changing atmosphere'. Within this 'peculiarly American nightmare' ('a sudden sense of the complete defamiliarisation of a site or terrain thought to be known and amenable') Hawthorne places what is probably the first fully analysed portrait of the American artist in Miles Coverdale and the conditions his words encounter. Foremost amongst these conditions (and what makes Coverdale so proto-typical of American artistry throughout the century) is the issue of counterfeit, prompted by the mysterious and unnamed crime of Old Moodie. Tanner makes it clear that the crime was forgery and notes the 'worryingly close similarity between writing fiction (or coining images) and counterfeiting the currency on which society depends'. It is perhaps because of this similarity that Coverdale's narration refuses to name the crime, and there is no doubt that it creates special pressure within a culture which advertises itself as new and aggressively self-invented. The story Coverdale tells has to be provisory, has to lack in confidence: the new inevitably works in the absence of established and sustaining structures, and equally inevitable raises questions about its own authenticity, its freshly minted reality (indeed, the creating of new writerly space means the risk not only of counterfeit but, in its most extreme forms, rape and murder: Melville's 'The Paradise of Bachelors and The Tartarus of Maids' and 'The Bell Tower' testify to each respectively). Making always comes close to faking here with a particular urgency that is not exhibited within other cultures – and faking is itself a form of making: forging applies to construction equally as to counterfeit (the distinctively American nature of Hawthorne's enterprise may be seen in a comparison with Dickens's *Great Expectations*). This problem of authenticity prompted by Hawthorne's fiscal metaphor additionally bears directly upon the novel's atmosphere of 'desubstantiation' in its invocation of the alarming financial instability that resulted from the bank wars of the 1830s, the concomitant debate over coined and paper money that continued through to the end of the century, and the epidemic of speculation in various forms (but particularly over land) that marked a further corollary. In all of these areas, what is at risk is confidence – in itself, not so stable an ideal as we might like to think (as Melville will demonstrate in *The Confidence-Man*, where he begins and ends with a blank cheque and the promissory note that is its counterpart), but nevertheless a necessary means of getting about.

How, then, to have confidence in a world of desubstantiation and counterfeit – or, rather, to give it authentic writerly shape when words may either imprison or remain themselves factitious? Counterfeit applies to people just as much as to bank-notes or art-works, and Tanner observes how the characters of Blithedale have a 'general tendency to lead a masked life' and a 'disposition towards "screening" of all kinds' (veils, false names, mysterious and mystified life histories). Karen Halttunen (in *Confidence Men and Painted Women: A Study of Middle-Class Culture in America, 1830–1870*) has documented how, by mid-century, the sentimental cult of sincerity had been obliged to find room for the necessity of performativeness in social manners and intercourse, and it is clear that counterfeit comes close to performance within the American exhortation to invent – be it the disavowal of Europe, the tinkering tradition of Franklin, or the self-engineering of Gatsby. No longer is it a matter of having the confidence to distinguish between the authentic and the fake, but of having the constructivist skill to maintain more confidence in some counterfeits (or representations) than in others (the issue becomes particularly compelling towards the end of the nineteenth century with the development of a culture of consumption – to which the novels of Henry James testify so richly). Since trust in all its forms (financial, social, and aesthetic) is so deeply embedded within the whole notion of representation, its fragility makes special demands upon the writer. For Tanner, these demands upon Hawthorne prompt him to create in Coverdale a new kind of figure in American literature – the artist as failed artist, and specifically as 'lodger', most at

home in 'places of transience' and 'truly at home nowhere'. The failure lies in 'forgetting the American past, while being disablingly sceptical about the American present' and in being 'dubious, undecided,
ambiguous, about the authentic validity or value of "fiction" and art in
general'. It is a clever trick, of course, for the presumably non-failed
artist to present such a figure since these are the very shortcomings
he will, by implicit comparison, lay claim to avoid. And it is a trick
(performance, fakery) we are intended to recognise – in claiming a
representative function for Coverdale, Tanner finds himself offering
further figures to add to the image of the lodger:

Inasmuch as he sees him as a true product of America, in his disorientation,
amnesia, and general sense of loss – *that* is what Hawthorne is doing with
Coverdale. Saying to American society, American history, American religion
and culture: *this* is the artist you have produced – intruder, lodger, spy.

We might go further still and complete 'intruder, lodger, spy' with
the confidence trickster, not only another American representative man
but a version of Hawthorne's knowingness about failed artistry. We
will confront this trickster in his fullest form of course in *The Confidence-
Man* itself, but first I want to look at Tanner's account of *Moby-Dick* in
order to develop some additional colours for the palette. Melville's
oceanic tale is insistently about words and their operations – 'as much
indebted to books as to whales' where 'the activities of writing and
fishing are curiously merged, teasingly mixed'. The catalogue of such
mergings is encyclopaedic and far too extensive to itemise here, but
the point I want to highlight is that particular merging of Melville's
lexicon, his 'assertive and allusive' style where 'words accumulate meanings and speculations accrue to words'. In short, words *work* for and in
a novel which takes human labour as its other principal theme, the
physical and the cerebral 'interweavingly working together'. Mergings,
interweavings, mixings, accretions, and allusions bring together style
and subject in a particularly expressive way to register what is perhaps
the main moral of the novel – what Tanner calls 'reversibility' whereby
'All things are potentially double, paradoxically mixed, oddly reversible. Opposites may turn out to be more like identities' and, crucially,
'rigid polarisation will not hold when applied to the swimming intermixedness of life'.

Reversibility is characterised by reciprocity and mutuality, is set
against 'the potentially disastrous, all annihilating effects of the kind of
Manichean, dualistic modes of thought based on notions of embattled
exclusivity'. So counter to the oppositional structures of Ahab, we have

Ishmael's 'tolerant inclusiveness, his disinclination for rigid partial versions and sectarian monocularity, his eroticised and playful porousness to the wholeness of life'. Osmosis combats bifurcation in Ishmael's 'survival through style', a style that is careless, inconsistent, resistant to closure, fond of 'careful disorderliness', and non-assertive: 'He digs and writes – moves on', as Tanner so economically puts it. This is also Melville's style and, for Tanner, that of America itself: 'In its vast assimilations, its seemingly opportunistic eclecticism, its pragmatic and improvisatory nonchalance, its capacious grandiloquence and demotic humour it is indeed a style for America – the style of America.' It is the 'widened range of sympathy' that Tanner had earlier associated with the stance of 'wonder' itself and its commitment to the *feel* of direction as against repose. In *The Confidence-Man*, this 'reversibility' of apprehension and understanding will be re-cast as 'interchangeability' (a term Tanner borrows from a later, more secular masquerader, Thomas Mann's Felix Krull) to register 'the multiplicity and the sheer ontological dubiety of the self', thoroughly in tune, I would add, with the shift from the cult of sincerity to the social necessity of performativeness I noted earlier. For Tanner, the Confidence Man is grounded in several of the abiding elements of American thought in the nineteenth century – Barnum the 'hoaxer showman', Franklin the 'self-technologist', Poe's 'diddler', and the Emersonian commitment to endless metamorphosis; all of which combine to underwrite, again, the peculiarly American faith in self-invention, 'the specialist in secondary, reproducible identities' (this composite figuration is one that Ralph Ellison will deploy to pessimistic effect at the behest of different social imperatives in *Invisible Man*). Melville now extends *Moby-Dick*'s critique of schismatic perception, the urge for fixed authority and absolute guarantees of authenticity, into a wider consideration of the fundamental novelistic strategies – ontological identity, the conception of character, and the conventions of representation. These preoccupations place additional pressure on the constructivist nature of language, on the capacity of words to make/fake. With a neatly punning slippage, the black cripple in the opening sequence hopes to find himself 'werry well wordy of all you kind ge'mmen's kind confidence'. The repetition of 'kind' is an awkward, and certainly fraught, reminder of those humanistic elements of reversibility we found in Ishmael. Here, interchangeability contributes a more abstract and damaging shade to the lexical experiment, the wordiness of the later novel where, as Tanner sees, rightly, 'the connection between words and "worth" or trustworthiness, indeed between language and value or integrity, is just what – in suitably various guises and disguises – this masquerade of a book is all about'.

The great thing about the masquerade of words (and, I suggest, one of the principal imperatives behind American Romanticism's fascination with the performative nature of words – endlessly manoeuvring and manoeuvrable, opening and closing, punning and literalising, various and singular) is that it displays so clearly language's constructivist function, its fresh capacity for making. One of the main reasons that *The Confidence-Man* is such a representative text, for all its adventurousness and its originality (a term profoundly questioned in itself by the novel), is that, as Tanner recognises, it 'is above all interested in the words men say – and write – as they attempt to relate or exploit, to communicate or manipulate, to enlighten or outwit, to tell the truth or insert a lie'. While we might tend to privilege the seemingly positive side of this list (communication and truth), in fact it is the putatively negative line (manipulation and lies) which I would suggest provides such a rich resource for Melville. This is so because it acknowledges the factitiousness of language (and, concomitantly, its variousness and variability, returning words to the generative and dispersive fluctuations of voice – the 'porousness' of Ishmael, perhaps, or more familiarly, the oral insistences of Whitman, the delight in dictating their works for the later Twain and James) at the same time as, paradoxically, it recognises its capacity for change and alterability. It is in these terms that we can trace the trajectory of Tanner's enterprise in the present collection (I'd probably want to insert Nietzsche and the Wilde of the 'truth of lies' as mediatory agents), the lexical inquiries which lead us from the radical experimentation of the American Romance to the nervousness of American postmodern fiction, from Hawthorne and Melville to DeLillo and Pynchon.

Arguably, *the* Romance of twentieth-century America has been the assassination of Kennedy, and it is striking that DeLillo, in his version of the story that is *Libra*, chose to ally the form of his enterprise (as we saw earlier) with Hawthornesque 'latitude'. And it is striking equally that Tanner, in thinking widely about the kinds of reading prompted by *Americana*, should find himself asking (in more contemporary terms) the sort of question he would have asked of *The Confidence-Man*: 'America – or Americana? What kind of "real" life people can shape for themselves in a mediated, consumer culture swamped in images and information, is an abiding concern.' The material conditions which enable and promote the confidence trickster and the advertising executive change – of course – but their words share a similar office, and anxieties over words resurface, for the writer, in more fevered form (particularly in competition with the 'news' which DeLillo sees as supplanting the novel, the 'news' diagnosed in a wonderful phrase by Tanner as 'atrocity tourism'). The nineteenth-century worry over meaninglessness becomes, in DeLillo, 'waste', and more strategically in Pynchon, the 'rubbish' which replaces the slightly earlier imagery of chaos (in Mailer most clearly) – the matter out of place, that which is rejected and neglected by systems of order; the people whom Pynchon calls 'preterite', those who, in Tanner's terms, are 'regarded by the System as human junk, to be overlooked, discarded'. In Pynchon again, the central issue of meaning and meaninglessness becomes translated into the problem of manyness and connection; of 'paranoia' where everything is connected and 'anti-paranoia' where nothing is connected to anything (in *Gravity's Rainbow*).

If *The Confidence-Man* presents the type of the American nineteenth-century Romance, then *Mason & Dixon* offers its twentieth-century counterpart, and it is entirely fitting that Tanner should conclude with this return to the earlier period of the Republic, with a literal and figurative landscape that may be released from images and conventional topographies into an ambiguous world of possibilities. Surveying provides a marvellous series of tropes whereby the grand themes of Tanner's trajectory can be incorporated: 'Lines become walls; differences become oppositions', he claims on behalf of Pynchon's larger distrust – 'either one great explanation of everything, or no meaning at all – Revelation, or nihilism' – and the oscillations between these two poles, thought through a rigorous scepticism about their tenability, reverberate both awkwardly and decisively within the entire trajectory to point to Tanner's fundamental conception of America's literary and ideational handling of America: 'The new country, the United States of America, depended for its existence both as entity and concept on two things – appropriated, surveyed, legally apportioned land; and a sense of an uncharted, inexhaustibly bounteous west, a plenitude of possibilities: measurement and dream.' To focus these large ideas, Tanner, quite brilliantly, relies upon style and celebrates above all the Subjunctive mood he discerns in Pynchon: 'The great subjunctive premiss underlying Pynchon's work is – *had* America taken a different path . . .' Opposed to this is the Indicative mood, seen as 'number'd and dreamless', and the Declarative mood 'reducing Possibilities to

Simplicities that serve the ends of Governments'. I'd like to suggest that the Subjunctive mood offered here is the honourable successor to the Wonder that Tanner has claimed already for the American literary stance. A key moment is a speech given to Cherrycoke in *Mason & Dixon*:

Who claims Truth, Truth abandons. History is hir'd, or coerc'd, only in Interests that must ever prove base. She is too innocent to be left within the reach of anyone in Power, – who need but touch her, and all her Credit is in the instant vanish'd, as if it had never been. She needs rather to be tended lovingly and honorably by fabulists and counterfeiters, Ballad-Mongers and Cranks of ev'ry Radius, Masters of Disguise to provide her the Costume, Toilette, and Bearing, and Speech nimble enough to keep her beyond the Desires, or even the Curiosity, of Government.

We come, in a sense, almost full circle here and might recognise Pynchon's counterfeiters, cranks, and masters of disguise as fit companions for Melville's Confidence Man or Hawthorne's play with the 'failed' artist as 'intruder, lodger, spy' – all figures who subvert and divert, resist through their variousness the singularity of an Ahab, a line on a map, or the appropriations of a government. Both DeLillo and Pynchon are alert to the transcendental possibilities of wonder (and both are alert equally to its proximity to dread), and the 'nimble' speech desired by Pynchon's Cherrycoke is close kin to the sympathy in the 'tolerant inclusiveness' and 'porousness' Tanner discovers in Melville's Ishmael. It is entirely right then that Tanner's account of Pynchon and his own trajectory in general should end with Emersonian flow, with that generosity towards the fluidity and reversibility of the world which resists mensuration and merely rational analysis. And if sympathy and generosity are Tanner's abiding American subjects, the present collection demonstrates abundantly and pleasurably how his own critical stance is particularly suited to their articulation, offering, as Emerson said of Carlyle's style, 'a sort of splendid conversation'.

Keele, 1999

CHAPTER 1

Lustres and condiments:
Ralph Waldo Emerson in his Essays

It is said that Nietzsche never travelled without carrying a volume of Emerson's essays with him. When I started reading American literature – some thirty years ago – the conjunction of those two names would have seemed not just incongruous but ludicrous. As the stereotypes of the time had it, on the one hand there was Emerson the Boston Brahmin, bland even to fatuity, contentedly ripening with the New England melons, benignly meditating on such vaporous notions as the Over-soul, serenely disengaged not only from politics and society but from all human relations, ideally winnowing himself down to a transparent eyeball. On the other hand, there was the European Nietzsche, savage even to madness, ferociously dismantling the belief systems and the hypocritically espoused values of the declining bourgeois Western world. What was *he* doing with Emerson in his pocket?

Born in 1803, Ralph Waldo Emerson, like his father before him, became a minister in the Unitarian Church, being ordained minister of Boston's Second Church in 1829. Unitarianism represented an extreme dilution of the rigidly Calvinistic Puritanism which had originally dominated New England. But it still retained a minimum of – comfortably unexacting – orthodoxy and ritual, for instance the communion service. The young Emerson soon found himself uneasy with this residue of formal religion which he saw as a symptom of rigidification and petrifaction. He had come to suspect all institutionalised prescriptions, anything enshrined and repeatedly imposed, all the drilled and regulated mediations of authority already in place. All this he saw as the tyranny of the past – as embodied in the father, the Church, Europe, or any tradition which seemed to claim the right both to guide and constrain the individual. 'Nature abhors the old . . . We call it by many names . . . rest, conservatism, appropriation, inertia; not newness, not the way onward. We grizzle every day. I see no need of it' ('Circles'). He did not want to install himself in, and subserviently

1

administer, any church, indeed any system, whatsoever. 'Up, down, around, the kingdom of thought has no enclosures, but the Muse makes us free of her city' ('Intellect').

In 1838 Emerson wrote that it seemed that 'the distinction of the new age' would be 'the refusal of authority'. In 1834 there had been riots at Harvard which started when a student said to a teacher, 'I do not recognise your authority.' In 1838 Emerson gave the famous, or infamous, 'Divinity School Address' at Harvard, in which he directly confronted and challenged established authorities. The address gave great offence and aroused fierce opposition – and no wonder. Emerson – *in* the Divinity School – speaks out against all formalisms and constituted mediations – 'we shrink as soon as the prayers begin'. He refers to 'the famine of our churches'; deplores 'the stationariness of religion'; and argues the need for an entirely new mode of revelation. Given the time and place, it was an explosively anarchistic performance. He was not invited back to Harvard for thirty years. In 1838 Emerson made his final break with the Church. He had resigned his ministry in 1832, but had continued preaching in Concord. Now he felt he had to disassociate himself from even the vestigial officialdom of the pulpit.

But if he was no longer a minister, what – up, down, and around – was he? This has been called Emerson's 'problem of vocation'. Over the ensuing years, he deployed a wide range of names or terms to designate what he was, or felt himself to be, or aspired to be – or, more generally, the kind of figure he felt America needed. The very proliferation of these names is an index to Emerson's uncertainty about the role – if any – he was playing, or could play, in society: he was variously Scholar, Seer, Reformer, Man of Genius, Contemplative Man, Hero, Poet, Transcendentalist, Student, Saint, Dissenter, Torch-bearer, Idealist, Aspirant, Radical. One might wonder why he could not simply have announced himself as a Writer, and have done with it. But things were not so simple in mid-nineteenth-century America. The idea that 'writing' could be a respectable full-time (male) occupation was regarded with particular suspicion. Fully explaining, or suggesting, the reasons for this would take us too far afield. Partly it was due to a Puritan deprecation of all fiction-making, all art, as potentially impious if not blasphemous. God was the only Maker. Then again, the whole ethos of America served to stress the importance of actual *doing* – pioneering, clearing, settling, building, inventing, mastering. The vast and growing new nation required men of action. Writers themselves often felt a deep ambivalence, if not actual guilt, about writing. Hawthorne's long introductory chapter to *The Scarlet Letter* is, among other things, a tortuous and often anxious justification of his embarking on the novel. A quotation from an earlier work, *Letters from an American Farmer*, by J. Hector St John de Crèvecoeur, exemplifies this American ambivalence about writing. In his introduction, the author records his wife as saying to him –

I would not have thee, James, pass for what the world calleth a writer; no, not for a peck of gold, as the saying is. Thy father before thee was a plain-dealing, honest man, punctual in all things; he was one of *yea* and *nay*, of few words; all he minded was his farm and work. I wonder from whence thee has got this love of the pen?[1]

To be sure, the *Letters* is a fiction, and there may be some comic exaggeration at work. But the wife expresses something both real and prevalent in pre-Civil War America: a feeling that writing was not, truly speaking, in and for itself, a proper, self-justifying activity.

Thus it is that we find Emerson often returning to the problematics of action. 'Besides, why should we be cowed by the name of Action? . . . We know that the ancestor of every action is a thought . . . The rich mind lies in the sun and sleeps, and is Nature. To think is to act . . . Action and inaction are alike to the true' ('Spiritual Laws'). Even more to the point, he writes: 'Words and deeds are quite indifferent modes of the divine energy. Words are also actions, and actions are a kind of words.' When he came to write his volume entitled *Representative Men*, Emerson was initially going to conclude (and thus climax) with 'Napoleon; or, the Man of the World' – Napoleon being for Emerson, as for so many nineteenth-century writers, the exemplary man of action of their age. But then Emerson came to question what was finally achieved by all Napoleon's activity – 'this vast talent and power . . . It came to no result. All passed away, like the smoke of his artillery, and left no trace.' So Emerson concluded the volume, triumphally as one feels, with 'Goethe; or the Writer'. The 'vast talent and power' of the great writer *does* leave traces.

A key word there, and for Emerson everywhere, is 'power' (perhaps this was part of his appeal for Nietzsche). 'The law of nature is, Do the thing, and you shall have the power: but they who do not the thing have not the power' ('Compensation'). Emerson's 'thing' was writing (and speaking) and he felt, had to feel, that he 'had the power'. 'The good soul nourishes me, unlocks new magazines of power and enjoyment to me every day' ('Spiritual Laws'). If, he says, you can really open the eyes of old and settled people to the truth, 'they are perfumed again with hope and power' ('Circles'). 'Perfumed with power' – the trope has an almost Shakespearean audacity. The 'real value' of great books 'is as signs of power' ('Art'). One can see why he should conclude his perhaps greatest essay, 'Experience', in this way: 'the true romance which the world exists to realise, will be the transformation of genius into practical power'. He refers easily to 'the direct splendor of intellectual power', and, rather remarkably, celebrates 'that *dream*-power which every night shows thee is thine own; a power transcending all limit and privacy' ('The Poet'). On the role of power in society, he affirms, in 'Manners', 'Power first, or no leading class.' Nietzsche would surely have approved of that. He would also have approved the belief that 'Power is in nature the essential measure of right.' And 'power' was inseparable from movement. 'Power ceases in the instant of re-pose; it resides in the moment of transition from a past to a new state; in the shooting of the gulf; in the darting to an aim' ('Self-Reliance'). 'Nothing is secure but life, transition, the energising spirit' ('Circles'). Writing, of course, fixes things – a written word is a word in repose. Emerson sought to find a mode of writing which, as it were, seemed to dissolve itself even as it began to settle, stiffen, and congeal – a writing seemingly in a state of permanent transition.

Thus crucial words for Emerson – in addition to 'power', 'force', 'energy' – are 'unfix', 'unsettle', 'upheave', 'antagonism'. He was against whatever was 'stationary'. Movement – transition – was what mattered. 'Every thing good is on the highway' ('Experience'). This is an apt enough aphorism for a literature which spends a good deal of its time 'on the road'. But it has more far-reaching implications for Emerson: 'all symbols are fluxional; all language is vehicular and transitive, and is good, as ferries and horses are, for conveyance, not as farms and houses are, for homestead' ('The Poet'). All Emerson's negative terms are to do with 'fixity' and arrest: all evil, he says, has to do with 'limit' ('the only sin is limitation' – 'Circles'). Throughout his essays, the image of the 'wall' serves as the most extreme abuse. 'Suffice it for the joy of the universe, that we have not arrived at a wall, but at interminable oceans' ('Experience'). Whatever makes for fluidity is seen as a positive force – he even makes 'flux' into an active – transitive – verb. 'Every solid in the universe is ready to become fluid on the approach of mind, and the power to flux it is the measure of the mind. If the wall remain adamant, it accuses the want of thought. To a subtler force, it will stream into new forms' ('Fate'). Life, for Emerson, was indeed 'a flux of moods', and for him it was a sign of health to go with the 'flux' and, since it is his verb, to keep on and on 'fluxing'. The risks and possible losses (even inhumanities) attendant on such a stance hardly need spelling out. But its potential for energising liberations is very great.

In this connection, it is worth considering the impact on Emerson of the death of his young son, Waldo, in 1842. Prior to this event, his essays were marked by an almost anarchistic confidence. One reviewer of the volume containing 'Self-Reliance' said that its doctrines 'if acted upon, would overthrow society, and resolve the world into chaos'. Certainly, with its attack on 'the smooth mediocrity and squalid contentment of the times', its view of society as a 'conspiracy against the manhood of every one of its members', its vigorous espousal of nonconformity ('whoso would be a man must be a nonconformist'), and what sounds like an unchecked, capricious arbitrariness ('I would write on the lintels of the door-post, *Whim*'), the essay does read as a licence for unhindered anti- or a-social individualism, overvaluing what he elsewhere calls 'the great and crescive self' (and thus, among other things, vulnerable to appropriation by supporters of a ruthless and unscrupulous self-aggrandising capitalism whom Emerson sought to excoriate).

Part of the problem is that, in a way, Emerson is writing against writing itself. He has to use sentences, and sentences, to the extent that they are semantically legible, look inexorably propositional. But Emerson purported not to believe in propositions ('essence refuses to be recorded in propositions'). He regarded language as potentially a trap which is liable to check us to the point of stagnation and even decay – indeed, 'stationariness'. That is why he had so little regard for 'foolish consistency'. Better to follow your own authentic impulses. Whim. 'Live ever in a new day.' 'The voyage of the best ship is a zigzag line of a hundred tacks.' And so it is with the voyage of his own writing. This is why it can be at times so exhilarating – always surprisingly on the move; and at times so exhausting to follow – it never stops tacking. But for good or bad, good and bad perhaps, this was something both extraordinary and new in American writing.

But four years later, in 1844, at the beginning of 'Experience', Emerson seems lost, or at least disorientated. 'Where do we find ourselves?' He found himself – lost himself – having to apprehend and assimilate the

sudden death of his adored young son. How he did so has been responsible for much of his later reputation as almost inhumanly unfeeling.
He only once wrote directly about this death:

The only thing grief has taught me, is to know how shallow it is . . . In the
death of my son . . . I seem to have lost a beautiful estate, – no more. I cannot
get it nearer to me. If to-morrow I should be informed of the bankruptcy of
my principal debtors, the loss of my property would be a great inconvenience
to me . . . but it would leave me as it found me, – neither better nor worse. So
is it with this calamity: it does not touch me . . . It was caducous. I grieve that
grief can teach me nothing, nor carry me one step into real nature . . . I take
this evanescence and lubricity of all objects, which lets them slip through our
fingers when we clutch hardest, to be the most unhandsome part of our
condition. Nature does not like to be observed, and likes that we should be
her fools and playmates.

This 'slippery, sliding', lubricious, caducous nature is very different
from the infinitely benign nature of Emerson's first essay, 'Nature'.
And Emerson's way of coping with grief seems preternaturally cool – a
supreme example of what he himself referred to as 'my old arctic
habits'. Clearly, when it came to the basic creatural passions and feelings, he was, by any reckoning, very repressed. (Sex and sexuality scarcely
figure in his copious writing, and John Jay Chapman once wrote that
a visitor from another planet, wishing to find out about human life on
this earth, would do better to go to the worst Italian opera than read
Emerson – because at least from the opera he would learn that there
are two sexes!) But 'arctic' males – and females – were, by all accounts,
common enough in nineteenth-century England and America; and
having initially found Emerson's dismissive composure in regard to his
son's death rather repellent, I now think it can be seen as manifesting
its own kind of bravery and strength. 'Providence has a wild, rough,
incalculable road to its end, and it is no use to try to whitewash its
huge mixed instrumentalities' ('Fate'). Confronted by the terrible results
of these 'huge, mixed instrumentalities' Emerson refused to be immo-
bilised by grief. 'Let us be poised, and wise, and our own, today.'

If life was 'flux' in constant 'metamorphosis' (another key word for
Emerson), then so should the writing of it be. 'Nature hates calcu-
lators; her methods are *saltatory and impulsive.* Man lives by *pulses*; our
organic movements are such; and the chemical and ethereal agents are
undulatory and alternate; and the mind goes *antagonising* on, and never
prospers but by fits. We thrive by *casualties* . . . The most attractive

class of people are those who are *powerful obliquely*' ('Experience'). The italics are mine, and while Emerson applies them to organic life, we can reapply them to his own prose – vehicular as opposed to stationary; more of a conveyance than a homestead; practising interminability in preference to giving a feeling of arrival; an ocean rather than a wall. Nature, he says, 'has set her heart on breaking up all styles and tricks' ('Nominalist and Realist'), so he tries himself to write in a style which gives the impression of constantly breaking *itself* up.

You do not read Emerson for information, nor – and this is where it sometimes becomes problematic – do you exactly read him for his sense. Two statements which reveal his own mode of reading – what he read *for* – may be helpful here. 'An imaginative book renders us much more service at first, by stimulating us through its *tropes*, than afterward, when we arrive at the *precise sense* of the author' ('The Poet' – my emphasis). Secondly, 'I find the most pleasure in reading a book in a manner least flattering to the author . . . I read for the *lustres*, as if one should use a fine picture in a chromatic experiment, for its rich colors' ('Nominalist and Realist' – my emphasis). Such a mode of reading of course risks promoting superficiality; and Emerson's own style at times courts the disaster of becoming almost meaningless. Emerson is neither a hard nor a deep thinker – nor does he aim to be. You read him for the tropes and the lustres, and allow their power, to adapt one of his own formulations, to 'slide into you as pleasure'. It is important to remember that he regarded himself as a serious poet, and it would be appropriate to say that many of his essays aspire to the condition of poetry.

It is also relevant to recall that Emerson's primary occupation was as a lecturer – in 1867, for example, he gave no fewer than eighty lectures. It is clear not only that he evolved his own highly original manner of speaking but also that that manner is behind his writing. Here is John Jay Chapman again, more admiringly: 'It was the platform which determined Emerson's style . . . The pauses and hesitation, the abstraction, the searching, the balancing, the turning forward and back of the leaves of his lecture, and then the discovery, the illumination, the gleam of lightning which you saw before your eyes descend into a man of genius, – all this was Emerson. He invented this style of speaking.'[2] As in the speaking, so in the writing. It is as if Emerson somehow seeks to escape from his own moments of utterance – as if speech, like writing, was a regrettable necessity. 'The waters of the great deep have ingress and egress to the soul. But if I speak, I define,

I confine, and am less' ('Intellect'). In much the same spirit he writes, 'The sentence must also contain its own apology for being spoken' ('Spiritual Laws'). The paradox of the great speaker and writer declaiming against the confining and diminishing effects of all forms of utterance and articulation is squarely faced by Emerson. 'No sentence will hold the whole truth, and the only way in which we can be just, is by giving ourselves the lie; speech is better than silence; silence is better than speech' ('Nominalist and Realist'). These perhaps rather too contented-seeming contiguous self-contradictions are of a piece with his belief that 'You are one thing, but nature is *one thing and the other thing*, in the same moment' ('Nominalist and Realist'). Emerson wanted to get some of that seamless doubleness of nature into his writing. He must then disappoint, if not infuriate, those whose expectations have been determined by more traditional modes of discourse – which seek to elicit clarifications and distinctions from the chaotic abundance of nature.

Nevertheless, the Emersonian voice is an important part of the affirmative strengths of that ongoing improvisation and experiment called America. It reminds us that 'society is fluid'; that institutions are not rooted in nature like trees; that all is 'alterable' ('Politics'). It is easy to fault or deride his optimism in the face of evil, suffering, and pain. Yet that power for persistence, that self-renewing energy and refusal of 'stationariness' for which he continually speaks, are essential things.

Like Nietzsche, he went 'antagonising on'; and society would stagnate without such bracing oppositional voices. But more than that, he knew that art was, and should be, not utilitarian and serviceable, but a supplement, an addition, an excess, something over and above; not our daily bread, but an added relish. 'We came this time for condiments, not for corn. We want the great genius only for joy' ('Nominalist and Realist').

NOTES

1 J. Hector St John de Crèvecoeur, *Letters from an American Farmer* (New York: Penguin Books, 1986), p. 48.
2 John Jay Chapman, *Emerson and Other Essays* (London: David Nutt, 1898), pp. 33–4.

CHAPTER 2

'A summer in the country':
Nathaniel Hawthorne's The Blithedale Romance

> True; if you look at it in one way, it had been only a summer in
> the country. But, considered in a profounder relation, it was part
> of another age, a different state of society, a segment of an existence
> peculiar in its aims and methods, a leaf of some mysterious volume,
> interpolated into the current history which Time was writing off.
> At one moment, the very circumstances now surrounding me –
> my coalfire, and the dingy room in the bustling hotel – appeared
> far off and intangible. The next instant, Blithedale looked vague,
> as if it were at a distance both in time and space, and so shadowy,
> that a question might be raised whether the whole affair had been
> anything more than the thoughts of a speculative man. I had
> never before experienced a mood that so robbed the actual world
> of its solidity. It nevertheless involved a charm, on which – a
> devoted epicure of my own emotions – I resolved to pause, and
> enjoy the moral sillabub until quite dissolved away.

By the end of this passage it is not entirely clear whether the 'dissolving
away' refers to the sillabub or the writer himself. Certainly in a text in
which the word 'melt' endlessly recurs and where dematerialisation,
attenuation, liquidation, vaporisation, and other modes of desubstantiation seem variously to dominate the changing atmosphere, the facility
with which a sweet dessert or a sentimental author might come to
share in the prevailing tendency to fade, no matter how stickily, away
could well come to seem about equal. We are certainly invited to
consider what kind of writer, and what kind of writing, are here involved. Yes, it is, from one point of view, all based on 'a summer in the
country' – the summer of 1841, to be precise, which Hawthorne himself spent at or in the experimental socialist (Utopian? perhaps Fourierist)
community at Brook Farm. But, looked at another way, and thus written
another way, it might become 'a leaf of some mysterious volume,
interpolated into the current history which Time was writing off'. It is
a somewhat curious formulation and one might wonder – who is doing

the writing here? Does Time both write current history and write it off at the same time? Is history somehow at once inscribed and erased? But Time only writes by a metaphor (though I suppose we would have to say that it erases in good earnest). The writing here is being done by the narrator, Miles Coverdale, and, in likening his summer experiences to 'a leaf of some mysterious volume' interpolated into the, presumably, unmysterious history being written, and written off, by Time, he must be suggesting that, whatever it is he is now writing, it is not history – or not history as currently conceived. And indeed he calls his non-historical history of that summer in the country a Romance. Hawthorne and Romance is a subject to drown in, but for the moment I want to make only a restricted point. Why is Miles Coverdale *not* writing history? Why does he, gesturally, leave that to Time or whatever? Or perhaps it is a more mysterious kind of history he is writing – devious, surreptitious, interpolatory? The matter is important because, as I shall try to suggest, problems involved in writing American history, the history of America (and in *not* writing it – writing off, writing out), are central to this novel. And whatever his relationship – non-relationship, sly-relationship – to history might be, the narrator has here reached a state of extreme reality-deprivation in which the 'actual world' has lost its solidity and he is collapsing into a state of solipsism – not to say infantilism – in which he has unashamed recourse to a kind of primal orality in which he sucks contentedly away on the (moral!) sillabub of the dissolving self.

What *is* Hawthorne doing?

When he returns to Blithedale after his sojourn in the city, Coverdale confessedly indulges in 'odd and extravagant conjectures'. The conjectures are 'spectral' and are all concerned with the evacuation of the real.

Either there was no such place as Blithedale, nor ever had been, nor any brotherhood of thoughtful laborers . . . or else it was all changed, during my absence. It had been nothing but dream-work and enchantment. I should seek in vain for the old farm-house . . . and for all that configuration of the land which I had imagined. It would be another spot, and an utter strangeness.

There is a peculiarly American nightmare or dread summed up in that last sentence – a sudden sense of the *complete* defamiliarisation of a site or terrain thought to be known and amenable. Coverdale looks for something to anchor him and finds it in the farm. 'That, surely, was something real.' (On another occasion he describes his determination to force Zenobia out of what he takes to be her continual acting. 'She should be compelled to give me a glimpse of something true; some nature, some passion, no matter whether right or wrong, provided it were real.' It is that same urgent need and desire for 'something real'. As in Frost's famous poem 'For once, then, something' (1923) which ends: 'What was that whiteness? | Truth? A pebble of quartz? For once, then, something.') The reality he finds is the very earth of the farm where, for a while, he had worked. 'I could have knelt down, and have laid my breast against that soil.' I am prompted to invoke Robert Frost again, and his powerful poem 'To Earthward' (1923), which ends:

> When stiff and sore and scarred
> I take away my hand
> From leaning on it hard
> In grass and sand,
>
> The hurt is not enough:
> I long for weight and strength
> To feel the earth as rough
> To all my length.[1]

– though it would have to be said that this longing stems from more powerful feelings than animate the always potentially dilettante Coverdale. Nor could the sybaritic Coverdale declare with the same authority as the austerely ascetic Thoreau, 'Be it life or death, we crave only reality.'[2] But it is an important aspect of him that he should at least intermittently experience this hunger for the real, undeveloped and undernourished an appetite as it may be. What might constitute the real or the Real are questions hardly to be addressed in this book, where reality, whatever and wherever it may be, is – it would appear – mainly to be known by the conviction that you have not got it.

What Coverdale does get, as he prowls around Blithedale looking for something real, is a 'concourse of strange figures' appearing and vanishing 'confusedly', consisting of, among others, an Indian chief, the goddess Diana, a Bavarian broom girl, a negro 'of the Jim Crow order', a Kentucky woodsman, a Shaker, Shepherds of Arcadia, grim Puritans, gay Cavaliers, Revolutionary officers, a gypsy, a witch, and so on – a disorderly medley of mythical and literary figures, national types, or stereotypes, and historical representatives. The chapter is called 'The Masqueraders' and that is what they are. The atmosphere of Blithedale has been saturated with artifice of all kinds from the start, as when Coverdale feels that the presence of Zenobia 'caused our heroic enterprise to show like an illusion, a masquerade, a pastoral, a counterfeit Arcadia, in which we grown-up men and women were making a play-day of the years that were given us to live in'. Noting the word 'counterfeit' we may just observe that all this pseudo-'masquerading' reveals itself to be pitifully self-conscious, juvenile, and fragile. Is *this* what has become of the deeply resonant pastoral and Arcadian images and visions of old Europe, when transplanted to the New World? It is a sort of ultimate trivialisation, and here the simple presence of the Yankee farmer Silas Foster, with his 'shrewd, acrid observation', is enough to 'disenchant the scene'. And yet there was a strong line of thought, or a persistent dream, that America might be the last best chance of, if not literalising Arcadia, then realising – Real-ising – Utopia. And that, surely, is not a trivial aspiration. I shall return to these matters.

Fleeing from 'the whole fantastic rabble' of masqueraders – 'like a mad poet hunted by chimaeras', he rather extravagantly puts it, given that it seems more like a romp at a picnic – Coverdale finally finds himself alone and effectively lost deep in the woods where

I stumbled over a heap of logs and sticks that had been cut for firewood, a great while ago, by some former possessor of the soil, and piled up square, in order to be carted or sledded away to the farmhouse. But, being forgotten, they had lain there, perhaps fifty years, and possibly much longer; until, by the accumulation of moss, and leaves falling over them and decaying there, from autumn to autumn, a green mound was formed, in which the softened outline of the wood-pile was still perceptible. In the fitful mood that then swayed my mind, I found something strangely affecting in this simple circumstance. I imagined the long-dead woodman, and his long-dead wife and children, coming out of their chill graves, and essaying to make a fire with this heap of mossy fuel.

This is, for me, one of the key moments of the book and to explain why I think so I want, once again, to invoke some lines by Frost from a poem called, indeed, 'The Wood-Pile' (1914). Frost describes going out for a walk in the woods and deciding at a certain point that, rather than turning back for home, he will 'go on farther' – a very Frostian moment. Soon he finds himself unable to 'mark or name a place' or 'say for certain I was here | Or somewhere else'. He is not exactly lost – 'I was just far from home.' And then he comes upon a pile of wood.

It was a cord of maple, cut and split
And piled – and measured, four by four by eight.
And not another like it could I see.
No runner tracks in this year's snow looped near it.
And it was older sure than this year's cutting,
Or even last year's or the year's before.
The wood was grey and the bark warping off it
And the pile somewhat sunken . . .
                                        I thought that only
Someone who lived in turning to fresh tasks
Could so forget his handiwork on which
He spent himself, the labour of his axe,
And leave it there far from a useful fireplace
To warm the frozen swamp as best it could
With the slow smokeless burning of decay.[3]

The two American poets – Coverdale is a poet, albeit a minor one – both find something almost namelessly pregnant and suggestive when they come across an abandoned wood-pile. Their somewhat disoriented, non-orientated state recapitulates – in little echoes if you like – the ontological situation of the original settlers of the land who would have found themselves, not lost exactly, but, with names and markers not yet affixed, definitely and definitively 'far from home', perhaps having to develop a sense of where they were from the knowledge of where they were not. The wood-pile, marked in both cases by 'decay', serves as both a sort of commemorial mound to 'some former possessor of the soil', and a reminder of the labour, the 'tasks', involved in the settling and domesticating (fuel essential for the 'useful fireplace' – the home) of the land. The 'axe' is the prime symbol of the pioneer and the advancing frontier. As an intentional object – in both cases the wood has been 'cut' and 'piled up square' – the wood-pile is a sign of culture in the wilderness; but a sign already mouldering away and being reclaimed by, reabsorbed into, nature, suggesting, a little, the pathos, transience, and ephemerality of the residual testimonies to the presence of human effort and constructive work. The wood-piles are inexplicably abandoned, suggesting that death – or distraction – always comes too soon; that man is everywhere outlasted by the poignant traces of his labour, leaving sundry edifices which he can no longer either tend or use. And with the 'softened outline' of the 'green mound', the pile is beginning – more specifically in Hawthorne – to resemble a grave. And it is this and all that it implies – call it mortality, call it mutability – which Coverdale has to face and his text, if it can, absorb. ET IN ARCADIA EGO.

In a much earlier scene, talking, somewhat banteringly, to Hollingsworth about the future of their new Community, Coverdale says:

I shall never feel as if this were a real, practical, as well as poetical system of human life, until someone has sanctified it by death . . . Let us choose the rudest, roughest, most uncultivatable spot, for Death's garden-ground; and Death shall teach us to beautify it, grave by grave. By our sweet, calm way of dying, and the airy elegance out of which we will shape our funeral rites, and the cheerful allegories which we will model into tombstones, the final scene shall lose its terrors . . .

And more in the same vein. His tone as always tends uncontrollably towards the facetious, so that, even if he wants to take something seriously, by the time he has finished talking about it he has either undermined, ridiculed, banalised, or vaporised it. In this scene, it is quite understandable that the grim, humourless Hollingsworth is irritated by what he feels is Coverdale's 'nonsense'. I will come to Coverdale and his hapless, or worse, errancies of tone. Here I just want to stress that, although the tone of this speech is all wrong, the content is half right. What he touches on banteringly, another American poet, Louis Simpson, formulates with more appropriate seriousness in the last stanza of his poem 'To the Western World' (1955):

> The treasures of Cathay were never found.
> In this America, this wilderness
> Where the axe echoes with a lonely sound,
> The generations labor to possess
> And grave by grave we civilize the ground.[4]

The treasures of Cathay, the fields of Arcadia, the phalansteries of Utopia – alike, never found – or founded. Though some people may have been the better for the searching. Maybe better, and then again maybe worse. That is a part of what this book is about. What Coverdale has to confront – and not as a matter for banter, or light literary conceits, or the pale, etiolated images of a Puvis de Chavannes – is that, yes, it *is* 'grave by grave' (his phrase as well as Simpson's) that we civilise the ground; that *death* is 'the real'; and that only by properly assimilating that will he – will we – find the real in anything else. By the end, of course, Blithedale has its grave. It contains the body of Zenobia, the figure accorded most physical, sexual, reality by Coverdale's account. Judging by the concluding chapter which follows her burial, she effectively, for Coverdale, takes 'the real' into the grave with her.

In Coverdale's story his primary involvement – if that is the word for his self-retentive, self-protective proximities to other people – is with Hollingsworth, Zenobia, and Priscilla. But he has a crucial conversation with the shadowy figure of Old Moodie, who is indeed the first person who speaks to Coverdale (with a request which Coverdale characteristically shrinks from complying with). The shadowy Moodie turns out to be the father, by different mothers (one brilliant and voluptuous, the other a 'poor phantom') of the allegorically opposed half-sisters, Zenobia and Priscilla. Late in the book, in a saloon (and I shall return to this setting), Moodie tells Coverdale his life story, which Coverdale then reconstitutes and writes down, with his customary speculative largesse ('my pen has perhaps allowed itself a trifle of romantic and legendary license'). For the purposes of his story – one might, following Melville's use of the phrase, term it an 'inside narrative' – Coverdale rebaptises Moodie and mystifies his origin. 'Five-and-twenty years ago . . . there dwelt, in one of the middle states, a man whom we shall call Fauntleroy.' Coverdale has a rather coy way with names which I shall look at later, but here I want to pause on the pseudonym – or is it the true name *behind* the name? (But then what *is* a *true* name?) – he has chosen.

And first I want to point to an important word he deploys on just two occasions. After recounting Zenobia's passionate words spoken at Eliot's Pulpit, Coverdale wonders if they amounted to no more than a 'stage declamation'. 'Were they formed of a material lighter than common air? Or, supposing them to bear *sterling* weight, was it not a perilous and dreadful wrong, which she was meditating towards herself and Hollingsworth?' (my italics). After they have recovered the corpse of Zenobia, rigid in an attitude of prayer but now disfigured and mutilated, Coverdale writes: 'A reflection occurs to me, that will show ludicrously, I doubt not, on my page, but must come in, for its *sterling* truth' (my italics). The reflection is that if she could have foreseen what a horrid spectacle she would present when recovered from the river, she would no more have done it than she would have appeared in public wearing a badly fitting garment – that is to say, that she was 'not quite simple in her death', that it contained 'some tint of Arcadian affectation'; acting, or counterfeiting, to the end we might say. 'Sterling' is of course the legal tender of what Hawthorne referred to as 'Our Old Home' (1863), and by extension came to be an epithet meaning 'authentic'. In using the word in these two contexts, Coverdale implicitly raises the problem of authenticity of both spoken and written words. How can we know if *any* words are, as it were, good currency, reliable 'scrip(t)'?

Now, 'Fauntleroy', it appeared, committed a crime which led him to flee to New England and live the shady, shadowy life of Old Moodie. And this crime 'was just the sort of crime, growing out of its artificial state, which society (unless it should change its entire constitution for this man's unworthy state) neither could nor ought to pardon. More safely might it pardon murder.' This heinous crime would seem to be literally unspeakable, or unwritable, since Coverdale never names it. But, since the appearance of an article by Charles Swann,[5] there can be no doubt that the crime was forgery. Henry Fauntleroy (1785–1824), a London banker who was also a spendthrift forger, became what one writer described as 'the prototypal forger for his contemporaries'. He was caught and executed, though there was a rumour that he had mysteriously escaped death (by inserting a silver tube in his throat to avoid strangulation) and gone abroad, where he lived for many years. All this was reported at length in the *Gentleman's Magazine*, which we know Hawthorne read (he was in any case an avid reader of newspaper accounts of criminal cases), and it is marvellously to his purpose. By seeming to pluck a pseudonym out of the air at random and actually fastening on the – at the time well-known – name of a notorious English forger, Coverdale releases suggestive resonances which permeate the whole book he is writing.

The worryingly close similarity between writing fiction (or coining images) and counterfeiting the currency on which society depends (which is why the crime was regarded as more socially undermining than murder since it abuses the trust – ruins by falsifying and thus depreciating the 'value' – which enables social exchange and coherence) has often occurred to artists. What is a 'true' copy? How can you tell the difference between 'forging' the uncreated conscience of your race, and the kind of forgery the police hunt down? You can, of course, but to a certain kind of writer it can seem that, at a certain level, both 'forgers' work by putting falsities/fictions into circulation. The matter has certainly worried more than one American writer (cf. *The Recognitions* by William Gaddis). But Hawthorne is effectively doing more than throw ironic light on the possible dubiety of his own writerly activity. Fauntleroy is a quintessentially European name, literally containing a recognition of that royalty (*le roi*) which America had violently repudiated in the process of asserting its own identity. Perhaps if Henry Fauntleroy *had* somehow escaped and come to live abroad – and where more obvious than America for his long declining years (he was thirty-nine when he was 'executed' and would have been fifty-six when the Blithedalers were forgathering)? – he would indeed be indistinguishable from Old Moodie. And *that* might suggest that, in addition to all the obvious beliefs and practices – in religion, law, literature – which America had inherited, or transplanted, from Our Old Home, it had latterly received a more sinister and unforeseen bequest – fakery. Dissimulation on an unknowably large scale. Or perhaps America replicated the English Fauntleroy with its own version engendered in those vague 'middle states'. Either way, Mr Fauntleroy has bequeathed to society, in the form of his children, not the customary patriarchal law and authority, but something catastrophically opposite – the seeds of paternal inauthenticity. Priscilla is more a void than a value (victim, too, perhaps): that she should 'triumph' or at least be the main survivor of the Blithedale experiment is by no means an unequivocally felicitous conclusion. While Zenobia, with her 'uncomfortable surplus of vitality', seemed to be the force which helped to drive Blithedale, Lady of the Revels, Queen of Arcadia. Was she all counterfeit? Was there *no* 'sterling' there? If so, the implications do not bear too much pondering – for that way lies the sort of scepticism, or distrust, which terminates in the nihilism of Billy Budd's posthumous rhetorical question – 'aren't it all a sham?'[6] This is the other end – or is it the other side? – of the quest for the Real.

All this goes some way to explaining Coverdale's, and the book's, obsession with veils and veilings of all kinds. But before addressing that, I want to revert to Coverdale's slightly teasing, slightly uncomfortable, way with 'names'. We may start with a short, jocular exchange between Coverdale and Old Moodie before he settles down to hear the life story or confessional reminiscences of the great forger – not that he is going to name *that* – to be recounted by, call him Fauntleroy, in the local saloon. A bottle of claret arrives. ' "It should be good wine," I remarked, "if it have any right to its label." "You cannot suppose, sir," said Moodie, with a sigh, "that a poor old fellow, like me, knows any difference in wines." ' Nor any differencies in currencies, in view of the story he is about to tell. More interesting is Coverdale's, perhaps habitual, suspicion. Does anything – anyone – have a 'right to its label'? What is it – what could it be – to have a *right* to a label? Take 'Zenobia'. What is the relationship between that 'label' and the intoxicatingly full-bodied wine of a woman who pours through these pages?

In chapter II Coverdale says, or writes, to us, concerning 'Zenobia':

This (as the reader, if at all acquainted with our literary biography, need scarcely be told) was not her real name. She had assumed it, in the first instance, as her magazine signature; and as it accorded well with something imperial which her friends attributed to this lady's figure and deportment, they, half-laughingly, adopted it in their familiar intercourse with her. She took the appellation in good part, and even encouraged its constant use . . .

Real name? Where might we find that? Not in this book, certainly. When Westervelt comes to Blithedale seeking information concerning 'Zenobia', Coverdale somewhat ineffectually hedges by replying: '"That is her name in literature . . . a name, too, which possibly she may permit her private friends to know and address her by; – but not one which they feel at liberty to recognise, when used of her, personally, by a stranger or casual acquaintance."' As it transpires, Westervelt is no stranger or casual acquaintance – though whether he is/was Zenobia's lover or husband is never named, or, perhaps we should say, spelled out – and here he replies, '"I am willing to know her by any cognomen that you may suggest."' Appellation, cognomen – what is the real name for a 'name'? Disliking Westervelt and wishing to get rid of him, Coverdale writes: 'I mentioned Zenobia's real name.' Mentions it to Westervelt, but never to us. You could say that Zenobia's real name in real life was Margaret Fuller and that Hawthorne, in his characteristically enigmatic way, is effectively saying: he who runs may read. But in terms of the novel as novel, that simply will not do. Coverdale as narrator is showing us that he is keeping something back – covering it indeed – leaving us with a very uncertain sense of the relationship, in his story, between labels and bottles, people and names. Call him Fauntleroy: call her Zenobia. This, after a famous neighbour had started a great novel: 'Call me Ishmael.' Westervelt admits to Coverdale that '"my business is private, personal, and somewhat peculiar"'. I think Coverdale, as writer, could say the same.

But the most interesting play with names occurs when a committee is formed 'for providing our infant Community with an appropriate name'. It is a more revealing moment than covering Coverdale lets on.

Blithedale was neither good nor bad. We should have resumed the old Indian name of the premises, had it possessed the oil-and-honey flow which the aborigines were so often happy in communicating to their local appellations; but it chanced to be a harsh, ill-connected, and interminable word, which seemed to fill the mouth with a mixture of very stiff clay and very crumbly pebbles. Zenobia suggested 'Sunny Glimpse' . . . too fine and sentimental a name . . . I ventured to whisper 'Utopia', which, however, was unanimously scouted down . . . Some were for calling our institution 'The Oasis', . . . others insisted on a proviso for reconsidering the matter, at a twelvemonth's end; when a final decision might be had, whether to name it 'The Oasis', or 'Saharah'. So, at last, finding it impracticable to hammer out anything better, we resolved that the spot should still be Blithedale, as being of good augury enough.

The alternatives are anodyne and cosy enough – the sort of names you could doubtless see on some middle-class homes and, in due course, on motels. But I wonder what that harsh and interminable 'old Indian name' was, the name given to the place by the, after all, ab-original inhabitants? That surely might be a label which, as it were, had a right to its bottle. Here we must 'go behind' a little, an activity particularly justified by this book, as I hope to show.

John Eliot, the famous apostle to the Indians and a leading founding Puritan, is a very important name in the book; more of that later. Crucially, he undertook to learn the language of the Indians, the better to preach to them. In *Magnalia Christi Americana* – almost a founding volume for America and one which not only Hawthorne but many of his readers would have known – Cotton Mather wrote the 'Life of John Eliot' and in particular animadverted on the great difficulties involved in mastering the Indian language:

but if their *Alphabet* be *short*, I am sure the *Words* composed of it are long enough to tire the Patience of any Scholar in the World; they are *Sesquipedalia Verba*, of which their *Lingua* is composed; one would think, they had been growing ever since *Babel*, unto the Dimensions to which they are now extended. For instance, if my Reader will count how many Letters there are in this one Word, *Nummatchekodtantamooonganunnonash*, when he has done, for his Reward I'll tell him, it signifies no more in *English*, than *our Lusts*, and if I were to translate, *our Loves*; it must be nothing shorter than *Noowomantammooon-kanunonnash*. Or, to give my Reader a longer Word than either of these, *Kummogkodonattoottummooetiteaongannunnonash*, is in English, *Our Question*: But I pray, Sir, count the Letters! . . . This tedious Language our *Eliot* (the Anagram of whose Name was TOILE) quickly became a Master of . . .[7]

Hellish difficult: why, says Mather, I tried it out on the *Daemons* of a possessed woman, and, although they had no trouble with Greek and Hebrew, they just could not cope with Indian. (Another justification, perhaps, for eliminating these tedious Lewis Carrolls of the forest.) Now perhaps the 'real name' of Blithedale was just such an 'ill-connected and interminable word' as the ones cited by Cotton Mather. Somewhat too harsh for the genteel New Englanders. Better change the label – something more soft and sweet. Something, too, which gets rid of the grating (and potentially embarrassing – whose Utopia was this?) otherness and Indianness of the original name. As a result, somehow the wrong book is being written. As a matter of fact, 'Our Lusts, Our Loves, Our Question' would have been no bad name for the site of this story, no bad title for the novel itself. I am suggesting, quite improperly, that the book we *should* have would have been *The History of Nummatchekodtantamooonganunnonash, Noowomantammooonkanunonnash, and Kummogkodonattoottummooetiteaongannunnonash* by Nathaniel Hawthorne. Instead we have *The Blithedale Romance* by Miles Coverdale – a sentimental over-writing of an earlier, uglier, and harsher reality which is unpronounceable, unhandlable, unwritable. The Devil himself would not understand it. 'Blithedale' is a cover: indeed it is a 'Coverdale' – the narrator is peculiarly well named.

Names then, or names as Coverdale and some of his characters use them, are veils (and I have added the suggestion that the book itself is a kind of veil). An article by Frank Davidson scrupulously notes the prolific references to veils and veilings throughout the novel. It has to be said, it would be hard *not* to notice them. The novel opens with a description of 'the wonderful exhibition of the Veiled Lady', and, in one way or another, the whole novel is a 'veiled exhibition'. In Frank Davidson's words, 'Almost everything in the romance except "the naked exposure" in Westervelt "of something that ought not to be left prominent" is partially hidden or totally obscured by a veiling medium or mask.'[8] Literal veils, false names, mysterious and mystified life histories (the whole Old Moodie/Fauntleroy family has an unpenetrated and perhaps impenetrable past – perhaps, in this, like America itself), and a general disposition towards 'screening' of all kinds – these are the hallmarks of the book. Old Moodie himself is, fittingly enough, particularly and literally self-effacing, as one might say – 'He had a queer appearance of hiding himself behind the patch on his left eye'; 'his upper part was mostly hidden behind the shrubbery'; in the tavern Coverdale 'recognized his hand and arm, protruding from behind a screen' – but his is only the most extreme case of a general tendency to lead a masked life.

The case of Westervelt is interesting. One should note that the characters seem to have differing ontological statuses – more real and less real in differing ways – and he is at once the most masked and the most exposed. Like his teeth, the man is *manifestly* 'a sham' – he is all 'humbug'; his face might be 'removeable like a mask'; there is 'nothing genuine about him', his visage is like 'polished steel' (reminding me of a Faulkner character whose face has 'the depthless brutality of stamped tin'). He leaves the tale as he enters it – mysteriously, independently, his power unassailed. Coverdale, in one of his frequent less than charitable moods, dismisses him, hoping that Heaven will 'annihilate him. He was altogether earthy, worldly, made for time and its gross objects, and incapable . . . of so much as one spiritual idea'. That is all very well, except that there is precious little 'idealism' in the book that is not badly compromised by the end. In all his fakery and falsity there is, nevertheless, that 'naked exposure of something that ought not to be left prominent' – unlike the river with its 'broad, black inscrutable depth, keeping its secrets from the eye of man'.

Coverdale does not attempt to put a name to that naked something Westervelt leaves indecently showing (he would rather cover than name), but we can perhaps suggest it is his shameless appetite and will-to-power. Although Hollingsworth rescues Priscilla from him, Westervelt – on his own terms – is the most powerful figure in the book. Of the male figures, it is only he, so we are allowed to gather, who has possessed Zenobia sexually. Man of mask he may be, but, looked at from one point of view, there is more *to* him than to the narrator. Coverdale's description of Christ, as 'One, who merely veiled himself in mortal and masculine shape, but was, in truth, divine', suggests that corporeality, sheer or mere physicality, is the unreal for Coverdale, an orthodox enough Transcendentalist tenet. Yet he is strangely drawn to the farm's pigs, 'involved, and almost stifled, and buried alive, in their own corporeal substance', and ponders 'the ponderous and fat satisfaction of their existence'. Hawthorne particularly disliked fat on women (you should be allowed to cut it off, he, let us hope jocularly, maintained), and perhaps some of his ambivalence to flesh and fleshliness has got into Coverdale, but it is hard to find in the book any very deep conviction of the existence of any divine, spiritual, or ideal realm of Reality. Perhaps the corporeal veil is all we have got – not a thought for Coverdale, or even Hawthorne, to be easy with. Zenobia's farewell declaration concludes: ' "When you next hear of Zenobia, her face will be behind the black veil." ' In the event it will be the black veil of the river, which now has another secret to keep.

More than anything else, veils ask to be looked behind, and Coverdale, who takes a 'back-room' in the hotel in town, makes a speciality of looking behind. Literally.

Bewitching to my fancy are all those nooks and crannies, where Nature, like a stray partridge, hides her head among the long-established haunts of men! It is likewise to be remarked, as a general rule, that there is far more of the picturesque, more truth to native and characteristic tendencies, and vastly greater suggestiveness, in the back view of a residence, whether in town or country, than in its front. The latter is always artificial; it is meant for the world's eye, and is therefore a veil and a concealment. Realities keep in the rear, and put forward an advance-guard of show and humbug.

Realities keep in the rear. Coverdale is interested (and excited by) 'posterior aspects' – in every sense, we may say. He announces his predilection – unambiguously enough we might feel – for getting acquainted with 'the backside of the universe'. His curiosity, not least his sexual curiosity, is high and easily inflamed. In his last recorded comment on Hawthorne (in a letter of 1904) Henry James summed up what he admired about Hawthorne with apt words: he saw 'the interest *behind* the interest'.[9] In an essay of 1896 he had spelt it out at greater length:

It was a question of looking behind and beneath for the suggestive idea, the artistic motive ... This ingenuity grew alert and irrepressible as it manoeuvred for the back view and turned up the under side of common aspects, – the laws secretly broken, the impulses secretly felt, the hidden passions, the double lives, the dark corners, the closed rooms, the skeletons in the cupboard and at the feast.[10]

'Behind and beneath' became one of James's favourite phrases as he grew more and more fascinated with 'the things *behind*', and one of the things behind was, awesomely and sometimes seemingly ubiquitously, the sexual.

Realities keep in the rear. All Coverdale's compulsive 'looking behind' – literally of houses, speculatively of people, their motives, their pasts, their relationships – suggests that, effete voyeur though he himself is, he has more than half a notion that he might find 'the real' in the sexual. Though, being the man he is, he is certainly not going to write like D. H. Lawrence! But he likes to imagine Zenobia naked and brood lasciviously on her past: ' "Zenobia is a wife! Zenobia has lived, and loved! There is no folded petal, no latent dewdrop, in this perfectly developed rose." ' And, talking of petals and roses, what is one to make of such a passage as the following, describing Priscilla's silk purses:

Their peculiar excellence, besides the great delicacy and beauty of the manufacture, lay in the almost impossibility that any uninitiated person should discover the aperture; although, to a practised touch, they would open as wide as charity or prodigality might wish. I wondered if it were not a symbol of Priscilla's own mystery.

One can only wonder at the sort of tacit cultural collusion which could maintain that no possibility of any *double entendre* and thus nothing remotely lubricious should attach to such writing, while being constantly ready to recoil in real or simulated horror if matters pertaining to sexual actualities were explicitly named. Coverdale, self-cosseting bachelor that he is, is not a passionate man, but he is a mighty prurient one; he is also a shameless fetishist: after Zenobia's corpse is recovered, he eagerly takes one of her shoes and has 'kept it ever since'. The original Coverdale was the first translator of the Bible, in a version reputedly pretty inaccurate but with some sudden arresting felicities. The same could be said of this Coverdale book, though what he translates is Fourier (likewise inaccurately if the one example we are given is anything to go by). Fourierism at that time was a codeword for free love and a byword for promiscuity – such as Coverdale more than hints obtained at Blithedale. (More than fifty Fourierist communities sprang up in America between 1840 and 1860, not all, of course, emphasising the need for the multiple sexual servicing of their members.) He admits to a certain male grossness of imagination, and, while we may choose not to place much credence on the concluding line of the book in which he claims that he was in love with Priscilla all along (a line opportunistically added by Hawthorne the day he dispatched the manuscript), we can feel fairly sure that he would not be above fantasising about fingering and opening the aperture to Priscilla's purse, running more to prodigality than to charity perhaps.

When he is outlining what they hoped to erect and achieve at Blithedale, Coverdale undermines the formulaic and programmatic optimism of their original intentions and expectations with an unusual metaphor.

Altogether, by projecting our minds outward, we had imparted a show of novelty to existence, and contemplated it as hopefully as if the soil, beneath our feet, had not been fathom-deep with the dust of deluded generations, on every one of which, as on ourselves, the world had imposed itself as a hitherto unwedded bride.

It is, characteristically, an erotic image; but it reveals much more than that. In an important essay Lauren Berlant glosses the passage as follows:

This 'people', according to Coverdale, sees the present moment as a hopeful fore-gleam of a future luminescence. But the scene of utopian fantasy is founded on the repression of histories that would, presumably, challenge the 'fact' of our present existence: Coverdale notes that his fellow workers act as if they are the land's first tillers and, by association, the nation's first utopians. But the community's historical amnesia with respect to the utopian projects that have preceded it reveals that American history has never been written or even thought. It has only been repressed, buried by new 'dirt', new stories. America, in this view, is always distinctively post-Utopian, but has never 'known' it.[11]

The image of the 'unwedded bride' suggests that Utopian dreams, hopes, and desires are dependent on, perhaps a function of, 'virginity' in every sense.

But when historical and sexual knowledge comes, when 'the world had imposed itself' upon us, we lose the clarity of utopian, libidinal perfection. The postvirginal bride who weds her demystifying knowledge to us is simultaneously the source of our historical consciousness, our historical amnesia, and our personal nostalgia for those moments before her 'knowledge' atomized our whole bodies and destroyed our utopian collective dreams.[12]

A striking example of such historical amnesia is given by Coverdale himself when Hollingsworth, describing his 'visionary edifice' for the reform of criminals, says: '"But I offer my edifice as a spectacle to the world . . . that it may take example and build many another like it. Therefore I mean to set it on the open hill-side."' The echo of John Winthrop's 'city on a hill' speech – a sort of foundational American declaration – could hardly be clearer. But it is lost on Coverdale. 'Twist these words how I might, they offered no very satisfactory import.' If he can forget *that*, what may not an American writer forget? And yet Coverdale sees the Blithedale venture as both a recapitulation and an extension of the first Puritan errand into the wilderness, and he and his friends as 'the descendants of the Pilgrims, whose high enterprise, as we sometimes flattered ourselves, we had taken up, and were carrying it onward and aloft, to a point which they never dreamed of attaining'. One may wonder if he has that original 'high enterprise' very clearly in his mind – and what it entailed for the original inhabitants.

This is the point of one of the slyest barbs, which Hawthorne releases through Coverdale when he describes the site of Eliot's Pulpit: 'as wild a tract of woodland as the great-great-great-great grandson of one of Eliot's Indians (had any such posterity been in existence) could have desired, for the site and shelter of his wigwam'. As here quite literally, the Indians have everywhere been 'bracketed out' of American history. This is why the name of John Eliot is important in the book. He was a figure who, as it were, tried to bracket the Indian *in* –

even while his contemporaries continued the work of dispossession. He set up 'praying towns' for numbers of Indians, and there is no reason to doubt the sincerity of his desire to transform, reclaim by converting, the manifestly un-Elect Indians. Coverdale 'romanticises' Eliot – that, after all, is what he is writing: 'I used to see the holy Apostle of the Indians, with the sunlight flickering down upon him through the leaves, and glorifying his figure as with the half-perceptible glow of a trans-figuration.' If he had historicised Eliot, Coverdale might have brought to mind, and written in, the fact that Eliot created in his Christianised Indians vulnerable hybrids who could never survive. They were wiped out in King Philip's War (1673–5), not least because they were not yet fully trusted by the whites, and no longer trusted by the Indians. This must be marked up as another Utopian project which ended in dis-astrous failure. Or rather, not marked up but left out. Coverdale takes (makes) the Romance – the saint in the wilderness – and forgets the history – the subsequent victims. Eliot trying to convert his Indians is clearly replicated in some way by Hollingsworth dedicated to reforming his criminals, another too fanatical attempt to assimilate the marginalised, or – to use a phrase of Bernard Schlurick – 'le verrouillage de l'autre dans le même' (the locking up of the other in the same).[13] It is another massive failure. No criminals are reclaimed; instead Hollingsworth feels he has been criminalised by causing Zenobia's suicide.

I am not, in this essay, going to discuss the characters and charac-terisation. Henry James's summary in his essay of 1896 can hardly be bettered:

The idea that he most tangibly presents is that of the unconscious way in which the search for the common good may cover a hundred interested impulses and personal motives; the suggestion that such a company could only be bound together more by its delusions, its mutual suspicions and frictions, than by any successful surrender of the self.[14]

Psychologically, Hawthorne was clearly still interested in how relation-ships could in fact be power struggles, contests of adverse wills, as he dramatised most clearly in chapter XIII of *The House of the Seven Gables*, 'Alice Pyncheon', in which Matthew Maule literally mesmerises the proud Alice in an agonistic contest of the eyes. 'She instinctively knew, it may be, that some sinister or evil potency was now striving to pass her barriers; nor would she decline the contest. So Alice put woman's might against man's might; a match not often equal on the part of the woman.' Indeed not. Matthew achieves total dominion, domination, saying to himself, ' "She is mine! . . . Mine, by the right of the strongest spirit."' Hawthorne had a strikingly adversarial and appropriative sense of human relationships – 'sharkish', Melville might have said – and this is again in evidence in the struggles between Hollingsworth and Zenobia, Hollingsworth and Coverdale, and the struggles over Priscilla. All this is clear enough in the book. But a word should be said about one of its central concerns – reform.

'In the history of the world the doctrine of Reform had never such scope as at the present hour' – thus Emerson in 1841 in 'Man the Reformer'.[15] There was an extraordinary proliferation, explosion indeed, of reform literature and movements in antebellum America. In his very interesting work, *Beneath the American Renaissance*, David Reynolds describes this vast literature and suggests very plausibly how it affected the now-regarded major writers. Initially this reform literature was conventional:

As time passed, however, there arose a strong subversive element, seen in a succession of vociferous reformers whose loudly announced goal was to stamp out various behavioral sins or social iniquities – intemperance, licentiousness, urban poverty, chattel and wage slavery, poor prison conditions, and so forth – but who described vice in such lurid detail that they were branded as dangerously immoral and sacrilegious. The *immoral* or *dark reformers*, as I call them, used didactic rhetoric as a protective shield for highly unconventional explorations of tabooed psychological and spiritual areas ... for both Hawthorne and Melville contemporary reform devices and themes provided an inroad toward literary ambiguity.[16]

'The dark reformers are largely responsible for transforming a culture of morality into a culture of ambiguity.'[17] The flood of this literature would seem to have had a destabilising effect on the old certainties, even the old ontologies. Reynolds quotes from *The Quaker City* by George Lippard (1845), in which a character, bewildered by the instabilities and amoralities surrounding him, complains: '"Every thing fleeting and nothing stable, everything shifting and changing, and nothing substantial!"' Reynolds comments: 'each of the major authors at one time or another expressed puzzlement and terror over the relativism implied by this fluid reform environment'.[18]

As we have seen at the start, this is certainly true of Coverdale, and he, of course, is surrounded by – up to his neck (though not his heart) in – reform movements of all kinds: prison reform, Associationism, temperance, feminism, spiritualism, mesmerism. Perhaps he does not directly confront the implication of his own writing (and non-writing) – namely that you cannot hope, and perhaps should hardly seek, to build a Utopia on a land stained by genocide and already replete with the dust of earlier failures. There is much talk of 'systems' in the book – throwing off old systems, devising new ones – but Coverdale finally finds that this talk is moving him towards a kind of vertigo of unreality.

I was beginning to lose the sense of what kind of world it was, among innumerable schemes of what it might or ought to be. It was impossible, situated as we were, not to imbibe the idea that everything in nature and human existence was fluid, or fast becoming so; that the crust of the Earth, in many places, was broken, and its whole surface portentously upheaving; that it was a day of crisis, and that we ourselves were in the critical vortex. Our great globe floated in the atmosphere of infinite space like an unsubstantial bubble. No sagacious man will long retain his sagacity, if he lives exclusively among reformers and progressive people, without periodically returning into a settled system of things, to correct himself by a new observation from that old stand-point.

After a quick good-bye to the pigs, he heads for town and some restabilising talk with a few Cambridge conservatives. So we may return to our opening question. What *is* Hawthorne doing with – through – Miles Coverdale?

From the start, commentators on the book have noted and stressed that, whatever else he is, Coverdale is pre-eminently an observer.

Coverdale is a picture of the contemplative, observant, analytic nature, nursing its fancies, and yet, thanks to an element of strong good sense, not bringing them up to be spoiled children; having little at stake in life, at any given moment, and yet indulging, in imagination, in a good many adventures; a portrait of a man, in a word, whose passions are slender, whose imagination is active, and whose happiness lies, not in doing, but in perceiving – half a poet, half a critic, and all a spectator.[19]

Thus Henry James, seeing Coverdale, we might think, in the most generous possible light. Not, perhaps, surprisingly, since his own subsequent work would turn out to be well-populated with just such slender-passioned imaginative spectators as he here describes. Writing nearly one hundred years later, Richard Poirier is more diagnostic and critical:

one consequence of an idealism gone sour can be the self-absorbed fastidiousness of a character like Coverdale . . . A somewhat sickly, somewhat even masturbatory quality in Coverdale's self-regarding retreat is evident even in the images describing it. It is as if he were retreating into a state not of heightened consciousness but of death . . . Hawthorne is here showing us the transformations of a sort of Emersonian man into a Dandy . . . a man incapable of human fellowship.[20]

James thought that Hawthorne had put himself into Coverdale ('Miles Coverdale is evidently as much Hawthorne as he is any one else in particular'), but that is necessarily imponderable. What is clear is that Hawthorne is attempting a kind of self-revelatory portrait of an American artist at a particular, and particularly problematic, moment of time – rather, artist *manqué*, just as Coverdale is also a lover *manqué*, idealist *manqué*, Utopianist *manqué*, communalist *manqué*, farmer *manqué*, citizen both of country and world *manqué*, arguably human *manqué* who comes to rest in metaphorical sillabubs and actual sherry-cobblers. After diaries of nobodies and confessions of superfluous men, not to mention notes from underground and men without qualities, we are quite familiar with self-marginalising, self-deprecating, even self-immolating narrators. But there is no narrator like him in earlier American literature (or in English, come to that) and I just want to ponder some of the possible implications of Hawthorne's handing over the telling of his novel to such a figure.

He is, we may say, bricked-in, bricked-up, from the start: 'a lodger – like myself – in one of the midmost houses of a brick-block; each house partaking of the warmth of all the rest'. Since he is a 'frosty bachelor', this generalised, anonymous communal warmth is no doubt welcome to him, and I shall return to his ambiguous need for heat. Here I want to note that Coverdale is in fact a generic 'lodger'. He is most at home in apartments, hotel rooms, taverns – places of transience. Even at Blithedale, for all his simulated commitment, he was only ever, really, passing through. He has a catlike knack of making himself comfortable, particularly in his own apartment, but he is truly at home nowhere. Taking the word with its broadest implications, the 'lodger' as failed artist, or the failed artist as 'lodger', was a new figure for Hawthorne to have introduced into American literature. And I think it has something to do with the spread of the 'brick-block' – let us call it the suburbanisation of America. I take the word from a very important sentence in the novel. It concerns the audience at the village Lyceum-hall where the (melo-)drama of the 'Veiled Lady' is to be enacted. Coverdale lists the varied occupations of this audience – farmers, shopkeepers, lawyers, students, and so on – and comments: 'all looking rather suburban than rural. In these days, there is absolutely no rusticity, except when the actual labor of the soil leaves its earth-mould on the person.' It was in quest of some such absolute 'rusticity' that Coverdale went to Blithedale, even to the extent of indeed getting 'earth-mould' on his person. And what he discovered is that it cannot be done. The attempt is *bound* to seem affected, factitious. The suburban lodger can never, despite or perhaps because of his sentimental pastoral nostalgia, reachieve or rediscover any absolute 'rusticity' – always supposing, of course, that there ever was such a thing. Suburban, not urban – suburbia as that indeterminate, homogenising area between the true town and the real country, which seeks to combine the comforts and amenities of the one with the beauties and felicities of the other, arguably, in the process, losing contact with the differing, dynamic energies of both. Hawthorne was astute enough to see that it was becoming increasingly difficult to avoid – ontologically, let us say – some variant of the suburban condition. Lodgers – in a sense – all, or most, of us.

This is why Coverdale's tone is so uncertain, veering always towards self-defeating facetiousness. He says he might join an Exploring Expedition up the Nile, or go and fight for Kossuth in Hungary, but just to formulate the notional possibilities is to become aware of their absurd unrealisability. 'Suburbanised' self-consciousness seems to corrode in advance any possibility of significant action and commitment. (In this, Coverdale is remarkably similar to the narrator figures of the poetry of Arthur Hugh Clough.) He tries to throw himself into Blithedale, and even seems to undergo some temporary re-birth there, but very soon he finds that he has, as it were, come out on the other side, floundering among failed hyperboles, bitter scepticism, and bathetic self-ridicule. But *is* there a right tone for Blithedale? Is it not from the start an impossible and doomed project? Economically – 'I very soon became sensible, that, as regarded society at large, we stood in a position of new hostility, rather than new brotherhood' – and socially; it seems soon to disintegrate into the centrifugality of unaligned power-plays – it is something of a disaster. Everybody is, more or less, posing (leaving aside Priscilla, who has something of an object status) and at least Coverdale *knows* he is posing. The motives of some of the other leading figures at Blithedale would not stand much scrutiny – particularly Hollingsworth's – and we may want to look again at Coverdale's motives, for at least he seems to have the virtue, even if it has curiously deleterious effects, of refusing to succumb to the lures of self-deception. At Blithedale and after, he is, indeed, the less – the least – deceived.

One thing he is not is an 'unreliable narrator', if by that we mean a narrator who, we somehow gather, is seeking to deceive the reader and probably him or her self, by disingenuousness, editing out, reformulation, or whatever (there are distinct traces of this in the narrative account of Gatsby by Nick Carraway, who otherwise is the American narrator who bears the greatest resemblance to Coverdale). Coverdale readily admits, when he does not positively flaunt the fact, that he has endless recourse to supplementation, speculation, fabrication, imagination, fantasy – the lot, you might say. 'I hardly could make out an intelligible sentence, on either side. What I seem to remember, I yet suspect may have been patched together by my fancy, in brooding over the matter, afterwards' – this is a characteristic admission. He is usually too far away in some sense or another – up the tree of his 'hermitage', in a distant hotel room looking through windows over which curtains are suddenly drawn – out of earshot and eyeshot. When he returns to Blithedale, he says: 'Had it been evening, I would have stolen to some lighted window of the old farm-house, and peeped darkling in' – a dark peeper, and a peeper usually in the dark. Such is the darkling voyeur who nevertheless writes – fabricates, forges – a narrative of some considerable length concerning matters of some considerable importance. Of himself, he writes in the last chapter: 'But what, after all, have I to tell? Nothing, nothing, nothing!' But, though there is a feeling of vacancy, vacuity, at the end, Coverdale has in fact told us a great deal about himself – not only his unreconstructible bachelorhood predilections, but the motivations behind his enquiry, his narrative.

That these motivations are deeply ambiguous he is well aware. The start of chapter ix is a long meditation on the unhealthiness of devoting oneself 'too exclusively to the study of individual men and women'. He makes the acute observation that, if we 'put a friend under our microscope, we thereby insulate him from many of his true relations, magnify his peculiarities, inevitably tear him into parts' and Coverdale knows that he may be doing Hollingsworth 'a great wrong by prying into his character . . . *But I could not help it*' (my italics). Blithedale and its inhabitants comprise both a 'problem' which it is his 'business', his 'vocation', to solve and also 'my private theatre', at once an obligation and a pastime. He often makes statements such as 'making my prey of peoples' individualities, as my custom was', and he can recognize that 'That cold tendency, between instinct and intellect, which made me pry with a speculative interest into people's passions and impulses, appeared to have gone far towards unhumanizing my heart.' Peep, pry, prey – these are not very pleasant words, and it becomes something of a question whether Coverdale can justify his uncontrollable speculative curiosity – he cannot help it, and will not – even to himself. When he talks about his 'experiments' on people, and collecting them as 'specimens', he is, morally speaking, in the most dangerous of areas as far as Hawthorne is concerned. Zenobia is quite certain of the culpability of his pursuits. ' "You know not what you do! It is dangerous, sir, believe me, to tamper thus with earnest human passions, out of your own mere idleness, and for your sport." ' She says she will hold him 'responsible' for any future 'mischief' that may follow, on account of his 'interference'. Since the main mischief will be her suicide, the charge is, in effect, a capital one. Again, when he spies on her in town, she indicts him for ' "following up your game, groping for human emotions in the dark corners of the heart" '. But what she calls his 'game', he also claims is his 'duty'. His main defence of his uncontrollable curiosity and obsessive observation is as follows:

For, was mine a mere vulgar curiosity? Zenobia should have known me better than to suppose it. She should have been able to appreciate that quality of the intellect and the heart, which impelled me (often against my own will, and to the detriment of my own comfort) to live in other lives, and to endeavour – by generous sympathies, by delicate intuitions, by taking note of things too slight for record, and by bringing my human spirit into manifold accordance with the companions whom God assigned me – to learn the secret which was hidden even from themselves.

This, we may think, is to make the best possible case for his compulsions – though there is a bit of a sting in the tail with the last words raising the matter of prying and preying. More generally, it reads like an artist's defence or apologia. The key claim is that the inquisitive spectatorial compulsion derives from, or crucially involves, 'generous sympathy'. It is Hawthorne's achievement, through Coverdale, to suggest just how many other derivations may be involved, what an inextricable cluster of motives may be determining the compulsion to watch, speculate, and 'narrativise' – or peep, pry, and prey.

An obvious comparison with Coverdale is the unnamed first-person narrator (*very* rare in Henry James) of *The Sacred Fount*, who is indeed James's Coverdale. To remind you, this narrator is a weekend guest at a country house party and he spends the time quite frantically speculating about the possible sexual relations – and their effects – among the guests. He may be right and he may be, as some think him, 'mad'. Whatever else, he is undoubtedly obsessive. I will run together some of his statements or claims.

My extraordinary interest in my fellow-creatures. I have more than most men. I've never really seen anyone with half so much. That breeds observation, and observation breeds ideas . . .

the best example I can give of the intensity of amusement I had at last
enabled my private madness to yield me . . .

the common fault of minds for which the vision of life is an obsession. The
obsession pays, if one will; but to pay it has to borrow . . .

it justified my indiscreet curiosity; it crowned my underhand process with
beauty . . .

I alone was magnificently and absurdly aware – everyone else was benightedly
out of it . . .

I struck myself as knowing again the joy of the intellectual mastery of things
unamenable, that joy of determining, almost of creating results . . .

Light or darkness, my imagination rides me . . .

The satisfaction of my curiosity is the pacification of my mind . . .

I couldn't save Mrs. Server, and I couldn't save poor Briss; I *could*, however,
guard to the last grain of gold, my precious sense of their loss, their disintegration and their doom.[21]

The key notion here is that of *guardianship* – not of the people involved, since they may be on their unarrestable way to doom and disintegration, but of the observer's *sense* of their experience, which is,
by comparison, pure gold. It is, in Jamesian translation, the translator
Coverdale's claim. It is somewhat akin to the Conradian notion of
art as a constant act of salvage from the perpetual wreckage of life.
To this extent, Coverdale, in all his ambiguity, hesitations, mixed
motives, and uncertainties of tone, embodies a flawed stance and
articulates an equivocal defence which would become increasingly
discernible and audible in the art, and among the artists, of the next
hundred years. He also reveals some of the dangers which attach to
the observer–speculator–empathiser stance.

I had given up my heart and soul to interests that were not mine. What had
I ever had to do with them? And why, being now free, should I take this
thraldom on me, once again? It was both sad and dangerous . . . to be in too
close affinity with the passions, the errors, and misfortunes, of individuals who
stood within a circle of their own, into which, if I stept at all, it must be as an
intruder, and at a peril that I could not estimate.

The artist as 'intruder' is another fine adumbration on Hawthorne's
part. And, while the figures he watches have 'absorbed my life into
themselves', he has also vaporised reality by too much thinking about
it. 'I spent painful hours in recalling these trifles, and rendering them
more misty and unsubstantial than at first, by the quality of speculative
musing, thus kneaded in with them.' Why do it? Why all this kneading
and losing? Why incur such pain and sadness? Why risk such danger?

Because he cannot help it. No wonder James spoke of 'the madness of art'.[22]

In his self-confessed 'frostiness', Coverdale clearly needs something to warm him up. There are many grateful references to actual domestic fires – his own apartment, we may infer, was warm even to fugginess – though even here a note of wariness enters, as when, at Blithedale, he speaks of enjoying 'the warm and radiant luxury of a *somewhat too abundant* fire' (my italics). Sex, not to put too fine a point upon it, would also seem to offer the possibility of thermal consolation, but here again a note of caution enters, as when, in reference of Zenobia, even Westervelt speaks of 'her *uncomfortable surplus* of vitality' (my italics). Just as Coverdale is drawn to, he draws back from, any heat which threatens to lead to excess, to involve him in a surplus abundance. At a, perhaps, higher level, the Transcendentalist excitations and Utopian warmth of Blithedale seem to hold out 'delectable visions of the spiritualization of labor'. But materiality remains coldly resistant. 'The clods of earth, which we so constantly belabored and turned over and over, were never ethereal-ized into thought. Our thoughts, on the contrary, were fast becoming cloddish. Our labor symbolized nothing.' This is only a disillusioning deflation if you feel it must symbolise *something* or else, in Melville's words, be of little worth. In an admittedly very diluted and attenuated way, Coverdale is still a late product of that Puritan–Transcendentalist line of American thought which requires a second order of justifying meaning behind the merely materially visible and palpable. If earth is only 'cloddish', if pigs in the 'fat satisfaction of their existence', have, as it were, got it right – well, says this kind of mentality, what really is it all about? Blithedale might turn out to be a cold comfort farm indeed.

But there is one thing which is guaranteed, and can be relied on, to afford an instant warmth, without involving the difficulties of engaging with other people or bothering about proto-religious convictions – 'a sherry-cobbler'. And, away from Blithedale, Coverdale seldom enters his apartment, or a hotel or tavern, without procuring one. Which makes his reference to himself, in the tavern scene, as 'we temperance people' a singular piece of effrontery. That scene (chapter xxi) again marks an innovation, for I can think of no earlier serious work of American fiction which situates one of its most important scenes in a tavern (temper-ance tracts with sensationalist accounts of the results of drink already abounded, as David Reynolds has documented,[23] but that is not quite the same thing; and T. S. Arthur's influential *Ten Nights in a Barroom* (1854) was still three years away). Coverdale's mild – let us assume –

solitary tippling perhaps only tells us something about his somewhat regressive, oral, narcissistic character – sucking on sillabubs, various. But references to alcohol play an important part in this novel. This is no place to attempt a brief history of alcohol. Suffice it here to remind ourselves that the word itself is Arabic and refers to the paint used to cover the eyelids of the dead – thus having connections with the 'spirit' world – and that in the early years of distilling alcohol in Europe (the fifteenth and sixteenth centuries) it was often closely associated with alchemy, which was involved in the attempts to distil other 'essences', and thus the attempt to produce what we call 'spirits' in some vague way carried overtones of a quest for higher 'spirit-ual' things, even when the searches set themselves in direct opposition.

It is these overtones which Hawthorne exploits. He will deliberately mix realms, as when, for instance, Coverdale imagines Zenobia's death-moment – 'her soul, bubbling out through her lips, may be'. Since we have had not a few references to the bubbles of sparkling wine previously, it is hard to say whether she died a Christian penitent, or went out like a bottle of opened champagne. Quite so, Hawthorne might say: not hard – *impossible*. Twice Coverdale comes across strangely – strangely in New England – luxuriant grape vines. There are grapes in his hermitage 'in abundant clusters of the deepest purple', and they provoke him to almost Dionysiac reveries.

Methinks a wine might be pressed out of them, possessing a passionate zest, and endowed with a new kind of intoxicating quality, attended with such bacchanalian ecstasies as the tamer grapes of Madeira, France, and the Rhine, are inadequate to produce. And I longed to quaff a great goblet of it, at that moment.

Methinks, if he was actually offered any such goblet, he would demur and settle for a sherry-cobbler, not being one actually to capitulate to bacchanalian ecstasies – as opposed to fantasising about them. In the tavern scene Coverdale attempts a cautious and measured defence of wine, if not of spirits: 'Human nature, in my opinion, has a naughty instinct that approves of wine, if not of stronger liquor.' (This sentence was crossed out, possibly by Sophia Hawthorne, so you can see what he was up against, and, in his sly Hawthorne way, writing against.)

There are various paintings on the walls of the tavern, all concerned with representations of food and drink, or drinking, and this permits Coverdale, and doubtless Hawthorne, to meditate on varying modes of representation, from low mimetic realism to a more etherealising kind of art. By situating the book's main discussion of *art* in a *tavern* Hawthorne is again doing something rather novel, or, rather, raising an old problem in a new way. Since the paintings concern food, drink, and 'revelling' (wenching?), we may say that in their varying ways – gross, life-like, noble, ideal, *too* real – they engage with our basic hungers and desires. Which implicitly points to the larger problem: what is, what can be, what should be, the relationship between art and appetite? Do such representations pander to our lowest, most basic and most powerful, wants and desires, courting and inflaming them? Or, by transposing such appetites and objects of desire into another medium, can such representations ideal-ise and spirit-ualise them? Hawthorne would not be one to resolve such a potentially infinite debate: characteristically, inasmuch as he hopes the latter, he fears the former – and vice versa. And, anyway, it is all just 'painted canvas'. But on this occasion, and in this setting, meditations about why men paint lead on to a discussion of why men drink. Art shades into alcohol. And Coverdale has a most interesting subversive thought. There is a fountain in the tavern and the basin or 'lakelet' in which it stands contains several 'gold-fishes'. Coverdale indulges a fancy:

Never before, I imagine, did a company of water-drinkers remain so entirely uncontaminated by the bad example around them, nor could I help wondering that it had not occurred to any freakish inebriate, to empty a glass of liquor into their lakelet. What a delightful idea! Who would not be a fish, if he could inhale jollity with the essential element of his existence!

Is the artist, perhaps, just such a 'freakish inebriate', subtly introducing his potent stimulants into the very cultural air his unsuspecting compatriots breathe? Is it a beneficence ('bringing warmth and cheer'), or a treachery ('intoxicating' people secretly and against their will)? Inasmuch as alcohol is known temporarily to raise the 'spirits', it may, with an ironic turn, be said to 'spiritualise' the consumer. But, despite its undoubted properties of bringing temporary consolation, short-lived feelings of gladness and hope, a brief illusion of restored 'youth and vigour', alcohol is far more likely to bestialise the one who turns to it too often. What clearly worried or preoccupied Hawthorne was the extent to which the questions and considerations raised in those last two sentences might exactly be applied to art.

Very near the end, Coverdale draws a 'moral' from what Hollingsworth's 'ruling passion' has done to him:

It ruins, or is fearfully apt to ruin, the heart; the rich juices of which God never meant should be pressed violently out, and distilled into alcoholic liquor, by an unnatural process; but should render life sweet, bland, and gently beneficent, and sensibly influence other hearts and other lives to the same blessed end.

A nice distinction, particularly in view of all the references to alcoholic drinks which have preceded it. Our heart's juices were not meant to be 'distilled' into strong liquor – certainly an unnatural and, if you will, a violent process; rather they should simply render life 'sweet' and 'bland' – a sherry-cobbler of a life (sherry is fortified but not distilled – a suitably equivocal potion), a sillabub existence. Coverdale is truly not a man of, or for, strong spirit(s) – in *every* sense of the word. But the most crucial play with this word occurs in the closing words of the narrative (excluding here the last short chapter which is a sort of postscript). Coverdale muses that, while Zenobia was alive, 'Nature was proud of her'. Now she is dead, will not 'Nature shed a tear?'.

Ah, no! She adopts the calamity at once into her system, and is just as well pleased, for aught we can see, with the tuft of ranker vegetation that grew out of Zenobia's heart, as with all the beauty which has bequeathed us no earthly representative, except in this crop of weeds. It is because the spirit is inestimable, that the lifeless body is so little valued.

Nature is the system which absorbs *all* the other systems, the provisional, partial, and ephemeral structures and social orderings which man attempts to erect. Nature simply waits for all human signs to fail, and Zenobia, like Conrad's Decoud, is 'swallowed up in the immense indifference of things'.[24] That being so, 'the spirit is inestimable' – but by this end-point of the book what on earth, literally on that cloddish earth, can 'spirit' signify? Throughout, Coverdale has revealed himself to be adrift in a lexicon of failed transcendence; a 'strayed reveller' (in Matthew Arnold's phrase) who has indeed lost his way, his home, his sense of history, his grasp of the real, any access to any ideal realm. That last appearance of the word 'spirit' gestures both pathetically to the final vagueness of a fading religious sense, and bathetically to those always available sherry-cobblers. Inasmuch as he sees him as a true product of America, in his disorientation, amnesia, and general sense of loss – *that* is what Hawthorne is doing with Coverdale. Saying to American society, American history, American religion and culture: *this* is the artist you have produced – intruder, lodger, spy.

As Michael Colacurcio and Richard Brodhead[25] have very well demonstrated, Hawthorne could use his fiction brilliantly to reinsert aspects of the American past which had been, or were being, assiduously left out and erased in the official versions – writing back *on*, as it were, what triumphalist American historiography was busy 'writing *off*'. But in *The Blithedale Romance*, though he does make his point about the occlusion and elimination of the Indians, he shows us an artist forgetting the American past, while being disablingly sceptical about the American present. Always dubious, undecided, ambiguous about the ultimate validity or value of 'fiction' and art in general, Hawthorne has written that uncertainty all through this book. Indeed one could say that he has taken that uncertainty, and a very far-reaching anatomy of it, and made it *into* a book. A curious dividend of this enterprise is that the book has more of the American nineteenth century in it than any other novel I know, and contains innumerable unforeseen and unforeseeable profundities and insights. In all its idiosyncratic inconsistencies of tone, its narrative vacillations and swerves, its inconclusiveness and loose ends, its unpredictable ranging through incongruously contiguous settings and scenes, its collocation of wildly dissimilar characters – in all these features, and indeed because of them, it is, almost despite itself, undoubtedly one of the great American novels. And, in its way, one of the saddest and most pessimistic. For by the end clearly America itself has become for Coverdale 'another spot, and an utter strangeness'. Perhaps for Hawthorne, too. For it was one of Henry James's late and considered characterisations of him that 'He is outside of everything, and an alien everywhere.'[26]

NOTES

1 Robert Frost, *The Poetry of Robert Frost*, ed. Edward Connery Lathem (London: Jonathan Cape, 1976), p. 227.
2 Henry David Thoreau, *Walden* (New York: Library of America, 1985), p. 400.
3 Frost, *Poetry*, pp. 101–2.
4 Louis Simpson, *Selected Poems* (London: Oxford University Press, 1966), p. 46.
5 Charles Swann, 'A Note on *The Blithedale Romance* or "Call him Fauntleroy"', *Journal of American Studies* 10 (1976), pp. 103–4.
6 Herman Melville, *Billy Budd, Sailor* (New York: Library of America, 1984), p. 1435.
7 Quoted in Perry Miller and Thomas H. Johnson (eds.), *The Puritans* (New York: American Book Company, 1938), p. 506.
8 Frank Davidson, 'Toward a Revaluation of *The Blithedale Romance*', *New England Quarterly* 25:3 (1952), p. 376.

9 Henry James, *Literary Criticism: Essays on Literature, American Writers, English Writers* (New York: Library of America, 1984), p. 471.
10 Ibid., p. 459.
11 Lauren Berlant, 'Fantasies of Utopia in *The Blithedale Romance*', *American Literary History* 1:1 (1989), pp. 31–2.
12 Ibid., p. 32.
13 Personal communication.
14 James, *Literary Criticism*, p. 464.
15 Ralph Waldo Emerson, *Essays and Lectures* (New York: Library of America, 1983), p. 135.
16 David S. Reynolds, *Beneath the American Renaissance: The Subversive Imagination in the Age of Emerson and Melville* (Cambridge: Harvard University Press, 1988), pp. 55–6.
17 Ibid., p. 59.
18 Ibid., pp. 84–5.
19 James, *Literary Criticism*, p. 419.
20 Richard Poirier, *A World Elsewhere* (London: Chatto and Windus, 1967), pp. 116, 120, 121, 122.
21 Henry James, *The Sacred Fount* (New York: Grove Press, 1953), pp. 147, 162, 23, 128, 177, 214, 276, 287, 273.
22 Henry James, *The Complete Tales of Henry James*, ed. Leon Edel, vol. 9 (London: Rupert Hart-Davis, 1964), p. 75.
23 Reynolds, *Beneath the American Renaissance*, pp. 65–73.
24 Joseph Conrad, *Nostromo* (London, 1904), p. 501.
25 Michael Colacurcio, *The Province of Piety: Moral History in Hawthorne's Early Tales* (Cambridge: Harvard University Press, 1984); Richard Brodhead, *The School of Hawthorne* (New York: Oxford University Press, 1986).
26 James, *Literary Criticism*, p. 467.

CHAPTER 3

'Nothing but cakes and ale':
Herman Melville's White-Jacket

This man-of-war book, My Dear Sir, is in some parts rather man-of-*warish* in style – rather aggressive I fear. – But you, who like myself, have experienced in person the usages to which a sailor is subjected, will not wonder, perhaps, at any thing in the book. Would to God, that every man who shall read it, had been before the mast in an armed ship, that he might know something himself of what he shall only read of.

(Melville to Richard Henry Dana, 6 October 1849)[1]

'Can't man ask a question here without being flogged?'

'No,' shouted the captain; 'nobody shall open his mouth aboard this vessel but myself'; and began laying the blows upon his back, swinging half round between each blow to give it full effect. As he went on his passion increased, and he danced about the deck, calling out as he swung the rope, 'If you want to know what I flog you for, I'll tell you. It's because I like to do it! – because I like to do it! – It suits me! That's what I do it for!'

The man writhed under the pain, until he could endure it no longer, when he called out, with an exclamation more common among foreigners than with us – 'Oh, Jesus Christ! Oh, Jesus Christ!'

'Don't call on Jesus Christ,' shouted the captain; *'he can't help you. Call on Captain T* – he's the man. He can help you! Jesus Christ can't help you now!' . . . 'You see your condition! You see where I've got you all, and you know what to expect! You've been mistaken in me – you didn't know what I was! Now you know what I am! I'll make you toe the mark, every soul of you, or I'll flog you all, fore and aft, from the boy up! – You've got a driver over you! Yes, a *slave-driver* – a *negro-driver!'*[2]

This is from the most famous – or sensational – scene in Dana's *Two Years Before the Mast* and perhaps the best-known, even notorious scene in nineteenth-century American fiction. The whipping to death of Tom in *Uncle Tom's Cabin* would subsequently arouse a more widespread public horror, but, appearing in 1840, Dana's scene seemed uniquely shocking. Not that flogging in the navy was news: the two 'institutions' had been for too long infamously inseparable. What Dana's account inscribes is an intolerable contradiction at the heart of the newly emerged – recently invented – republic of America itself. This new country, as much a conceptual construct as a land, as much an abstraction as a terrain, was founded on proclaimed ideas and ideals of liberty and equality, yet it was economically quite substantially grounded in slavery. Whereas the axe – the instrument of land-clearance, agriculture, settlement, and thus culture – was the symbol of its public triumph and the ever-advancing frontier, the whip was the mark of its secret shame, the cancer of a slavery always seeking to spread. The shock of Dana's scene is the spectacle of a white American seaman being flogged like a slave, and of a white American captain glorying in his blasphemous tyranny and sadistically identifying with a slave-driver with unashamed pleasure. Of that flogged sailor it could be said, as Melville was to write in *White-Jacket*: 'For him our Revolution was in vain; to him our Declaration of Independence is a lie.' This dread possibility was a nerve which Dana's scene electrically touched on. Melville's work probes relentlessly deeper.

Melville certainly had Dana's book well in mind when he wrote *White-Jacket*. In a letter to Dana of 1 May 1850, he refers to 'those strange, congenial feelings, with which after my first voyage, I for the first time read "Two Years Before the Mast", and while so engaged was, as it were, tied and welded to you by a sort of Siamese link of affectionate sympathy'.[3] Dana, a Harvard student of law who embarked on his adventure 'before the mast' (that is, with the common sailors of the forecastle) partly for health reasons and for a strictly limited period ('two years'), never forgets in his book that he is a gentleman-sailor – an oxymoron for the time. A large part of his satisfaction derives from the discovery that 'I – home-bred, gentleman-bred, college-bred – could stand it as well as the roughest of them', but while he is indeed initiated into the seaman's life, achieves (or proves) his manhood, and is accepted as a genuine member of the crew, he never forgets and never wants to forget his 'difference'. This is not simply snobbery or élitism. It has more to do with wishing both to share in immediate common experience – the sailor – and to retain the reflective privilege of detachment and commentary – the lawyer-writer. It is also related to the more general problem felt with especial urgency by many American writers (among others): how to hold on to some individualising specialness or distinctness without seeming to support un-American notions of hierarchy, class, privilege, and rank; how to be a Gentleman and a Democrat? All these considerations, barring some modifications, apply to Melville as well. He gives a very direct nod to Dana at the start of *Moby-Dick*: 'When I go to sea, I go as a simple sailor, right before the mast' says Ishmael; but when Melville goes to write, he goes as a complex writer, to some lonely space of his own. (Other writers would use Dana's phrase as a metaphor to gesture towards direct experience unmediated by tradition or convention, as for example Thoreau at the end of *Walden*: 'I did not wish to take a cabin passage, but rather to go before the mast and on the deck of the world, for there I could best see the moonlight amid the mountains.'[4]) And these words from *White-Jacket*: 'Virtue must come down from aloft, even as our blessed Redeemer came down to redeem our whole man-of-war world; to that end, mixing with its sailors and sinners as equals', might be compared to Dana's assertion: 'We must come down from our heights . . . if we would learn truths by strong contrasts.'

There are a number of similarities, and revealing differences, between Dana's book and Melville's. Dana, seeking both to learn and control a whole new experiential world, limits himself as far as possible to information – facts and figures, 'the life of a common sailor as it really is'. The weather, the sails, the different jobs, the shipboard routine, the longitude and latitude, the wages, the quantities of goods – all these – and more – are matters for almost itemising report. The surfaces of things are, as it were, meticulously inventoried. Melville engages in a lot of this as well, but invariably with some Melvillian twist or elaboration. We cannot imagine Dana writing, as Melville does, of 'serenely concocting information into wisdom'. When Melville writes about rounding Cape Horn he pays specific tribute to Dana's own account ('But if you want the best idea of Cape Horn, get my friend Dana's unmatchable *Two Years Before the Mast* . . . His chapters describing Cape Horn must have been written with an icicle'); but we cannot imagine Dana adding after his account, as Melville does: 'But, sailor or landsman, there is some sort of a Cape Horn for all.' Some of Dana's characters almost seem to prefigure some of Melville's – for instance Bill Jackson, 'the best specimen of a thoroughbred English sailor that I ever saw', seems to anticipate the figure of Jack Chase. Again, just as Captain Thomas threatens to turn Dana's ship, the *Pilgrim*, into 'hell afloat' so Melville tells us that men-of-war are known among sailors as 'Floating Hells'. Dana is interested in 'manliness' as it is defined or determined at sea, just as Melville has an eye for the 'manhood-testing conjuncture', though here again Melville's speculations range more widely. One final similarity involving a yet greater difference: near the end of his voyage Dana describes a 'narrow escape' when he is almost 'thrown violently from the height of ninety or a hundred feet overboard, or, what is worse, upon the deck'. He regains his footing and this effectively ends the voyage, for there are only two incident-free chapters to follow. Melville makes the final climax of his voyage a terrifying account of a tremendous fall which never happened to him but is instead his own amplification of a more prosaic account of a somewhat less tremendous fall which he found in Nathaniel Ames's *Mariner's Sketches*. Following which there are, indeed, two incident-free chapters to conclude before – like Dana – he is back in home harbour.

That Melville was well aware of the crucial difference between his writing and Dana's – in spite of the many similarities and 'congenialities' – is clear from another passage from the letter last quoted:

About the 'whaling voyage' – I am half-way in the work, and am very glad that your suggestion so jumps with mine. It will be a strange sort of book, tho', I fear; blubber is blubber you know; tho' you may get oil out of it, the poetry runs as hard as sap from a frozen maple tree; – and to cook the thing up, one must needs throw in a little fancy, which from the nature of the thing, must be ungainly as the gambols of the whales themselves. Yet I mean to give the truth of the thing, spite of this.[5]

Throwing in fancy to cook things up and indulging in ungainly gambolling in pursuit of poetry was just exactly what Dana would never do: he stayed squarely – and powerfully – within the known and knowable longitudes and latitudes of experience. He was, after all, a lawyer and he kept scrupulously to the brief he had set himself. Melville was a writer and in 1849 – when he wrote *Redburn* in two months and then, incredibly, *White-Jacket* in two more – he was a writer at odds with himself, or with what he imagined was his public, and in trouble. While he was writing *Mardi* in 1848, Melville wrote to John Murray: 'proceeding in my narrative of *facts* I began to feel an incurable distaste for the same; and a longing to plume my pinions for a flight, and felt irked, cramped and fettered by plodding along with dull common places, – So suddenly standing [abandoning?] the thing alltogether, I went to work heart and soul at a romance which is now in fair progress' (25 March).[6] *Mardi* came out on 14 April 1849 and was what might be called an instant unsuccess. With a young family Melville now needed money badly and immediately turned to a different mode of writing. As he explained to Richard Bentley:

I have now in preparation a thing of a widely different cast from *Mardi*: – a plain, straightforward, amusing narrative of personal experience – the son of a gentleman on his first voyage to sea as a sailor – no metaphysics, no comic-sections, nothing but cakes and ale. I have shifted my ground from the South Seas to a different quarter of the globe – nearer home – and what I write I have almost wholly picked up by my own observations under comical circumstances. (5 June)[7]

This 'widely different' type of writing resulted in *Redburn* and *White-Jacket*, and, if we are to believe a letter he wrote after their publication to his stepfather Lemuel Shaw, it was writing against the grain:

They are two *jobs*, which I have done for money – being forced to it, as other men are to sawing wood. And while I have felt obliged to refrain from writing the kind of book I would wish to; yet, in writing these two books, I have not repressed myself much – so far as *they* are concerned; but have spoken pretty much as I feel. – Being books, then, written in this way, my only desire for their 'success' (as it is called) springs from my pocket, and not from my heart. So far as I am individually concerned, and independent of my pocket, it is my earnest desire to write those sort of books which are said to 'fail'. – Pardon this egotism.[8]

By Melville's relatively modest standards, these two '*jobs*' were quite successful; and we need not decide that his turn to a more 'cakes and ale' sort of writing was wholly uncongenial to him, nor a complete, cynical–financial perversion of his instincts as a writer. As we have seen in his letter to Dana, he was fully resolved to add poetry to blubber in his next book – *Moby-Dick* of course; but in a letter to Evert Duyckinck of 12 February 1851, in the course of some unstinting praise for the work of Hawthorne, he adds a slight reservation which indicates that he sensed that writing which aimed too directly for the 'deeper meanings' might suffer from its own kind of impoverishments and attenuations. 'Some of those sketches are wonderfully subtle. Their deeper meanings are worthy of a Brahmin. Still there is something lacking – a good deal lacking – to the plump sphericity of the man. What is that? – He doesn't patronise the butcher – he needs roast-beef, done rare.'[9] In *White-Jacket*, in more ways, I am sure, than he intended by his use of the image, Melville did indeed 'patronise the butcher'. But the butcher turned out to be the American Navy.

The biographical facts are as follows. Herman Melville first went to sea in June 1839 when he was nineteen. He joined a trans-Atlantic packet sailing between New York and Liverpool (see *Redburn*). He subsequently joined the whaling ship *Acushnet* on 31 December 1840 at Fairhaven, and deserted in the Marquesas (see *Typee*). He joined another whaling ship and again deserted, this time in Tahiti (see *Omoo*). He made his way to the Hawaiian Islands in May 1843, and worked in a store in Honolulu until August, when he signed on in a United States frigate called, indeed, *United States*. There followed fourteen months of naval service before he reached Boston on 14 October 1844. It was his last voyage and is, of course, the one described – along with a number of invented or interpolated episodes – in *White-Jacket*. In June 1851 he wrote to Hawthorne: 'Until I was twenty-five, I had no development at all. From my twenty-fifth year I date my life.'[10] That twenty-fifth birthday occurred shortly before the end of his voyage on the *United States*. During that voyage 163 floggings are reported as having taken place – all hands always summoned to witness punishment – and, as in Dana's book, the horrific flogging scene provides the explosive emotional centre of *White-Jacket*. But this final similarity between the two books serves to bring into focus their most important difference. Dana's first reaction to the flogging is a mixture of sickness, anger, and excitement. 'A man – a human being, made in God's likeness – fastened up and flogged like a beast! The first and almost uncontrollable impulse was resistance. But what was to be done?' And gradually the lawyer in him, we might say, becomes uppermost. 'But beside the numbers, what is there for sailors to do? If they resist, it is mutiny; and if they succeed, and take the vessel, it is piracy . . . Bad as it was it must be borne. It is what a sailor ships for.'[11] Elsewhere he supports and justifies the captain's absolute authority and the necessity for corporal punishment. As a gentleman he averts his eyes from the scene of the flogging: 'Disgusted, sick, and horror-struck, I turned away and leaned over the rail and looked down into the water.' As a lawyer he 'vows' that 'if God should ever give me the means, I would do something to redress the grievances and relieve the sufferings of that poor class of beings, of whom I then was one'.[12] And he seems to think that more intelligence and efficiency in running ships will gradually make flogging obsolete.

Melville's reaction is different by 180 degrees, as it were. He attacks man-made law on all sides. He attacks the 'arbitrary laws' by which a human being can be 'scourged worse than a hound . . . for things not essentially criminal'. He attacks the laws – or legalism – of the land which serves to legitimate and support that so-called naval law, which is in fact a 'tyranny' that is permitted to 'convert into slaves some of the citizens of a nation of free-men', and he invokes the 'Law of Nature' with a supporting quotation from Blackstone. This law is 'coeval with mankind, dictated by God himself, superior in obligation to any other, and no human laws are of any validity if contrary to this'. Dana exhibits the spirit of functionalism which was coming to mark American law. He respects the law already in place and considers how it might be modified and its codifications adjusted. Melville cuts through these constructs and appeals to a quite different order or level of reality. The Founding Fathers – Jefferson certainly – believed in Natural Law, and indeed that what they were doing (writing 'America') was grounded in it. But during the first half of the nineteenth century the discourse of law in America was becoming more instrumental and local, and less given to general statements and ideal claims. In his excellent book *Law and Letters* Robert Ferguson has considered some of the implications of this and comments very illuminatingly on the difference between Dana and Melville:

The narrowing professionalism of the mid-century lawyer is the visible side of a curious reversal in American literature. For even as leaders of the bar reject natural law in the name of a more technical expertise, a new breed of literary intellectual arises to seize the abandoned legacy. Few have noticed how frequently the writers of the American Renaissance resort to higher law as a mode of explanation, and no one has appreciated the continuities involved. Melville, Emerson, Thoreau, and Hawthorne are reacting against the past, against the civic tones and themes of early republican literature; nonetheless, it is Melville, the romantic novelist, who reaches back to natural law to condemn flogging, and not Dana, the student of law.[13]

The difference – it is the difference between two Americas and two American discourses – is nicely illustrated, as Ferguson points out, by the fact that one year after *Two Years Before the Mast*, Dana published what he called 'purely a business book', namely *The Seaman's Friend: Containing a Treatise of Practical Seamanship with Plates; A Dictionary of Sea Terms; Customs and Usages of the Merchant Services; Laws Relating to the Practical Duties of Master and Mariners*; while one year after *White-Jacket* Melville published – *Moby-Dick*.

But the treatment of flogging in *White-Jacket* is not quite as uncomplicated a matter as might at first appear. When Melville intimated to Dana that his book was 'man-of-*warish*' and 'aggressive' he probably had in mind his ringing denunciations of the practice of flogging in the American Navy – passages such as this:

Irrespective of incidental considerations, we assert that flogging in the Navy is opposed to the essential dignity of man, which no legislator has a right to violate; that it is oppressive, and glaringly unequal in its operations; that it is utterly repugnant to the spirit of our democratic institutions; indeed, that it involves a lingering trait of the worst times of a barbarous feudal aristocracy; in a word, we denounce it as religiously, morally, and immutably *wrong*.

However impeccable the sentiments expressed in them, these somewhat stilted and sonorous declamations hardly show Melville's style at its most imaginative or forceful. Melville is happier undermining – or at least problematising – than univocally advancing a cause, and some of these propagandist passages ring curiously hollow in spite of – or more likely because of – their strident rhetoric. *White-Jacket* has acquired the vague reputation of having brought about the abolition of flogging in the American Navy, but this is both entirely unsubstantiated and highly unlikely. Flogging in the United States Navy had been debated in Congress throughout the 1840s and an act to abolish it was finally passed on 28 September 1850. ('I am offering up devout jubilations for the abolition of the flogging law' wrote Melville to Evert Duyckinck on 6 October 1850.[14]) But it should be noted that *White-Jacket* was not even mentioned in the congressional debate, and indeed its publication only preceded the conclusion of the long debate by a few months. The fact is, not to put too fine a point upon it, that Melville was on fairly safe ground when he vociferated so loudly, and with such righteous indignation, about an indisputable barbarism that was about to disappear. This is in no way to question the sincerity of Melville's outrage, nor the depths of his outraged repugnance. Rather, it is to raise the question of whether this apparently fearless and principled rhetoric, so loud and clear in its support of a cause that had almost ceased to be contentious, against an abuse about to be eradicated, might not be some kind of compensation for an uneasy silence elsewhere: a strategy to deflect attention from another abuse that was growing yearly *more* contentious, an abuse that, far from being eradicated, seemed to be trying to consolidate itself in the Union to the point of threatening the union of that Union – namely, slavery. Melville is clear enough that it is entirely abhorrent that white men should be flogged like black slaves. He is not quite so clear that it is equally abhorrent for blacks to be whipped – or to be slaves either for that matter. Again, this is not to suggest that within Melville's rightly famous democratic and humane heart there lingered traces of a toxic racism, but rather that this work of 1849 contains within it some of the crucial tensions, ambivalences, and contradictions that were to tear the nation to pieces little more than a decade later. Far from pointing out black spots in Melville, I am suggesting that this work is most interesting in the way that works of great writers often are – that is, seemingly in spite of themselves. Let me just consider briefly the way the book touches on three phenomena, which were inseparably and constitutively involved in the origin of the United States: revolution (or rebellion), slavery, and egalitarianism.

Because the arbitrariness of the martial law that operated at sea was so utterly at variance with American institutions which 'claim to be based upon broad principles of political liberty and equality', Melville feels that – according to the Natural Law he invoked – 'every man-of-war's-man would be morally justified in resisting the scourge to the uttermost; and, in so resisting, would be religiously justified in what would be judicially styled "the act of mutiny" itself'. This is quite in line with the justification of America's act of mutiny or rebellion against the oppressive tyranny of its parent country, or 'captain'. Melville was consistently a supporter of great political revolutions of the past, from the Greeks against the Thirty Tyrants, to the Puritans against the English king, to the French Revolution, and of course to America's own throwing off of the feudal yoke. He is also sympathetic to more specifically naval mutinies, as for example those of Spithead and Nore.[15] Given this spirited sympathy with cases and instincts of justified mutiny it is curious that two of the fabricated incidents in the book (that is, with *no* basis in Melville's own experience) start with the provoking and arousing of mutinous feelings, but end in incredible appeasement and limp dispersal. The first is Melville's fantasy about nearly being flogged when he imagines White-Jacket unjustly condemned to the cat. This enables him to imagine how he might have felt if about to be whipped: 'I cannot analyse my heart, though it then stood still within me . . . I felt my man's manhood so bottomless within me, that no word, no blow, no scourge of Captain Claret could cut me deep enough for that. I but swung to an instinct in me – the instinct diffused through all animated nature, the same that prompts even a worm to turn under the heel' (ch. LXVII). And he resolves to clasp the Captain and drag him overboard in a combined murder-suicide. Then a 'gentlemanly corporal of marines', Colbrook, mildly speaks up on White-Jacket's behalf, and Jack Chase – that model of prudence and circumspection – seeing that the Captain takes no action against Colbrook, ventures also to put in a good word for White-Jacket 'in a manly but carefully respectful manner'. The Captain listens, then strolls away telling White-Jacket *'you may go'*. White-Jacket, understandably, nearly bursts 'into tears of thankfulness'. Now this is all very incredible. In Dana's scene when a man mildly questions the reason for the flogging he is instantly put in irons and then flogged himself, and it would have been infinitely more plausible if the fairly sadistic, and completely autocratic, Captain Claret had done the same. Yet Melville's scene transforms the bloody decks of the man-of-war into a site of almost courtly decorum with good manners, mild speaking, and mutually attentive respect all round. Even stranger is the fact that Melville almost certainly took this episode from a story by William Leggett entitled 'Brought to the Gangway', in which a seaman is also unjustly condemned to be flogged but does indeed carry his despotic persecutor to death with him in a way which White-Jacket only fantasises about.[16] Melville's episode is the emasculating fiction of a fiction, quite against the grain of the book – or at least much of the book. But we may consider it together with another failed or aborted mutiny – 'The Great Massacre of the Beards'.

Again this has no basis in anything that Melville experienced (though there had been an order sent out from Washington in 1841 to similar effect), which means that Melville was under no constraints of historical accuracy or verisimilitude to make it into what in effect it is – the climactic event of the voyage. Indeed, quite the contrary. Once again we have a strange, imagined interpolation, and one which finds Melville as tonally adrift as he is ever likely to get. The men decide to let their beards grow. A 'cruel thought entered into the heart of our captain' and he orders them to have their beards cut (that technically he has the naval law on his side is made secondary; it is presented as yet another example of the cruel caprice and arbitrary edicts of the tyrannous captain). Melville first pretends to feelings of inexpressible melancholy prompted by the memory of what happened: 'Such a heartless massacre of hair! Such a Bartholomew's Day and Sicilian Vespers of assassinated beards! Ah! who would believe it!' This sort of mock-epic inflation (possibly a burlesque of Carlyle, as Priscilla Zirker has suggested)[17] would seem to preclude any high seriousness in what follows. And yet the indubitably serious language of mutiny soon begins to stir.

Train your guns inboard [my italics], let the marines fix their bayonets, let the officers draw their swords; we *will not* let our beards be reaped – the last insult inflicted upon a vanquished foe in the East! Where are you, sheet-anchor men! captains of the tops! gunners mates! mariners, all! Muster round the capstan your venerable beards, and while you braid them together in token of brotherhood, cross hands and swear that we will enact over again the mutiny of the Nore, and sooner perish than yield up a hair!

The mutiny has really begun to look potentially serious when it is effortlessly scattered and defused by a few words from Mad Jack – for which Melville admires him: 'Therefore, Mad Jack! you did right . . . you perhaps quelled a very serious affair in the bud, and prevented the disgrace to the American Navy of a tragical mutiny, growing out of whiskers, soap-suds, and razors.' It is hard to see what has happened to Melville's credentials as a principled mutineer at this point (remember it is all his invention: Mad Jack's effortless and even contemptuous mastery over the would-be mutineers is Melville's own). And the crew – save one – all submit to have their beards cut. Under some sort of protest, to be sure: 'Captain Claret . . . I yielded to your tyranny – by this manly beard, I swear it was barbarous.'

Now there is a certain kind of word play of which Melville is particularly fond and it is quite possible that one reason for the interpolation of this episode was the opportunity it offered him to juggle with the barbarous/barber-ous treatment of men who are symbolically castrated by the whim of a tyrant. (The incident starts in a chapter entitled 'Man-of-War Barbers' and many details of barbering are given.) The etymologies of the two homonymous words are of course quite distinct – *barba* (beard) having nothing to do with the 'bar-bar' noises which the Greeks thought that non-Greeks made. But Melville was seriously interested in what exactly was 'barbarous', and throughout his work it is clear that he recognised that barbarities could issue from the heart of the United States – just as they are to be found at the centre of *United States* with its barbarous floggings – which could equal if not surpass in savagery the barbarities of so-called primitive peoples. So the barbarous/barber-ous edict of the Captain could have become a serious matter. But Melville lets, or makes, it all turn silly and even sentimental with the barber being absolved and, in turn, treating the shorn beard of Jack Chase (who had of course 'deemed it but wisdom to succumb') almost as a sacred relic.

Then it all turns most unpleasantly serious. Old Ushant, the 'sea-Socrates', refuses to comply with the order and the Captain orders him to be flogged, showing again a sadistic fury which hardly conceals its pleasure. There is the tiniest ripple and murmur of incipient protest and resistance, which is stilled and silenced even as it indulges in its carefully *sotto voce* expression. ' "By heaven!" thrillingly whispered Jack

Chase who stood by, "it's only a halter; I'll strike him!" "Better not" said a top-mate, "it's death or worse punishment, remember." ' And that is the full extent of the protest. Jack Chase instead turns away 'with moist eyes'. It is impossible to estimate how much irony Melville intended by the phrase 'thrillingly whispered', but as far as the 'match-less and unmatchable Jack Chase' and his pretensions to any kind of heroic status are concerned, it is effectively the *coup de grâce*. And it cannot be a coincidence that the words he uses as he forces his way away from the flogging, 'I can't stand it', are exactly echoed by the cowardly slave Guinea, who also pushes away from the sight of a flogging with the words 'I can't 'tand it'. As Melville shows, Jack Chase can only be a 'hero' in the amateur theatricals, in which he plays the 'chivalric' character of Percy Royal-Mast and rescues 'fifteen oppressed sailors' to great applause (ch. xxiii). It is impossible even to sense how far the mockery of handsome Jack Chase's empty theatrical posturing and actual faint-hearted circumspection is meant to go. But looked at closely, he is, in Melville's larger vocabulary, as much a 'slave' as anyone on the ship.

Meanwhile, old Ushant takes his dozen lashes and is standing 'as the Dying Gladiator lies'. Still refusing to shave his beard, he spends five more days in irons. He becomes the one figure on the ship who has held fast to his principled refusal to comply with the arbitrary dictates of a tyrannous captain or to succumb to his brutality. In this sense he is the only hero: the one true mutineer-martyr to stand out and stand firm. At this point, almost madly one might feel, Melville seems to offer a kind of defence of Captain Claret: 'Let it not be supposed that it is here sought to impale him before the world as a cruel, black-hearted man. Such he was not.' Certainly not, says Melville; why 'it has been related what privileges he accorded to the seamen respecting the free playing of checkers'. By which time it is becoming impossible to have any sure sense of what Melville might be trying to do with the whole episode. At the end of it all he seems to return to a firm conviction that the men were right in the first place to make it a matter of principle, and thus potentially a matter for mutiny. 'And that our man-of-war's-men were right in desiring to perpetuate their beards, as martial appurtenances, must seem very plain, when it is considered that, as the beard is the token of manhood, so, in some shape or other, has it ever been held the true badge of the warrior.' Which would seem to lend honour and vindication to the figure of Ushant, sea-Socrates and Dying Gladiator. But then Melville's tone changes yet again as he veers off into his own kind of inscrutable jocularity: 'Most all fighting creatures sport either whiskers or beards; it seems a law of Dame Nature. Witness the boar, the tiger, the cougar, man, the leopard, the ram, the cat – all warriors, and all whiskerandos. Whereas, the peace-loving tribes have mostly enamelled chins.' Ushant as just another of Dame Nature's 'whiskerandos' is a much reduced figure.

I will return to these failed, or stylistically subverted and tonally betrayed, mutinies shortly. But first I want to draw attention to the sequence of chapters and subjects with which Melville proceeds to conclude his book after that final episode. In his next chapter he returns to flogging in its most horrific form – 'Flogging through the Fleet' – which is indeed a 'Golgotha' of a chapter. This leads him on to extending the 'catalogue of evil' to be found in 'The Social State in a Man-of-War', and here we move from Golgotha to Gomorrah: 'The sins for which the cities of the plain were overthrown still linger in some of these wooden-walled Gomorrahs of the Deep. More than once complaints were made at the mast in the *Neversink*, from which the deck officer would turn away with loathing, refuse to hear them, and command the complainant out of his sight. There are evils in men-of-war which . . . will neither bear representing, nor reading, and will hardly bear thinking of.' Whether Melville himself questioned the arguable perversity of conventions of representation which allow him to describe sadistic floggings at detailed length while preventing him from even writing the word 'homosexuality' is not here clear. But the proximity of the two things in his text gives some weight to those who detect a suggestion of incipient sexual excitement in the flogging scenes; 'sodomy and the lash', as Winston Churchill used to say, always going closely together in the Navy. Melville's apparent horror at the very idea or word 'homosexual', feigned or real, is a far cry from the at times almost outrageous homo-erotic playfulness to be found in *Moby-Dick*. But at this point Melville is following a line of evil. In 'The Manning of Navies' we are among the 'many moral monsters' to be found in the 'Floating Hells' at sea. The chapter concludes with the sketch of Landless, a man who has, as it were, been flogged into a state of 'invincible indifference' during ten years in the Navy. Apparently happy-go-lucky and popular with the officers, he represents for Melville a kind of ultimate degradation: 'A fellow without shame, without a soul, so dead to the least dignity of manhood that he could hardly be called a man.' The following chapter aspires to be more cheerful but can only conclude that a man-of-war is but a microcosm of the world's badness – 'though boasting some fine fellows here and there, yet, upon the whole, charged to the combings of her hatchways with the spirit of Belial and all unrighteousness'. After the chapter describing his 'imagined' fall we soon move on to the concluding words of the book: 'For the rest, whatever befall us, *let us never train our murderous guns inboard* [my italics]; let us not mutiny with bloody pikes in our hands. Our Lord High Admiral will yet interpose; and though long ages should elapse, and leave our wrongs unredressed, yet, shipmates and worldmates! let us never forget, that,

> Whoever afflict us, whatever surround,
> Life is a voyage that's homeward bound.'

This, by any other name, is quietism, and a comparison of the italicised words with those italicised earlier marks the inversion of the discourse of mutiny into the discourse of pacifism. (Melville is hardly known for his belief in the beneficent supervision of a 'Lord High Admiral', or indeed in His existence.) Guns turned inboard were often crucial in mutiny, and of course – given Melville's use of the ship as microcosm – could easily signify a state of civil war. Priscilla Zirker, to whose crucial article I owe this and other points, shows that the fear of the possibility of national disunity and the sense of impending crisis, if not worse, was growing throughout the 1840s and was 'probably at its height in 1849' when Melville was writing his book (the fear intensified, of course, by the revolutions in Europe during 1848).[18] It was that fear, it would seem, that led Melville to radically muffle his mutineering instincts in such strange, dissonant ways.

The fear of national disunity was of course precipitated by the problem of slavery. It has to be remembered that many of the liberals who were against slavery and opposed its extension – including Lincoln himself – had little respect for negroes as men and no doubt at all about white superiority. The Democrats – and Melville was a Democrat at this time – regarded themselves as the 'Party of Equality'. They thought, as did many others, that it should be possible to reconcile their proclaimed political ideals of freedom and equality with at least a tolerance – in the name of national unity – of the 'peculiar institution' of the South. Priscilla Zirker comments:

But the conciliatory gesture, upholding the sacred rights of property in slaves and denying the Negroes status as men, which began with the Compromise of 1850 and continued with the Fugitive Slave Act, the Kansas–Nebraska Act and the Dred Scott decision, only forced the opponents of conciliation into new and irrevocable paths or into underground activity . . . the Democratic Party transformed itself from the 'party of Equality' into the party of slavery. And even then the Union could not be saved except through war and the conquering of one section by another.[19]

In the event, nothing finally could stop the training of the murderous guns inboard. And there was another issue that was making it increasingly difficult to keep the question of slavery somehow separate from the central political problems facing the United States: the debate concerning flogging in the navy. Inevitably, since to all but the most benightedly racist eye the flogging of a black man must seem mighty similar to the flogging of a white one, the connection between the issues of flogging and slavery becomes obvious and irreversible. Priscilla Zirker again: 'The alignment of congressmen on the issues of flogging and slavery was clear in the 1840s; it would have taken no prescience of the final severing of these members into opposing parties and then into opposing nations, as was to happen, to see that the abolition of flogging and slavery were related, that egalitarianism must inevitably proceed like water, to cover the lowest depths.'[20]

Priscilla Zirker is right, I think, to say that Melville was frightened by the whole matter and problem of slavery; meaning not a general metaphysical or ontological condition ('who aint a slave?' asks Ishmael, cheerfully enough, in *Moby-Dick*), but the black slaves, rapidly increasing in numbers – and volatility – in mid-century America. When, apropos the gunpowder kept in the depths of the ship, Melville characteristically generalises the fact into a trope and says 'it is pretty certain that the whole earth is a vast hogshead, full of inflammable materials, and which we are always bestriding', we may take it for some of his off-the-cuff metaphysics; but it is also in line with a recurring image which can be found in other writing of the period which suggests that America is a volcano waiting to erupt, and that the 'inflammable material' is slavery. When Melville wants to convey a sense of the difference between a 'sham fight' which is used for training the men, and a 'real cannonading' he suggests that '*then* our bulwarks might look like the walls of the houses in West Broadway in New York, after being broken into and burned out by the negro mob'. '*The* negro mob': Melville is being specific, and there was indeed a slave revolt in 1741 in which fires were started in New York. But Melville suppresses the history and instead offers an apocalyptic scenario of hideous butchery, rivers of blood, and terrifying destruction. He hardly needed to reach back to 'the negro mob' for such a scene of generalised carnage (there was after all the French Revolution – but of course he approved of that), but it came to him. In *Benito Cereno* he would subsequently offer an incomparable study of the myopic, self-deceiving, and cruel complacencies of a white, American, racist, imperialist consciousness – but the slave revolt is still frightening. White-Jacket feels some sympathy with the black Rose-Water when he is flogged, and pities him as 'one of an oppressed race', which prompts the unashamed exclamation 'Thank God! I am white.' However, being white is no protection against being flogged in the Navy, and immediately after this White-Jacket is himself sentenced to be flogged. Clearly his expressed relief at being white is meant to be ironically undercut. But this does not lead to a sense of *identification* with the black. And the negroes on board hardly enjoy the full reach of Melville's humanism. They are given minstrel names – Sunshine, May-Day, Old Coffee, Rose-Water – and if Melville does not degrade them like the Captain, who makes them engage in head-bumping contests for his amusement, he does rather ridicule them. About Guinea, the one slave on board who paradoxically enjoys an ease and freedom denied the sailors, White-Jacket is positively resentful. And when Melville writes 'the lieutenants from the Southern States, the descendants of the old Virginians, are much less severe, and much more gentle and gentlemanly in command, than the Northern officers, as a class' he sounds almost like an apologist for the old South and its peculiar institution. He was, of course, nothing of the kind; but at this point the figure of the black slave (or freed slave) provokes ambivalent feelings which confuse him.

This is one reason, I think, why Melville felt much easier making sweeping general statements about the Rights of Man: when a writer engages in universals he absolves himself from having to confront local, historical, and political problems – like the status of the black slave in the America of 1849. Elsewhere in the book Melville displays the kind of enlightened cultural relativism which is a consistent feature of his writing. Thus when the Polynesian figure, Wooloo, confronted by western and ship-board phenomena which are quite new to him, makes all sorts of amusing mistakes, Melville comments: 'In our man-of-war, this semi-savage, wandering about the gun-deck in his barbaric robe, seemed a being from some other sphere. His tastes were our abominations: ours his. Our creed he rejected: his we. We thought him a loon: he fancied us fools. *Had the case been reversed* [my italics]; had we been Polynesians and he an American, our mutual opinion of each other would still have remained the same. A fact proving that neither was wrong, but both right.' It is a quintessentially Melvillian observation, and indeed 'reversibility' – of function, category, culture, belief – becomes a major motif in his later work, at times threatening to obliterate 'difference' altogether. That is another story. In terms of this book it must be said that the figure of the black American slave worries Melville a good deal more than that of the Polynesian servant. (It should perhaps be noted here that later in his life Melville spoke unambiguously of the evil of slavery; but I am trying to identify some of the tensions which are present in *White-Jacket*.) Quite apart from anything else, the presence of slaves in America placed an added strain on his not always unequivocal egalitarian principles and beliefs. According to those principles, of course, the American slave should have been an impossible contradiction in terms. Yet there he was, staring him, and countless other worried white liberals, frighteningly in the face.

Melville's proclaimed and doubtless sincere egalitarianism is the third problematical area of this book I wish to touch on, and it is of course intimately involved with the previous two. In 1851 he wrote to Hawthorne: 'When you see or hear of my ruthless democracy on all sides, you may possibly feel a touch of a shrink, or something of that sort. It is but nature to be shy of a mortal who boldly declares that a thief in jail is as honorable a personage as Gen. George Washington.'[21] At an abstract or idealistic level Melville's democracy is fervent and ruthless enough. But the account of his voyage on the *United States* seethes with matters of rank, class distinction, and hierarchy. The arbitrary tyranny of the captain prompts Melville to make comparative references to feudalism, sultanism, Czars, emperors, Caesar, Charles the Fifth, and so on – understandably, since one of Melville's constant questions and concerns is 'by what monstrous grafting of tyranny upon freedom' did the *American* Navy acquire such a barbaric and despotic code while sailing in protection of the nation which had produced the Declaration of Independence. At the other extreme there are recurrent references to '*the people*', that generically classless class of common humanity for which Melville the democrat regards himself as the spokesman. But there are other terms for the common people – such as 'mob', 'desperadoes', 'gang', 'miscellaneous rabble', and so on. This is absolutely in line with a common ambivalence to be found in republics in which 'the people' are the honoured abstraction, 'the masses' the ambiguous unadmired reality, and 'the mob' the dreaded nightmare. In chapter forty-five there is a revealing exchange between Lemsford (who like Melville is both a 'gentleman' and a writer) and Jack Chase. Lemsford is a notably unsuccessful writer who despises the 'mob and rabble' who ignored his book: 'What they call the public is a monster, like the idol we saw in Owhyhee, with the head of a jackass, the body of a baboon, and the tail of a scorpion.' Jack demurs, pointing out that on shore he is, inevitably, part of that public. Not so, says Lemsford: 'You are then part of the people, just as you are aboard the frigate here. The public is one thing, Jack, and the people another.' Jack instantly approves of the distinction: 'Ay, ay, my lads, let us hate the one, and cleave to the other.' Whether these are exactly Melville's own sentiments we may hardly ponder, but it seems likely; and on board ship White-Jacket shows himself to be keen to mark himself off from the common crew ('the people').

He is very aware of a kind of 'aristocracy' among the sailors – one based on an appreciation of literature, good manners, sensitivity, and a certain nonchalant elegance of style, epitomised of course by Jack Chase – with which he identifies and to which he soon belongs. For the official insignia of rank and its attendant ceremonies he has little time, and indeed he talks of the need for 'levelling downward' and getting rid of the differentiating pomp of official hierarchy: 'To gain the true level, in some things, we must *cut* downward; for how can you make every sailor a commodore? ... by bringing down naval officers ... without affecting their legitimate dignity and authority, we shall correspondingly elevate the common sailor.' But White-Jacket's aspirations are distinctly upward, and when he is accepted into the élite of the topmen, he regards himself as being both literally and figuratively at the top of the unofficial hierarchy among the crew. 'We accounted ourselves the best seamen in the ship; and from our airy perch, literally looked down upon the land-lopers below, sneaking about the deck, among the guns.' There is always a touch of humour in White-Jacket's account; but there is no doubt that he enjoys his promotion, his being accepted into the best 'club', his 'elevation' and the feeling of 'aboveness' it affords him. When he is in fact 'blackballed' from an earlier and much less prestigious 'club' his comment is: 'I was shocked. Such a want of tact and delicacy'; and he shows his highly developed fastidiousness early on when he realises the dangers of 'indiscriminate intimacy'. He admires those who somehow retain an aura of distinction and difference while still being part of the crew – like Nord: 'How he managed to preserve his dignity, as he did, among such a rabble rout was ... a mystery.' By the end of the voyage one certainly has the sense of the crew as being more a rabble – lazy, coarse, even depraved – than 'the people'.

Perhaps the most significant lexical symptom is the frequent occurrence of the word 'gentlemen'. The history of that word is a large piece of social history in itself. Suffice it here to note that by the Victorian period it had become both crucial and indefinable as a word. In an increasingly secular and democratic society it was used to signify some sort of human distinction, style, and worth. Yet just what made someone a gentleman was not easy to say. Trollope, for whom the figure and the concept is absolutely central, confessed that he had no idea what a gentleman really was. One advantage of this vagueness was that the word was not tied to social rank or status (or, by this time, to birth or wealth) so that any one might turn out to have those mysterious qualities which made him a gentleman wherever he might find himself. (The disadvantage was the possible dilution, diffusion, and general distribution of the term to the point of meaninglessness – as is arguably the case today.) Melville takes advantage of the relatively free-floating status of the word (in his vocabulary it would be a 'loose fish') to make it clear that while many of the officers were quite decidedly *not* gentlemen, a rare and precious few among the crew (conspicuously Jack Chase of course) most definitely were. To what extent being a gentleman might militate against one's being a democrat – or indeed vice versa – might be said to be another problem which vexes the book.[22]

Finally, the title merits some comment. Not the subtitle: 'The World in a Man-of-War' is self-explanatory and after Melville's extraordinarily rich and varied evocation, analysis, and probing, not only of the men and activities of the ship, but also of their possible emblematic significance and figurative suggestiveness, we readily recognise that when he writes at the end, 'Outwardly regarded, our craft is a lie; for all that is outwardly seen of it is the clean-swept deck, and oft-painted planks comprised above the water-line; whereas, the vast mass of our fabric, with all its store-rooms of secrets, forever slides along the water far under the surface', he is referring not only to the ship, but to the individual, to society, and perhaps to the cosmos itself. But why *White-Jacket*? Melville's father imported fine clothes and accessories for a possible American aristocracy (his business failed) and Melville was always peculiarly aware of the varying extents (laughable or appalling) to which social, if not human, identity was a sartorial construction (Carlyle's *Sartor Resartus* was a favourite book). In *White-Jacket* he satirises dandyish officers and overdressed monarchs with rich Melvillian humour. But what sort of garment is that white jacket, and what might it be suggesting, over and above the possible fact that it was, as Melville claimed to Dana, an actual garment he had? It has been seen variously as the sign of his alienation or estrangement or proud isolation or aristocratic pretensions or egotistical self-absorption; thus the final episode, when he rips himself out of it after his fall into the water and 'bursts . . . free', can be seen as a self-procured rebirth into society, 'the people', communality, maturity, or some other new lease of life now that he has freed himself from his self-imposed, self-isolating incubus. Clearly Melville does intend it to do some special work since, apart from the title, he starts the book describing how he made this 'outlandish garment of my own devising' and ends it by describing his desperate liberation from a garment which threatens to become his shroud. The jacket sinks from sight as the sailors harpoon it, mistaking it for a shark. It figures in nine chapters in all and is responsible for involving him in various, usually unpleasant, incidents. It tends to turn the crew against him. He is humiliated when no one even bids for it when he tries to auction it off. He often berates and regrets his 'horrible jacket' and indeed 'had it not once jeopardized my very existence?' It does inevitably serve to 'individualize' him in the 'mob of incognitos' and while that means he is often singled out for a task, one comes to feel that being individualised from the mob, no matter what pains and penalties it may incur or prejudices it might arouse, is something that White-Jacket greatly desires. The fact that, with all its secret places and private pockets, it is on one occasion likened to both an 'old castle' and 'a confidential writing desk' must give it some sort of special token value for Melville, with his aristocratic heritage and his writer's vocation. An ambiguous garment of his own making which marks him as an odd-man-out with frequently socially unpleasant results – this is surely no very unapt vestment for sailor-writer Melville on his last voyage. That it finally becomes a hampering garment from which he must break free may indeed be interpreted in many ways. But it certainly does not initiate him into any new-found solidarity with the crew or 'the people'. We last see him where he has always been most comfortable – above, with his élite: 'We maintop-men are all aloft in the top; and round our mast we circle, a brother-band, hand in hand, all spliced together.' What he breaks out to is life on the land, and commitment to a full-time career as a writer.

White-Jacket was well received and reviewed on the whole. Melville's friend Evert Duyckinck set the favourable tone by pointing to the 'union of culture and experience, of thought and observation, the sharp breeze of the forecastle alternating with the mellow stillness of the library, books and work imparting to each other mutual life',[23] though this makes the book sound a more serene performance than in fact it is. Indeed, it is possible to sympathise with the reviewer who found a 'want of continuity of interest', a 'want of motive', and a want of 'that quality which in painting we term composition' (*Britannia*, 2 February 1850) in the book,[24] and it is even possible to understand, if not actually to share, the impatience of Charles Gordon Brown for what he felt bound to designate as the 'autobiographical twaddle' to which Melville has recourse (Boston *Post*, 10 April 1850).[25] It is a rich book written with self-amplifying energy, but deeply uncertain of its direction, apart from the minimal linearity of the voyage being 'homeward bound'. At times Melville seeks to pull his intentions together with bursts of what might fairly be called 'Manifest Destiny' rhetoric, such as:

The Past is dead, and has no resurrection; but the Future is endowed with such a life, that it lives to us even in anticipation . . . Let us leave the Past, then, to dictate laws to immovable China . . . There are occasions when it is for America to make precedents, and not to obey them . . . we Americans are the peculiar, chosen people – the Israel of our time; we bear the ark of the liberties of the world . . . We are the pioneers of the world; the advance-guard, sent on through the wilderness of untried things, to break a new path in the New World that is ours.

But to some extent this sort of thing reads rather like those clean-swept decks and oft-painted planks which made, so he said, 'our craft . . . a lie'. This is the official, outward-looking rhetoric of American triumphalist optimism. But Melville is always better in seeking out those 'store-rooms of secrets' which slide along 'far under the surface', and it is in the exposure and exhibition of some of those secret and secreted evils – the corruptions and degradations, the amputations and flagellations – that *White-Jacket* tears itself free from any hampering orthodoxy and achieves a true Melvillian unsettling power. For clearly Melville's experiences on the *United States* took him to the heart of some of the most profound problems, which were troubling not only Melville himself, but the unity, stability, and indeed the meaning of America itself.

NOTES

1 Herman Melville, *Correspondence*, ed. Lynn Horth (Evanston: Northwestern University Press, 1993), p. 140.
2 Richard Henry Dana, Jr, *Two Years Before the Mast* (New York: Penguin Books, 1986), pp. 155–6.
3 Melville, *Correspondence*, p. 160.
4 Henry David Thoreau, *Walden* (New York: Library of America, 1985), p. 579.
5 Melville, *Correspondence*, p. 162.
6 Ibid., p. 106.
7 Ibid., p. 132.
8 Ibid., pp. 138–9.
9 Ibid., p. 181.
10 Ibid., p. 193.
11 Dana, *Two Years Before the Mast*, pp. 153–4.
12 Ibid., pp. 155, 157.
13 Robert A. Ferguson, *Law and Letters in American Culture* (Cambridge: Harvard University Press, 1984), p. 266.
14 Melville, *Correspondence*, p. 171.
15 There is also a familial aspect to this sympathy with mutineers. In chapter LXX he refers in passing to 'three sailors on board an American armed vessel . . . who once were alive, but now are dead', which is an allusion to three seamen who were executed without trial for suspected mutinous intentions on board the brig-of-war *Somers*. Melville heard of this while he was sailing on the *United States*. The officer who presided over the court which sentenced the men was Melville's cousin, Guert Gansevoort. Melville himself had been taking part, fairly marginally, in a somewhat less serious mutiny on the *Lucy Ann* at about the time the other men were hanged (see *Omoo* in which Melville generously promotes himself to being the ring-leader of the untragic mutiny). Melville's family was a distinguished one and his ancestors included Scottish nobles, Dutch patricians, and heroes of the American Revolution. His cousin represented the kind of filocidal autocratic exercise of power against which Melville was rebelling. He was, as it were, the self-styled mutineer within the family. For the rich story of Melville's deeply ambivalent relationship to his illustrious family – and the way that relationship feeds and informs his fiction – see the excellent book by Michael Paul Rogin, *Subversive Genealogy: The Politics and Art of Herman Melville* (New York: Alfred A. Knopf, 1983).
16 See P. S. Proctor, 'A Source for the Flogging Incident in *White-Jacket*', *American Literature* 22 (May 1950), pp. 176–7.
17 Priscilla Zirker, 'In Evidence of the Slavery Dilemma in *White-Jacket*', *American Quarterly* 18 (Fall 1966), pp. 477–92.
18 Ibid., pp. 480–1.
19 Ibid., p. 483.
20 Ibid.

21 Melville, *Correspondence*, pp. 190–1.
22 Apropos Melville's problematical attitude to egalitarianism, see Larry J. Reynolds, 'Anti-Democratic Emphasis in *White-Jacket*', *American Literature* 48.1 (March 1976), pp. 13–28.
23 Quoted in Brian Higgins and Hershel Parker (eds.), *Herman Melville: The Contemporary Reviews* (Cambridge: Cambridge University Press, 1995), p. 312.
24 Ibid., p. 307.
25 Ibid., p. 334.

CHAPTER 4

'All interweavingly working together': Herman Melville's Moby-Dick

'This is an odd book, professing to be a novel; wantonly eccentric; outrageously bombastic; in places charmingly and vividly descriptive' (*Literary Gazette* 1851). The first reviewers of *Moby-Dick* knew that a remarkable and highly original text had been put before the world. It is, indeed, '*sui generis*', as an anonymous critic recognised. The reviewers all noted that it was a strange mixture of genres, a 'singular medley', which appealed to some more than to others. An early London review hailed it as reflecting more credit on America than any previous publication and aptly applauded its 'liberal feeling', 'soaring speculation', and (the phrase is very felicitous) 'playful learning'. Another found it an 'ill-compounded mixture of romance and matter-of-fact', sourly deprecated its 'mad English', 'frantic invention', and 'salad-wise patchiness', and dismissed it as 'trash', a species of 'Bedlam literature'. But although quite a number of reviewers baulked at what was perceived as 'purposeless extravagance', most recognised Melville's 'almost unparalleled power over the capabilities of language'. William Butler, a contemporary American lawyer and biographer, lucidly described the book as 'a prose Epic on Whaling' (Epic is exactly the right word) and generously marvelled that 'language in the hands of this master becomes like a magician's wand'. And he makes one singularly pertinent observation: 'Mr. Melville has a strange power to reach the sinuosities of a thought.' In the key chapter in *Mardi* entitled 'Sailing On', Melville had written: 'But this new world here sought, is stranger far than his, who stretched his vans from Palos. It is the world of mind; wherein the wanderer may gaze around, with more of wonder than Balboa's band roving through the golden Aztec shades.' In *Moby-Dick* Melville gazes and roves – and hunts and plays – in that world even to its furthest reaches. Here indeed we find, as another early reviewer noted, 'an intellect working with muscles which seemed not likely soon to tire'. The bodily metaphor is fitting, since in this work Melville does unsurpassed justice to the world of human labour, the unimaginable expenditure and application of human physical energy involved in the mastery and maintenance of, and struggle with, the world men live – and sail – in. It is a book which could only have been written in America and, arguably, only in the mid-nineteenth century, when America seemed to stand at a new height, or new edge, of triumphant dominion and expansionary confidence in the western world. The seas had been conquered, prairies and forests increasingly tamed; the frontier was receding so rapidly that America seemed about to inflate and extend itself to its natural geographic size, while industry and the railways were colonising and subjugating the vast and bountiful continent in hitherto inconceivable ways. The parent country had been decisively beaten and dismissed, and the fratricide of the Civil War was hardly dreamed of. If ever there was a moment when the New World might have been expected to generate its own epic and myth – in effect to find its own Homer – it was surely around 1850. And so it did. 'He had a pull to the origin of things, the first day, the first man, the unknown sea, Betelgeuse, the buried continent. From passive places his imagination sprang a harpoon. He sought prime . . . It gave him the power to find the lost past of America, the unfound present, and make a myth, *Moby-Dick*, for a people of Ishmaels.'[1] Charles Olson's words hit the right note.

The epic, according to Georg Lukács, aspires towards achieving a 'totality of objects', as opposed to drama which aims for a 'totality of actions'. Melville's imagination, as Newton Arvin has noted, was 'profoundly undramatic', but there is an extraordinary feeling of totality – of immensity, range, inclusiveness – in *Moby-Dick*. The simple geographical vastness is unmissable, but the oceans of history are trawled as well. We encounter figures such as Perseus, Alexander and Hannibal, Tamerlane and the Crusaders; czars, sultans, and kings; names from the Bible; famous ocean-voyagers, navigators, and explorers. We are referred to cathedrals and ruins: 'the great dome of St Peter's', the unfinished tower of Cologne, the remains at Lima, the halls of Thermes below the Hôtel de Cluny. We are reminded of far-flung events, from the Mexican War and the Erie Canal to the flooding of the Netherlands; of empires and imperialism ('What was America in 1492 . . . What was Poland to the Czar? What Greece to the Turk? What India to England? What at last will Mexico be to the United States?'); of armies and warfare and the unrelenting carnage of the past. All these enter the book through analogy, the equivalent of epic simile by which the epic poet gradually draws in the circumambient universe and the prelusive ages to amplify his particular narrative. So we also have generous representation of the animal kingdom – often the strange, the splendid, the rare; elephants, anacondas, tigers, bears, the moose, the white albatross, and many others prowl and fly or majestically proceed in and out of the imagery of the book, thus bringing in the wondrous creatures of the land to set beside the sharks, squid, and whales we meet in the story – just as the sea is constantly described in terms of the prairie. Melville wants the whole world in – particularly the human world; hence the slightly improbable spectrum of the crew of the *Pequod*: in addition to the various white Americans we have a Gayhead Indian, a Negro, a Polynesian, a bunch of Parsees, as well as a Maltese, a Tahitian, an Icelander, a Chinaman, a Dane, and so on. The ship itself is made to seem inherently international, multi-national (e.g. 'her old hull's complexion was darkened like a French grenadier's, who has alike fought in Egypt and Siberia' – a perfect example of epic simile). And not only men, but what men do – often what they have to do, to eat, build, survive. Carpenters, blacksmiths, hunters, harpooners, as well as the commercial adventures of speculative capitalism are to be met with. Warner Berthoff has very aptly noted that 'the long succession of passages describing the crew at its jobs makes up a "song of occupations" as comprehensive and ecstatic as Whitman's'.[2] We are led to recall that the European migration to America and the gradual conquest of the continent (and the Indians – not forgotten by Melville; the exploitive Quaker owner of the *Pequod*, Captain Peleg, sits with his profits in a 'wigwam' on the quarter-deck, a little reminder of the dark depredations and expropriations on which America built itself) effectively saw a return to conditions associated with an archaic, 'heroic' age – the raw individualism, the violence, the brawling and boasting, the story-telling, the superstitions, the unsocialised conditions of life (signalled not least by the minimal role played by – allowed to – women), all these were to be found on the American frontier as on the American whaling ship up to the time of Melville's writing and indeed beyond. And they are all to be found in his book. In addition the book echoes with reminders of the new industrial America which was emerging. References to the railway are crucial, particularly in connection with Ahab, but there are also images of drilling and blasting, and mining, of cogged wheels, mechanical looms, and magnetic wires dissonantly mixing with more primitive crafts and archaic arts and handicrafts. As Newton Arvin has eloquently said: 'It is not Bronze Age warfare or hunting that is Melville's subject, as it was Homer's and the others', but it is an industry that had some of the aspects of warfare and certainly of the archaic hunt', so that in his book 'there is a shade of feeling that carries one far out of the nineteenth century and recalls again the epic minstrel and the way he lingered over his imagery of javelin and sword, shield and breastplate, chariot and ship, and such practical activities as sailing, hunting, plowing, and the performance of obligatory rites'.[3]

Though the book centrally concerns a voyage (a hunt, a quest) and is thus most extensively involved with the nonhuman, forever uncivilisable sea, life on land and in cities is not forgotten. The first fifth of the book is set on dry land (only a little less than its share of the earth's surface) and we are made vividly aware of the streets and harbours, offices and chapels, inns and chowder shops, fellowship and loneliness, to be found in cities and settlements such as New York, New Bedford, and Nantucket. And even at sea we are constantly reminded of the sites and institutions which men build in their attempts to live and work together, of the signs and structures of their attempts at corporate, communal existence. Thus the *Pequod* is also a parliament, a guildhall, a fortress, and, perhaps most notably, a factory. There are other worlds in the universe (the multiverse) of Melville's epic. There is the whole world of world literature, for this most graphically physical and material book is also an exceedingly bookish book: not for nothing does it start with pages of 'Etymology' and 'Extracts'. And then, of course, there is the world of all the world's religions and myths, philosophies, and beliefs, the realm in which Melville engages in what he called his 'ontological heroics' and, I might add, his ontological 'ludics' as well. I shall come back to these two worlds, but I just want to remark on one more epic characteristic of *Moby-Dick*. One recurrent feature of epic narratives is the presence of a major hero and of a secondary hero who is something of an anti-hero, something of a clown. The secondary hero is like the hearers, like the readers, like us. He can and does assume that he and we share the same basic attitudes, values, general sense of life. He also shares with us a similar range and type of information and perspectives, and assumes (and thus assumes us into) a common discourse. The major hero is remote from us, remote from everybody. He is almost solipsistically enclosed in his own self-sealing discourse, his own realm and range of information and ideas, which may be obsessions, fantasies, driving delusions, as well as heroic aspirations. The secondary hero tries to mediate between this figure and us, between the singular 'heroic' and the communal and commonly known familiar. Thus Enkidu and Gilgamesh; thus Sancho Panza and Don Quixote; and thus the 'survivor' Ishmael and the 'monomaniac' Ahab.

The first chapter is entitled 'Loomings', a word with at least two senses. As a verb, 'loom', according to the *OED*, means 'to rise and fall, as the sea does . . . to come indistinctly into sight as over the horizon, hence appear impressively or exaggeratedly in enlarged, or distorted, and indistinct form, often because of atmospheric conditions'. The book is full of objects (and related thoughts and speculations) which loom in just this way, the changing 'atmospheric conditions' including Ishmael's moods which, as he knows, influence perception. All the things which 'loom' in this impressive but often distorted or indistinct form centre finally on the whale which, when it does loom above the waters, almost defeats and annihilates the watching human consciousness. 'Loom' as a noun signifies a tool, mainly 'a frame for weaving'. In this sense as well as in the other, it is one of the key recurring words in the book and I will just note some of its occurrences and their contexts to give some idea of the accretive and allusive way in which Melville works, the way words accumulate meanings and speculations accrue to words. In 'The Mat-Maker', when Ishmael and Queequeg are weaving a sword-mat, the activity becomes so dream-like that 'it seemed as if this were the Loom of Time, and I myself were a shuttle mechanically weaving and weaving away at the Fates . . . This warp seemed necessity; and here, thought I, with my own hand I ply my own shuttle and weave my own destiny into these unalterable threads.' And so, he thinks, it is like 'chance, free will and necessity – no wise incompatible – all interweavingly working together'. Notice here the characteristic provisionality of the speculations – 'as if', 'seemed', 'like'; Ishmael is weaving his web of tentative thoughts while weaving the actual mat, the physical and the cerebral, as usual, 'interweavingly working together'. Immediately after this, whales are sighted: the other kind of 'looming'. Later in the book, when Pip is left alone in the sea, 'the infinite of his soul' is drowned. Carried down to mysterious and wondrous depths 'he saw God's foot upon the treadle of the loom, and spoke it; and therefore his shipmates called him mad'. For such a glimpse of the very loom of creation, weaving out its multiple shapes, is a vision which cannot be brought back from the depths and 'spoken'. Language does not reach so far and Pip seems mad because he has dropped out of intelligible human discourse. The loom is now associated with the secret source of all life, as it is, with ever richer implications, in a spectacular passage in 'A Bower in the Arsacides'. Ishmael describes seeing the skeleton of a great Sperm Whale situated, incongruously, in a bower on land – a characteristic confounding or conflating of only apparently discrete and opposed realms.

It was a wondrous sight. The wood was green as mosses of the Icy Glen; the trees stood high and haughty, feeling their living sap; the industrious earth beneath was as a weaver's loom, with a gorgeous carpet on it, whereof the ground-vine tendrils formed the warp and woof, and the living flowers the figures. All the trees, with all their laden branches; all the shrubs, and ferns, and grasses; the message-carrying air; all these unceasingly were active. Through the lacings of the leaves, the great sun seemed a flying shuttle weaving the unwearied verdure. Oh, busy weaver! – pause! – one word! – whither flows the fabric? what palace may it deck? wherefore all these cease-less toilings? Speak, weaver! – stay thy hand! – but one single word with thee! Nay – the shuttle flies – the figures float from forth the loom; the freshet-rushing carpet for ever slides away. The weaver-god, he weaves; and by that weaving is he deafened, that he hears no mortal voice; and by that humming, we, too, who look on the loom are deafened; and only when we escape it shall we hear the thousand voices that speak through it. For even so is it in all material factories. The spoken words that are inaudible among the flying spindles; those same words are plainly heard without the walls, bursting from the opened casements. Thereby have villanies been detected. Ah, mortal! then, be heedful; for so, in all this din of the great world's loom, thy subtlest thinkings may be overheard afar.

From pastoral metaphysics to reminders of modern factory conditions. Is the 'weaver-god', like the submissive mechanical automata produced by the industrial revolution (or the crew of the *Pequod*, mechanised and automatised by the relentless manipulations of 'iron Ahab'), deafened by his own processes and products? Nature produces man but does not answer his questions. The forms *of* things are woven endlessly by the loom of nature; the words *for* things are woven endlessly by man. But there is no converse, no conversation, between them. Is nature saying something which may be heard once we are outside the factory of creation? But only the human worker-writer speaks. The whole book is an endless (and thus unfinishable) weaving from the loom of signs, while the objects and wonders of nature are forever 'looming' before man – tantalising but wordless, indefinable, unarrestable; unuttering and unutterable. And who knows what is the relationship between the products of the two looms – man's tapestry of signs and nature's carpet of wonders? Elsewhere Stubb gives trenchant voice to one of the deep worries of the book and of Melville's age. 'Signs and wonders, eh? Pity if there is nothing wonderful in signs, and significant in wonders!' How close can words really come to things – things in their living reality? You can, as Ishmael does, measure a dead whale. But that is precisely to miss and lose the real *whaleness* of the whale. In 'Cetology' Ishmael tries to 'systematize' the whale in every available detail and from multiple perspectives, an effort he likens to 'the classification of the constituents of a chaos' (remember that the nineteenth century was the great age of ambitious, comprehensive, exhaustive philosophical and taxonomic 'systems'). It is an informed and informative effort: there really is a lot of information about whales in the book. But the categorisations proliferate impossibly, perhaps even parodically, as if to show the hopeless arbitrariness of all our categorisings, the hopelessness of our categorising ambitions. Ishmael leaves his 'system' deliberately and wisely 'unfinished'. 'God keep me from ever completing anything. This whole book is but a draught – nay, but the draught of a draught.' And, of course, a draft of a draft. Ishmael, the whaler-writer, knows that the great Sperm-Whale, 'scientific or poetic, lives not complete in any literature . . . his is an unwritten life'. And Ishmael-Melville's is a written book. We must not expect to find Moby-Dick in *Moby-Dick*.

Shortly before the final chase and the climax of the voyage, Ishmael describes a wondrous, soothing calm and this occasions one of the most important passages in the book. It occurs in 'The Gilder'.

Would to God these blessed calms would last. But the mingled, mingling threads of life are woven by warp and woof; calms crossed by storms, a storm for every calm. There is no steady unretracing progress in this life; we do not advance through fixed gradations, and at the last one pause: – through infancy's unconscious spell, boyhood's thoughtless faith, adolescence' doubt (the common doom), then scepticism, then disbelief, resting at last in manhood's pondering repose of If. But once gone through, we trace the round again; and are infants, boys, and men, and Ifs eternally. Where lies the final harbor, whence we unmoor no more? In what rapt ether sails the world, of which the weariest will never weary? Where is the foundling's father hidden? Our souls are like those orphans whose unwedded mothers die in bearing them: the secret of our paternity lies in their grave, and we must there to learn it.

Here the loom of the book weaves together some of the deepest organising and engendering concerns of the book. These include the destinationless circularity of all human efforts – a dis-teleological vision which ran exactly counter to nineteenth-century versions of unilinear Progress and Evolutions; a sense of the repetitious nature of human existence composed, as it inescapably is, of endless 'retracings'; the tentativeness and provisionality which inhere in the conclusions of all human inquiry so that we can never really transcend the conditionality of 'If'; and, perhaps most important of all, a sense of lost origin (of paternity unknown) so that it is the condition of modern man to feel he is an ontological orphan. Nietzsche, some twenty years later, was to fix on this sense of disorigination as the constituent plight of modern man, deploring contemporary society as 'a culture without any fixed and consecrated place of origin, condemned to exhaust all possibilities and feed miserably and parasitically on every culture under the sun'. And here is one of his central assertions: 'Man today, stripped of myth, stands famished among all his pasts and must dig frantically for roots, be it among the most remote antiquities. What does our great histor-ical hunger signify, our clutching about us of countless other cultures, our consuming desire for knowledge, if not the loss of myth, of a mythic home, the mythic womb.'[4] In many ways *Moby-Dick* demon-strates and diagnoses this condition, this mythic bereftness and desper-ate cultural eclecticism, this denudation and digging, this loss and desire. Melville can well be seen as anticipating some of Nietzsche's most vital and challenging insights and ideas. For instance, that crucial 'perspectivism' which enabled Nietzsche to demonstrate that contest-ing systems of values and beliefs were simply different interpretations of the same text is exactly adumbrated in a comment made by Stubb on the quarter-deck as he watches the various characters interpret the 'strange figures and inscriptions' on Ahab's doubloon. 'There's another rendering now; but still one text.' It could be Nietzsche's guiding motto.

Given the radically orphaned condition of modern man (Ishmael ends as an 'orphan', which is the last word of his book), a danger that Melville could see was the accelerating drift into disconnectedness of the non-affiliated contemporary individual. Like the 'scattered con-gregation' Ishmael sees in the Whaleman's Chapel in New Bedford, people were becoming 'insular and incommunicable'. Melville clearly felt this to be a particular problem in America which, like his *Pequod*, seemed increasingly to be manned by '*Isolatoes*' ('not acknowledging the common continent of man, but each *Isolato* living on a separate continent of his own'). The 'centripetal isolation' of the serenely 'self-reliant' new

American individual was optimistically welcomed and celebrated by, for example, Whitman and Emerson. The devastating and ruinous loneliness, estrangement, and lostness which was always the potential obverse (or result) of this splendid independence – the latent sterile solipsism of self-reliance – was not lost on other American writers, pre-eminently Melville. How, therefore, men might move from isolation to connectedness was a matter of great moment to him and it pervades the book. Let me trace another set of suggestive incremental echoes. With reference to his arrival at the Spouter Inn where he is told he will have to share a room (and a bed), Ishmael says that a man would 'a good deal rather not sleep with [his] brother' and speaks of the advantage of being able to 'cover yourself with your own blanket, and sleep in your own skin'. Alone in the bedroom he is to share with an as yet unknown person, he turns down 'the counterpane' of the bed, and then tries on 'the poncho' which he finds (and which of course belongs to Queequeg). Now these ordinary sounding words are picked up and brought together in a later context, thus: 'the whale is indeed wrapt up in his blubber as in a real blanket or counterpane; or, still better, an Indian poncho slipt over his head, and skirting his extremity'. In skin, in clothes, under blankets and counterpanes – there is undeniable comfort and security in our self-protecting singularity. But no man is self-sufficient. Ahab may curse our 'mortal inter-indebtedness' – it is indeed a symptom of his self-isolating monomania that he should do so – but Queequeg is in the right of it when he says 'It's a mutual, joint-stock world, in all meridians.' Melville himself certainly believed that all men are united by the bond of reciprocal dependence, by a community of function and responsibility.

So what kinds of contact can we make when we emerge from under our blankets or from our covered and cherished separateness? Can we in any way assume another's poncho? The statement about the whale occurs in the chapter called 'The Blanket'. If we look back to the chapter entitled 'The Counterpane' (in which Ishmael wakes to find Queequeg's arm around him) we find Ishmael's account of an episode in his childhood when his stepmother shut him up in his room on the longest day of the year. In desperate solitude he finally drifted off to sleep, only to wake in a state of horror: 'nothing was to be seen, and nothing was to be heard; but a supernatural hand seemed placed in mine. My arm hung over the counterpane, and the nameless, unimaginable, silent form or phantom, to which the hand belonged, seemed closely seated by my bedside.' Here is the question. What does a man touch when his hand comes out from underneath the counterpane? Ishmael's early nightmare experience seems to have been a sense of being held by the hand of pure Non-Being, Nothingness, a contact with utter vacancy. Note that this desolation was precipitated by his stepmother, for Ishmael is careful to call Ahab's world a 'step-mother world', as who should say, a world in which the sense of natural connectedness is missing; in which, as it were, the spontaneous instincts of love and attachment have been evacuated, the erotic replaced by a heartless volition. That is one phenomenon that the outreaching hand can encounter – a palpable, freezing negation. At first Ishmael compares Queequeg's unsolicited embrace with this experience, but he soon learns that it is a loving embrace, 'a bridegroom clasp', as Queequeg hugs him 'as though naught but death should part us twain'. There is also a hand of love which may take hold of ours. The bridal imagery is crucial. It might seem rather daring or problematical used in this way, for the sense or suspicion of homosexuality, or at least of homo-eroticism, is unavoidable. This is even more the case in the chapter 'A Squeeze of the Hand'. This follows 'The Castaway' which concerns Pip's abandonment and crazing isolation in the sea and is (designedly one must feel) about the experience of merging with other men – 'The Cast-togethers' perhaps. The Crew are sitting around a bath squeezing whale sperm. ('A Squeeze of the Hand' precedes a chapter about the whale's penis, 'The Cassock'.) Erotic feelings are engendered to a point which reads like a mixture of orgasmic ecstasy and comic exaggeration. 'Come; let us squeeze hands all round; nay, let us squeeze ourselves universally into each other; let us squeeze ourselves universally into the very milk and sperm of kindness.' Articulated in an all-male community, the exhortations are so outrageous as to be effectively innocent of any possible perversion. But in his ludic, hyperbolic way Melville is inscribing a reminder of how the erotic impulse is crucial in generating instincts and impulses towards inter-connectedness, inter-subjectivity – indeed, inter-penetration. No man is an island – certainly not while squeezing sperm.

In 'The Cassock', the mincer gowns himself in the skin of the whale's penis, and thus 'arrayed in decent black' looks like a 'candidate for an archbishoprick' (the archaic 'k' emphasising the deliberate phallic pun). This is in line with Melville's belief, or sense, that phallus-worship is somewhere at the source of all religions. The whale's phallus is explicitly compared with Queequeg's little phallic idol, Tojo, and the erotic instincts fuel Queequeg's loyalty and friendship just as their extinction in Ahab, who 'lack[s] the low enjoying power' ('few thoughts of Pan stirred in Ahab's brain'), not only leads him to abandon his wife and family but also drives him, who drags his crew, to a ferocious self-destruction. *His* ultimate idol is Thanatos. (I would just note that Ishmael's presence on the *Pequod* is determined by two opposing influences. He goes to sea as a substitute for committing suicide when he is depressed and death drawn, but the choice of the actual ship is traceable to the imperious ruling of the phallic Tojo. Before Freud, Melville could see how Eros and Thanatos might be 'interweavingly working together' – or in opposition – in our motivations. The open, susceptible, flexible, impressionable, sympathetic Ishmael is, life-savingly, ready to recognize and admit both.) Ishmael's relationship with Queequeg is characteristically described in terms of a wedding after that initial 'bridegroom clasp'. This is emphasised in 'The Monkey Rope', where Ishmael sees them as 'wedded' by the life-line which joins them – 'my own individuality was now merged in a joint stock company of two' (he appropriates Queequeg's own metaphor). Ishmael is, then, 'wedded' to Queequeg. But he is also, for a time, 'welded' to Ahab. It is worth looking a little at that word in connection with that figure.

'I, Ishmael, was one of that crew; my shouts had gone up with the rest; my oath had been welded with theirs; and stronger I shouted, and more did I hammer and clinch my oath, because of the dread in my soul.' Ahab works through welding. He calculates how to coerce and use what he revealingly thinks of as 'manufactured man'. His carpenter is 'a stript abstract . . . an unfractioned integral . . . a pure manipulator', a perverse triumph of self-reification, almost an 'automaton'. (Note – almost. That is the Melville touch: he can identify a 'subtle something', the 'unaccountable, cunning life-principle in him', although for the most part he is 'an unreasoning wheel'.) It is the carpenter who, along with the blacksmith, manufactures a new leg for Ahab. It is through them that Ahab has a new harpoon 'welded', though he insists that 'he would weld his own iron'. As with his body, so with his crew. ''Twas not so hard a task. I thought to find one stubborn, at the least; but my one cogged wheel fits into all their various wheels, and they revolve' – so muses Ahab. And the crew become indeed increasingly 'mechanical', as they succumb to Ahab's monomaniac drive and 'iron way'. As they obey his perverse orders they seem to be 'ground' in 'the clamped mortar of Ahab's iron soul. Like machines, they dumbly moved around the deck.' As the climactic chase commences, 'they were one man, not thirty . . . all the individualities of the crew . . . all varieties *were welded into oneness*, and were all directed to that fatal goal which Ahab their one lord and keel did point to' (my italics). In every way associated with iron force, mechanisation, manipulation, Ahab may indeed be seen (as some critics have suggested) as, among other things, a figure embodying the ruthlessness of power released in the contemporary industrial revolution. He is also, and not coincidentally, a homogenising force; one of the possible nightmares of the brave new society of America, as foreseen by Alexis de Tocqueville for example, was that its enriching hospitality to variety and tolerance of difference might paradoxically result in a terminal indistinction, a great flat 'dead level' expanse of human sameness.

What is at stake here is precisely Democracy – its meaning, truth, justice, feasibility, and fate. This was very close to Melville's heart, and indeed to the heart of Melville's America. Ahab is most notably not a democrat. He tends to regard the plurality of men as 'a mob of un-necessary duplicates'. He claims equality with whatever gods there may be, but not with the people. As Starbuck pertinently meditates, 'he would be a democrat to all above; look, how he lords it over all below!' Melville-Ishmael is quite explicit about Ahab's totalitarianism, describing how that 'certain sultanism of his brain' on the ship becomes 'incarnate in an irresistible dictatorship'. Clearly our author-witness feels some respect and awe confronted with this brooding, imperious, autocratic figure. But to feel that he is somehow to be admired as a heroic Faustian Overreacher seems to me to be a wrong reaction – an inappropriate sentimentalisation. Melville, I am sure, is speaking for himself when Ishmael writes of 'that abounding dignity which has no robed investiture. Thou shalt see it shining in the arm that wields a pick or drives a spike; that democratic dignity which, on all hands, radiates without end from God Himself! The great God absolute! The centre and circumference of all democracy! His omnipresence, our divine equality!' Melville was not a Christian but believed, I think, in the diffused divinity – and centrality – of human equality. But he recognised the possible power and authority of another kind of cen-trality, for instance when 'the ringed crown of geographical empire encircles an imperial brain'. As in the case of Nicholas the Czar, 'then, the plebeian herds crouch abased before the tremendous centraliza-tion'. Ahab uses the 'tremendous centralization' of the power of the ship's captain like the czar and treats his crew as serfs and tools. Clearly he has charisma and there is a certain romantic aura in his dark, deranged defiance, amplified as it is by liberal Shakespearean and Carlylean echoes. But he represents a refusal, a dismissal, a blasphemy, of every belief, aspiration, and commitment which nourish the democratic ideal.

And he is not just some fine old archaic warrior-aristocrat who has somehow fallen in the wrong age. Ahab is just such a man as the American nineteenth century was producing, a man who could and did ruthlessly exploit and manipulate the land and the people for his own grandiose, self-aggrandising ends. This too is explicit. Ahab knows how to seem to respect the 'forms and usages' of the ship's community. But he uses them as 'masks', incidentally making use of them 'for other and more private ends than they were legitimately intended to subserve'. The legitimate and legitimizing purpose of the voyage of the *Pequod* is to obtain oil which will then illuminate the communities of the land. It is a cultural quest. And Ahab subverts, perverts, inverts this quest to satisfy the destructive imperatives of his insane lust for vengeance. (See, for example, his trick with the reverse compass, a piece of shabby 'magic' which fascinates the crew but from which Starbuck turns away in disgust. Among other things, Ahab is a disgrace to his calling and position.) His 180-degree perversion of the intent and purpose of the voyage also has sexual implications. The only happy heterosexuality in evidence in the book (if we discount the lovely description of the 'wondrous world' of 'the nursing mothers of the whales') would seem to be on board the ship *Bachelor* where there is 'lively revelry' as the mates and harpooners dance with 'olive-hued girls who had eloped with them from the Polynesian Isles' as the ship heads happily for home. The Captain does not even 'believe' in 'the White Whale' and is clearly very happy in his unbelief. Ahab is heading in exactly the opposite direction. Moby-Dick is no Polynesian girl and whatever Ahab is after it is manifestly a more serious (if manifestly a less pleasant) business than the deck-dancing on the *Bachelor*. Moby-Dick may be seen – and felt, as evoked in some of the greatest prose of the nineteenth century – as simply Nature itself. We might say *herself* as there is much that is seductive and maternal about Moby-Dick; or *himself* since it has the terrifying power of an omnipotent god. It is both. It is the wholeness of Nature in all its beauty, danger, and mystery. Ahab's insane violence is turned against the all-parenting, all-potentiating power of Nature. That this involves some very radical derangement or displacement of the erotic drive is sufficiently intimated throughout, even up to his final cry as he lunges with the hysterical fury of an impotent child at the 'damned whale': '*Thus*, I give up the spear!' The perverse and mutilating sacrifice of the phallus started long before and Ahab has long been unable to relate to Nature in any other way than with hatred, negativity, resentment – and an ingenious, ruthless, ultimately destructive manipulation. In some lights he might seem to be a figure of some tragic grandeur. But it seems to me that he clearly represents a profound inquiry and concern on Melville's part. To what extent was the nation America becoming like, behaving like, the mad captain of the *Pequod*? Mad, but also danger-ously and successfully dominating. Ishmael himself is welded into that helpless and hapless oneness. He only survives, we may feel, because of his prior 'wedding' to Queequeg who showed him the sustaining real-ity of love. It is more than fitting that Queequeg's coffin should also serve as Ishmael's lifebuoy. But Ishmael is a lone survivor. What would, or could, save the ship America if she should follow the *Pequod*? Melville's epic is also a warning – perhaps a prophecy.

Cesare Pavese characterised Melville as 'above all a man of letters' and *Moby-Dick* is as much indebted to books as to whales: indeed, Ishmael, a self-styled 'whale author', continually keeps the problemat-ical relationship between the two in play: as, for instance, when he attempts to classify and 'divide the whales into three primary BOOKS (subdivisible into Chapters)' – Folio, Octavo, Duodecimo. 'I have swam through libraries and sailed through oceans', he says, and the book contains almost as many descriptions of people reading as of people whaling. The large question continually looms – what does it mean that man both writes and fishes? What, if any, is the connection be-tween what we haul up in words and haul up in nets? What, in short, is the relation between text and world? 'You books must know your places', muses Stubb, the shrewd materialist. The more capacious specu-lations of Ishmael turn that sentiment into a question – what *is* the place of books? The proper place, that is, for, in literal terms, they are simply everywhere – pulpit, bedroom, cabin, deck. Beyond the books, men's signs and inscriptions are to be found on all the surfaces of the world. Queequeg's body is covered with the tattooing of a 'departed prophet' who 'had written out on his body a complete theory of the heavens and the earth' in 'hieroglyphic marks'. Queequeg sets about carving the lid of his coffin with figures derived from those on his body. He is both written upon and a writer – an inscribed scribe. In this he is a representative figure – 'a wondrous work in one volume'. So, exactly, is man. Elsewhere Ishmael recalls having the dimensions of a whale's skeleton 'tattooed' on his right arm, from which he now copies them 'verbatim', though, as he explains, he has to conserve space since he needs 'the other parts of my body to remain a blank page for a poem I was then composing'. Well, he is a comical lad, but as usual the joking glimpses at deeper matters. What is all this compulsive marking, recording, copying? Queequeg and Ishmael alike copy signs recording important data on their respective skins, so authorship becomes a sort of secondary tattooing. And what does that make Melville's work? Confronted by a Queequeg, how can you say what is text and what is body? How can you differentiate the skin from the sign? These are not questions to be answered, but questions raised in order to make us think again about our relationship to some of our most basic activities – and, if nothing else, marvel. Having chased the whale at sea, Ishmael is out to catch it in words. 'But when Leviathan is the text, the case is altered.' There is some kind of exchange going on here. If the whale is now textualised, Ishmael must accordingly 'leviathanise' his text. How he might do that is one of the ongoing quests and questions of the book. Certainly, for a book of a whale you must write a whale of a book. And it is among other things a very bookish whale. Much work has been done on the books in which Melville fished for *Moby-Dick*: they include Thomas Beale's *Natural History of the Sperm Whale*, Revd Henry T. Cheever's *The Whale and His Captors*, William Scoresby's *Journal of a Voyage to the Northern Whale Fishery*, and, crucially, Owen Chase's *Narrative of the Most Extraordinary and Distressing Shipwreck of the Whale-Ship Essex*. Plagiarism is not in question. Melville wants to communalise his quest for the whale, and shows the writings of other 'whale authors' 'interweavingly' – we would now say inter-textually – working with his own. Ishmael refers to volumes, commentaries, quartos, lexicons, as often as (indeed, more often than) he refers to harpoons. Words are most certainly not things, at least in no very obvious way, yet the activities of writing and fishing are curiously merged, teasingly mixed – as, for example, when the mates cry out to the man mincing the blubber, 'Bible leaves! Bible leaves!', which, Melville explains, is an exhortation to keep the slices as thin as possible, thus increasing both quantity and quality. The playful interchanges between whale and book which are possible in spite of (or is it because of?) their manifest differences offer Melville-Ishmael the opportunity for some of his most searching and provocative hints and speculations.

'Interchangeability' may indeed be said to be a major theme of the book. When, because he does not know its use, Queequeg carries the wheelbarrow which someone has lent him to transport his belongings, Melville is making a joke about the interchangeability of functions and agents – more widely, reversibility – which operates and modulates throughout the book. Queequeg's tomahawk-pipe which kills and soothes is, like his coffin which becomes a lifebuoy, a representative object. All things are potentially double, paradoxically mixed, oddly reversible. Opposites may turn out to be more like identities. The *Pequod*'s owners are 'Quakers with a vengeance'; Queequeg shows himself to be a most Christian cannibal; the god of democracy chooses his champions from 'the kingly commons'; the culture-vessel *Pequod*, garnished with whales' teeth 'like one continuous jaw', comes to seem uncannily like its nature-prey Moby-Dick. During 'Stubb's Supper' when there is eating above and below decks (thanks to the sharks), Ishmael considers the similarities with a sea-fight. On deck men butcher each other with their swords while underneath the sharks, 'with their jewel-hilted mouths', are similarly engaged with the corpses that come their way and, on occasions, even devouring their own insides: *'were you to turn the whole affair upside down, it would still be pretty much the same thing,* that is to say, a shocking, sharkish business enough for all parties'. The words I have italicised succinctly convey an attitude, a discovery, a belief which is right at the heart of *Moby-Dick*.

At the end of the first day of 'The Chase', Ahab bursts out to his mates: 'Ye two are the opposite poles of one thing; Starbuck is Stubb reversed, and Stubb is Starbuck; and ye two are all mankind.' Ahab's fury at discovering this unexpected reversibility, this underlying similarity in apparent difference is consistent with his ferocious desire – Manichean, Calvinist – to divide the world into starkly opposed categories of good and bad. Above all he wants to identify the whale with all Evil – malevolence, negation, darkness, death; and thus, himself as the heroic, defiant, 'good' opponent. But here again, Melville's book shows that this rigid polarisation simply will not hold when applied to the swimming intermixedness of life. Many of the characteristics and features which Ahab wishes to locate and identify in Moby-Dick are in fact manifest projections of his own temperament – for who or what is more blind, vengeful, sterile, dark, and destructive than he? Conversely, the whales (in general) are associated with light (from their oil), life and sexuality (their sperm spreads a contagious lovingness), family and regeneration (the nursing mothers), and finally an awesome beauty which must command reverence. 'A gentle joyousness – a mighty mildness of repose in swiftness invested the gliding whale' – set this

against the fretful, hindered gait of the crippled Ahab and it is irresist-
ibly clear that his determination to mythify the hunt, the fight, the
antagonism – to make it a proto-religious matter – recoils fatally,
shatteringly on him. The whole book is thick with references to myths
and religions – classical, Hindu, Christian certainly, but most importantly Egyptian. Critics have shown how references to Egyptian history
and mythology permeate the book. The words 'Sphinx', 'pyramid'
(and note that *both* Ahab and Moby-Dick are described as being, in
different ways, 'pyramidical', another hint of opposites melting towards
identity), and 'hieroglyph' occur in many contexts. In connection with
the last word we may note a reference in the book to 'Champillon'
who deciphered Egyptian hieroglyphic writing in the 1820s with the
aid of the Rosetta stone. Excited speculations triggered by his interpretations had an important influence on the nineteenth-century
renaissance in American writing and its interest in symbolism. (Thus,
for example, little Pearl in Hawthorne's *The Scarlet Letter* is described as
a 'living hieroglyph', and thus the markings on the side of the sperm
whale are 'hieroglyphical'. Hermeneutics and matters concerning all
aspects of 'interpretation' were of quite particular interest to American
writers, and to none more than Melville.)

But he did not go to the Egyptians only for their hieroglyphics. Of
all the religious and mythic references in the book, undoubtedly the
most important are those which refer to the myth of Osiris and Typhon.
For details of this myth consult Plutarch's 'Isis and Osiris', as Melville
undoubtedly did, or Bruce Franklin's *The Wake of the Gods: Melville's
Mythology*. In brief, Osiris is a priest-king-god who sails the seas hunting
Typhon, an aquatic monster. Once a year Typhon dismembers Osiris
who then disappears from the earth, and the land is infertile. In a
vernal phallic ritual Osiris is healed and the fertility of the land is
restored. There is every reason to believe that Melville regarded this as
the Ur-myth, and that he subscribed to the then central notion of
comparative mythology that Egypt was the birthplace of the gods, the
original ground of religion. The similarities between Osiris–Typhon
and Ahab–Moby-Dick are obvious. What is crucial is what Melville
has done with the original mythic distributions. There is, obviously, no
inclusion of a vision of resurrection, restoration, regeneration – though
no exclusion of its possibility. More importantly, Melville has mixed,
blurred, and duplicated the traditional features and virtues attached to
the king-god and the monster respectively so that there is much that is
Typhon-like about Ahab and a good deal of the majesty and potency

of Osiris in Moby-Dick – an extension, this, on a cosmic scale of the possible interchangeability and reversibility of role and function which was adumbrated in a lowly way when Queequeg shouldered his wheelbarrow and the aid became the load. What Melville is showing is that the apparently opposing elemental powers and drives which go to make up life – good and evil, light and dark, love and hate, potency and negation, Osiris and Typhon – are not absolutely separable or starkly opposed. Rather, they are reciprocal, mutually constitutive, 'interweavingly' mixed. The significance and importance of this demonstration of the potentially disastrous, all-annihilating effects of the kind of Manichean, dualistic modes of thought based on notions of embattled exclusivity, exemplified in extreme form by Ahab, can hardly be overstressed. As against this we have the example of Ishmael's tolerant inclusiveness, his disinclination for rigid partial versions and sectarian monocularity, his eroticised and playful porousness to the wholeness of life.

Ishmael is his style. 'I try all things; I achieve what I can.' He is careless about 'narrative', offhand about consistency, resistant to completion or closure. He does not care to approach his writing task 'methodically', maintaining that 'there are some enterprises in which a careful disorderliness is the true method'. He likes to 'hypothesize' but rarely asserts. Somewhat like 'The Hyena' he 'bolts down all events, all creeds, and beliefs, and persuasions, all hard things visible and invisible, never mind how knobby', and disgorges them in his richly mixed writing. He can change mood like the weather, going from the potentially suicidal gloom of his 'hypos' (hypochondria) to a truly cosmic sense of the absurd which 'takes this whole universe for a vast practical joke': he has read his Descartes, Locke, and Kant but seems more at home with the 'free and easy sort of genial, desperado philosophy' bred by his whaling experience at sea. His land tasks always seem to have involved digging down – ditches, canals, wells, wine vaults, cellars, cisterns – and he certainly likes to probe into matters material and immaterial. But he never rests content or secure with anything, any thought, he finds. He digs and writes – and moves on. When he writes his 'last will and testament' at sea he feels effectively resurrected, reborn, afterwards: 'I survived myself.' His survival is, in effect, through writing, for *Moby-Dick* is, in effect, another 'testament' and testimony to his survival through style. I have been speaking of Ishmael but in this matter of style he is, of course, indistinguishable from Melville. In its vast assimilations, its seemingly opportunistic eclecticism, its pragmatic and improvisatory nonchalance, its capacious grandiloquence and demotic humour it is indeed a style for America – the style of America. In *Mardi* there is a discussion of the strange work of the writer Lombardo (who claims to have 'created the creative'), called the Koztanza. Abrazza objects that it 'lacks cohesion; it is wild, unconnected, all episode' – as some early reviewers said of *Moby-Dick*. Babalanja defends the work in these terms: 'And so is Mardi itself: – nothing but episodes; valleys and hills; rivers, digressing from plains; vines, roving all over; boulders and diamonds; flowers and thistles; forests and thickets; and, here and there, fens and moors. And so, the world is Koztanza.' 'Mardi' is Polynesian for 'the world' and we may take this defence to suggest something of both the scope and the ambition of *Moby-Dick* – the topography of its topics, the terrain of its style. I could put it another way. In his journals, Emerson noted that 'genius . . . finds its end in its means'.[5] In *Moby-Dick* Melville's 'end' may be said to be a history of the whaling industry, a study in comparative mythology, the epicalising of America, the meaning or unmeaning of life. And all this would be true enough. But his 'means' was writing. And it was in the processes, possibilities, and procedures of writing, explored and exploited with an inventiveness and to an extent no other American writer has matched, that Melville's genius found its true and proper and infinitely rewarding end.

NOTES

1 Charles Olson, *Call Me Ishmael* (New York: Grove Press, Inc., 1947), p. 15.
2 Warner Berthoff, *The Example of Melville* (Princeton: Princeton University Press, 1962), p. 81.
3 Newton Arvin, *Herman Melville* (New York: William Sloane Associates, 1950), p. 159.
4 Friedrich Nietzsche, *The Birth of Tragedy*, section xxiii, tr. Francis Golffing (Garden City, NY: Doubleday & Co., 1956), p. 137.
5 Ralph Waldo Emerson, *Journals and Miscellaneous Notebooks*, ed. William H. Gibson *et al.*, 16 vols. (Cambridge: Harvard University Press, 1960–82), III, 221.

CHAPTER 5

Melville's counterfeit detector:
The Confidence-Man

In 1855 P. T. Barnum published his autobiography, *Life*. He started his career as a showman by exhibiting an aged negress, fraudulently claimed to have been George Washington's childhood nurse. His successful career as showman and entrepreneur was based on pioneering work in developing modes of extravagant publicity and advertising. Later he was to organise his famous circus which he advertised quite simply as 'the greatest show on earth'. He quite shamelessly admits, indeed brazenly boasts, that from the start, when he worked in a store, deception was the spirit, if not the name, of the game. 'The customers cheated us in their fabrics: we cheated the customers with our goods. Each party expected to be cheated, if it was possible.'[1] He describes a life devoted to hoaxing (and entertaining) a public, perhaps excessively gullible or perhaps content enough to be deceived if it also meant being amused.

Also in 1855 Herman Melville published *Israel Potter: His Fifty Years of Exile*. Israel is an American loser – a failure and a victim. After fighting for his country he spends years of exile in England and Europe. When he finally manages to return to America he finds his family homestead burnt down and being ploughed over, while he himself is spurned by his ungrateful country and left to die in poverty and obscurity. 'He was repulsed in efforts, after a pension, by certain caprices of law. His scars proved his only medals. He dictated a little book, the record of his fortunes. But long ago it faded out of print – himself out of being – his name out of memory.' His is a case of total obliteration and erasure – he is one of those many Americans whom Thomas Pynchon was to designate as 'the praeterite', all those discarded, passed over, negated, or otherwise junked by the dominant power systems. But Melville also includes in this novel a portrait of the man who was the most successful American of them all – Benjamin Franklin. He perfectly catches that mixture of cunning and innocence which seems to have been the

81

essence of the man. 'The diplomatist and the shepherd are blended; a union not without warrant; the apostolic serpent and dove. A tanned Machiavelli in tents.' And Melville goes on to describe him as, effectively, *the* archetypal American:

Having carefully weighed the world, *Franklin could act any part in it*. By nature turned to knowledge, his mind was often grave, but never serious. At times he had seriousness – extreme seriousness – for others, but never for himself. Tranquillity was to him instead of it. This philosophical levity of tranquillity, so to speak, is shown in his easy variety of pursuits. Printer, postmaster, almanac maker, essayist, chemist, orator, tinker, statesman, humorist, philosopher, parlor-man, political economist, professor of housewifery, ambassador, projector, maximmonger, herb-doctor, wit: – Jack of all trades, master of each and mastered by none – *the type and genius of his land*. (my italics)

In his *Autobiography*, itself a calculated product, a piece of publicity, an advertisement, Franklin displays a curiously instrumental attitude towards himself – as if the image of himself can be made, constructed, always with an eye on the public. It is as though he is always detached from the self that acts and performs in the world, manipulating it with a cool and calculating amiability which is not quite cynicism, not quite hypocrisy, but which does suggest a degree of smooth and protean adaptability. This can make one wonder about the core morality, the determining values and the commitments, the emotional capacities, of the internal manager, promoter, producer of all his fluent, sometimes devious, adjustments, his opportunistic, often brilliant, improvisations. Who, or what, is in charge of the show? One might have asked the same thing of P. T. Barnum. Both men, certainly, showed an uncanny promotional flair.

In his essay in 'The Poet', published in 1844, Emerson repeatedly deploys a word which is at the centre of his thinking – 'metamorphosis'. The poet 'sees the flowing or metamorphosis'; his speech 'flows with the flowing of nature'; his mind 'flows into and through things . . . and the metamorphosis is possible'; 'the metamorphosis once seen, we divine that it does not stop'. This emphasis on 'incessant metamorphosis', on the 'fluxional', the 'flexible', the 'plastic', the 'ductile', the 'fluid and volatile' is everywhere in Emerson. It stems from his root conviction that the real evil in the world is everything that can be subsumed under the notion of 'fixity': 'There are no fixtures in nature'; 'The quality of the imagination is to flow, and not to freeze'; 'The only sin is limitation.' A lot of this reiterated stress on the supreme value of endless metamorphosis stems from his antipathy to the past, to all institutions, to previous authorities, to social structures, indeed to the 'jail-yard of individual relations' – to anything that binds, limits, constrains, commits. Indeed, in his seminal essay 'Self-Reliance' – seminal for America – he rather alarmingly announced 'I will have no covenants but proximities.' From one point of view this could seem like a willingness, indeed a determination, to dissolve identity in present contingency and certainly Emerson seems willing to embrace an extreme discontinuity of self: 'A foolish consistency is the hobgoblin of little minds . . . live ever in a new day'; 'Our moods do not believe in each other.' We should take our cue from nature, and nature, as Emerson sees it, is perpetual change: 'this surface on which we now stand is not fixed, but sliding'. So slide with it: 'we live amid surfaces, and the true art of life is to skate well on them'. Everything is 'flowing' – so 'go with the flow'. That Californian injunction of the 1960s is pure Emerson. For Emerson metamorphosis was evolutionary, ascensional, a constant move towards higher and ever higher forms. Clearly this overlooks or minimises the possibility of regressive or degenerative metamorphosis, a devolution or degradation to lower forms – the Kafka vision. And whatever else, the emphasis on sliding, skating, flowing could suggest an enthusiastic endorsement of a self a good deal more adaptive and protean than Franklin's deft self-technologist. And was there any enduring depth of self under this eager notional capitulation to shifting surface and incessant transience? Emerson had his own answer to this problem of the ultimate identity of the fluid, mutating self:

Man is not a farmer, or a professor, or an engineer, but he is all. Man is priest, and scholar, and statesman, and producer, and soldier. In the *divided* or social state these functions are parcelled out to individuals, each of whom aims to do his stint of the point work, whilst each other performs his . . . The state of society is one in which the members have suffered amputation from the trunk, and strut about like so many walking monsters – a good finger, a neck, a stomach, an elbow, but never a man. Man is thus metamorphosed into a thing, into many things.[2]

Individuation is amputation; socialisation is fragmentation. There is, after all, bad metamorphosis – from a mystical unitary totality into partiality and reification. Emerson can solve his problem – or conjure it away – by positing a transcendental identification of the real self with the All. Meanwhile, in the 'divided' state which is society, all those fingers and elbows can go on sliding and skating around on the shifting surface of things, abjuring consistency, refusing covenants, eluding relations. It can be seen that there is a high potential for anarchy in Emerson's descriptions and prescriptions. Certainly, there is not the slightest interest in what might make for and sustain any kind of community or communality. The self-reliant Emersonian self is determinedly anti-social.

So, in his own very different way, is Edgar Alan Poe's 'diddler'. In 1843 Poe wrote an essay entitled 'Diddling Considered as One of the Exact Sciences'. Jeremy Diddler was in fact a character in an English play (*Raising the Wind*, 1803, by James Kenney) who borrowed small amounts of money with no intention of repaying them, but Poe sees something more profound in the art to which he gave his name: 'A crow thieves; a fox cheats; a weasel outwits; a man diddles.'[3] He is indeed a self-reliant self – against the world: 'He regards always the main chance. He looks to Number One. You are Number Two, and must look to yourself.'[4] But Poe's diddler is not just a generic cheat, though cheating is all he does. He has very distinctive characteristics. 'Diddling rightly considered, is a compound, of which the ingredients are minuteness, interest, perseverance, ingenuity, audacity, *nonchalance*, originality, impertinence, and *grin*.'[5] Poe was himself a unique sort of literary diddler, playing every kind of trick and hoax on his readers and indeed manifesting in his art just those qualities he ascribed to the more overtly financial diddler. And his portrait seems almost prophetic. In July 1849 the *New York Herald* carried an item headed 'Arrest of the Confidence Man' which began:

For the last few months a man has been travelling about the city, known as the 'Confidence Man;' that is, he would go up to a perfect stranger in the street, and being a man of genteel appearance, would easily command an interview. Upon this interview he would say, after some little conversation, 'have you confidence in me to trust me with your watch until to-morrow;' the stranger, at this novel request, supposing him to be some old acquaintance, not at the moment recollected, allows him to take the watch, thus placing 'confidence' in the honesty of the stranger, who walks off laughing, and the other, supposing it to be a joke, allows him so to do. In this way many have been duped . . .[6]

This reads exactly like one of the examples Poe gives of successful diddles. And, of course, it gave Melville the title – even perhaps the idea – for his last novel.

Later in the same year, Melville's friend Evert Duyckinck, writing in the *Literary World*, commented on an editorial in another paper concerning the 'Confidence Man':

The Confidence Man, the new species of the Jeremy Diddler recently a subject of police fingering, and still later impressed into the service of Burton's comicalities in Chambers Street, is excellently handled by a clever pen in the *Merchants' Ledger*, which we are glad to see has a column for the credit as well as for the debit side of humanity. It is not the worst thing that can be said for a country that it gives birth to a confidence man: – '. . . It is a good thing, and speaks well for human nature, that, at this late day, in spite of all the hardening of civilization and all the warning of newspapers, men *can be swindled*. The man who is *always* on his guard, *always* proof against appeal, who cannot be beguiled into the weakness of pity by *any* story – is far gone, in our opinion, towards being a hardened villain. He may steer clear of petty larceny and open swindling – but mark that man well in his intercourse with his fellows – they have no confidence in him, and he has none in them. He lives coldly among his people, he walks an iceberg in the marts of trade and social life – and when he dies, may Heaven have that confidence in him which he had not in his fellow mortals!'[7]

These cogent and eloquent – and perceptive – comments raise profound issues which are at the heart of Melville's novel, issues concerning the crucial role of 'trust' in society – not to say in humanity. I note in passing that the two men who most notably *cannot be swindled* in the novel (Mark Winsome and Egbert) are based on Emerson and Thoreau and in their casuistical impermeability to pity they are just as ice-cold as the writer in the *Merchant's Ledger* predicted such a type would be.

Clearly by running together descriptions of Poe's diddler, Emerson's sliding self-reliant metamorphoser, Franklin's craftily adaptable self, P. T. Barnum the hoaxer–showman, and the historically actual American confidence man of 1849, I am suggesting that they have something in common, and something which is peculiarly American. I stress this because, while there seem to be trickster figures in every culture's mythology or folk-lore, so that Hermes has innumerable relations and descendants, and while Proteus, too, is only one of many 'shape-shifters' in world narrative, and while some people have no doubt abused other people's trust since at least the time when there were signs and signals with which to deceive them, the 'confidence man' is a figure of quite special – and central – importance in American culture and history. To appreciate better what Melville is doing in his extraordinary novel, it is really essential to try to see it in its historical context – that is, as being very specifically concerned with matters and phenomena generated in and by the conditions of American society, or lack of it, in the first half of the nineteenth century when the euphoria of Independence had not yet been sobered by the Civil War. Of course the novel touches on matters of universal importance and concern, but some of these universal problems first began to emerge in their modern form in the America of this time.

In the chapter entitled 'American Ideals 1800', in his magisterial *History of the United States of America During the Administrations of Thomas Jefferson and James Madison*, Henry Adams contrasts the animating spirit of these times with the aims and aspirations of the first colonists:

In the early days of colonization, a very new settlement represented an idea and proclaimed a mission . . . No such character belonged to the colonization of 1800. From Lake Erie to Florida, in long, unbroken line, pioneers were at work, cutting into the forests with the energy of so many beavers, and with no more express moral purpose than the beavers they drove away. The civilization they carried with them was rarely illumined by an idea; they sought room for no new truth, and aimed neither at creating, like the Puritans, a government of saints, nor, like the Quakers, one of love and peace . . . To a new society, ignorant and semi-barbarous, a mass of demagogues insisted on applying every stimulant that could inflame its worst appetites, while at the same instant taking away every influence that had hitherto helped to restrain its passions. Greed for wealth, lust for power, yearning for the blank void of savage freedom such as Indians and wolves delighted in, – these were the fires that flamed under the cauldron of American society, in which, as conservatives believed, the old, well-proven, conservative crust of religion, government, family, and even common respect for age, education, and experience was rapidly melting away, and was indeed already broken into fragments, swept about by the seething mass of scum ever rising in greater quantities to the surface.[8]

Adams was a conservative, and a pessimist, and doubtless there is some personal feeling behind these patrician words, but it clearly did seem to many observers that, having as it were slipped the leash of England – broken free of old ties – America in the nineteenth century was becoming a place of both vertiginous activity and radical uncertainty of direction. And the Americans themselves: what kind of people were these citizens of this new republic turning out to be like? Alexis de Tocqueville saw them as dissolvers of the past, endlessly transforming their heritage, their environment, themselves:

Under their hand, political principles, laws, and human institutions seem malleable, capable of being shaped and combined at will. As they go forward, the barriers which imprisoned society and behind which they were born are lowered; old opinions, which for centuries had been controlling the world, vanish; a course almost without limits, a field without horizon, is revealed: the human spirit rushes forward and traverses them in every direction.[9]

This of course is exactly what Emerson would praise and prescribe for the new American individual, but de Tocqueville draws out some of the possible pains and problems in this new, seemingly almost anarchic, state of society: 'Thus not only does democracy make every man forget his ancestors, but it hides his descendants and separates his contemporaries from him; it throws him back forever upon himself alone and threatens in the end to confine him entirely within the solitude of his own heart.'[10] It is one thing to break up old, repressive hierarchies and jettison a tyrannous and burdensome past. But if the process goes on to sever all generational and social ties – call them chains, call them bonds, or covenants – then self-reliance might turn into a self-sealing solitude. It is no doubt good to get rid of imperious marks of rank and cruel badges of class division, but again new problems may arise: 'As each class gradually approaches others and mingles with them, its members become undifferentiated and lose their class identity for each other.'[11] We know very well how insidious class distinctions, in every sense, can be – and de Tocqueville is another conservative. But when all signs of 'class identity' are erased, social identity itself can become endlessly problematical. This may be an exhilarating freedom from restrictive and coercive classifications, but it might make it harder and harder to know just whom you are talking to, as Melville – a very emphatic and passionate democrat – shows in his novel. And one may drown in undifferentiation, as one may indeed suffocate in hierarchy. What de Tocqueville could see was that in this America there was bound to be something like a permanent crisis of authority. There was so much fluidity, so much movement, that it might be impossible, and would certainly be very difficult, to locate or establish or recognise any stable guide-posts. 'Paternal authority' was notably weakened and this could be taken as a paradigm of the waning and dimming of all previous sources of directional influence. Movement and expansion can mean progress and development, but when 'the whole of society is in motion' it can become increasingly difficult to orient, or focus, or even locate, yourself. It is important to remember that what was happening in America was not the sudden upheaval and dislocation of a previously stable and relatively settled society. Immigration and a moving frontier meant an endless inpouring of strangers, who in the general movement became endlessly re-estranged. Melville's description of the embarking and disembarking passengers on his Mississippi steamer *Fidèle* makes it exactly a microcosm of America, the frontier of America in particular, at this time: 'though always full of strangers, she continually, in some degree, adds to, or replaces them with strangers still more strange'. In a society made up completely of strangers and perpetually stirring itself, problems of communication, recognition, identification, and, above all, trust and confidence become *particularly* acute. And the problem may have a further, and more worrying, twist: 'for in democratic times what is most unstable, in the midst of the instability of everything, is the heart of man'. It may be difficult and confusing trying to work out who, or what, your neighbour, or contiguous stranger, is. But what if you should find that you have become a stranger to yourself? Such a society was, of course, peculiarly liable to produce 'confidence men'. To someone with an eye as searching as Melville's it might become a matter of more moment whether it would – or could – produce anything else.

There was another characteristic of these early nineteenth-century Americans identified by Adams which gives an added meaning or dimension to the notion of 'confidence':

the hard, practical, money-getting American democrat ... was in truth living in a world of dream, and acting a drama more instinct with poetry than all the avatars of the East, walking in gardens of emerald and rubies, in ambition already ruling the world and guiding Nature with a kinder and wiser hand than had ever yet been felt in human history ... Even on his practical and sordid side, the American might easily have been represented as a victim to illusion. If the Englishman had lived as the American speculator did, – in the future, – the hyperbole of enthusiasm would have seemed less monstrous.[12]

And Adams then describes the sort of visionary enthusiasm which could already see – or imagine – 'magnificent cities' where there were actually only 'tremendous wastes, swamps and forests' – exactly the kind of wild 'confidence' in the future which Charles Dickens satirises in *Martin Chuzzlewit* when a land agent describes the 'flourishing' city of Eden to an impressed Martin, who gradually discovers that it is 'not quite' built yet; Melville glances at this when his Confidence Man tries to arouse interest (and contributions) with his evocation of the 'thriving city' of New Jerusalem. Clearly this kind of visionary enthusiasm could make it difficult to distinguish between the imaginative prophet – say, Whitman – and the fraudulent speculator. Of both it might be said that 'his dream was his whole existence', as Adams said of the generic American of 1800, adding of this 'class of men' that 'whether imagination or greed led them to describe more than actually existed, they still saw no more than any inventor or discoverer must have seen in order to give him the energy of success'.[13]

The result of all this living in, and on, and indeed off, the future was the emergence of America as a 'confidence culture'. The phrase is Gary Lindberg's, who describes how 'the visionary tradition has been one of the major continuities in American culture, linking land boomers and poets, prophets and profiteers'. Indeed, 'in the general atmosphere of boosterism and mutual congratulation, "America" itself came to exist primarily in the imagination'.[14] Lindberg demonstrates that 'the confidence man sees more opportunities in New World fluidity, not merely to improve his lot by cleverness and technical proficiency but actually to recast the self through cunning imitation. He becomes the specialist in secondary, reproducible identities.'[15] The very idea of 'the self-made man' (the phrase dates apparently from 1832) is peculiarly American since, aptly ambiguous, it suggests both the independent achievement of success and a more radical act of self-parenting. Jay Gatsby, who 'sprang from his own conception of himself', is only one of the more memorable of the many figures in American literature – and indeed history – who dismiss and erase or ignore their actual biological point of origin in favour of some more desirable, or profitable, or marketable, fabricated identity. Following other critics (R. W. B. Lewis, Kenneth Lynn, Daniel Hoffman), Lindberg puts together such figures as Franklin, Jefferson, William James, and more generic American folk types like the Yankee Peddler, the booster, the gamesman, the healer, along with writers such as Emerson and Whitman, as figures who all, in their very different ways, traffic in 'belief', or peddle in 'confidence'. And in his survey he shows how prevalent the figure of the confidence man is in American literature, from the earliest years of the republic, before he had been named, up to the present day. Carwin and Arthur Mervyn in Charles Brockden Brown's *Wieland* and *Arthur Mervyn*, Richard Jones in James Fenimore Cooper's *The Pioneeers*, Holgrave in Hawthorne's *The House of the Seven Gables* ('putting off one exterior, and snatching up another, to be soon shifted for a third'), Johnson J. Hooper's Simon Suggs ('It is good to be shifty in a new country'), the Duke and the Dauphin on Huckleberry Finn's raft, and Huckleberry Finn himself (not to mention Tom Sawyer), William Faulkner's Flem Snopes, Ralph Ellison's Invisible Man, Saul Bellow's Augie March – the list is indefinitely extendable: all these figures, in various ways, trade in and on trust and belief – in different ways and, of course, for widely different ends. It may be for the most ruthless exploitation and self-aggrandisement, as in the case of Flem Snopes; or it might be for sheer survival, as with Huck Finn. But in one way or another 'confidence' is the name of the game, and it is a peculiarly (not exclusively, but peculiarly) American game. And no book both demonstrates and explores this fact more profoundly, memorably, disturbingly than Melville's novel, which indeed confronts the Confidence Man in all his singularity and multiplicity.

I use the words advisedly since a reader coming to the novel for the first time would almost certainly think that there was no one confidence man, as the title suggests, but a whole series of them. Critics, most notably Bruce Franklin,[16] have shown that a number of the figures who appear in very different dress are probably avatars of one 'original' confidence man – though even here there has been disagreement as to whether, for instance, the deaf mute of the first chapter is one of these avatars or not. And there is certainly more than one confidence man on board the *Fidèle*, indeed often two are present at the same time trying to 'con' each other, as in the long central exchange between Francis Goodman and Charlie Noble, so that it must be uncertain how many of the characters are in fact one man in several disguises and how many are simply other confidence men at large. It is important to recognise that this uncertainty – are they all one, or all different people? – cannot be resolved, since this is central to the novel's deep intention: namely, to question whether man has a core self, whether there is any consistency or continuity-through-change of character; or whether man is indeed serial and partial, a plurality of fragmentary and momentary roles? Spreading outward through the book is growing doubt about the ontological status of individual identity, which means that it does not read like other novels of its time, precisely because it calls into question the conception of character and the conventions of representation which were current then and which, indeed, for many readers and writers, still prevail today.

Contemporaries certainly had trouble with it. 'A novel it is not, unless a novel means forty-five conversations held on board a steamer, conducted by passengers who might pass for the errata of creation, and so far resembling the Dialogues of Plato as to be undoubted Greek to ordinary men' (*The Literary Gazette*, 11 April 1857).[17] Actually, that is no bad description. The forty-odd characters are so pastless, so unfamilied, so devoid of interiority, such strangers strange and estranged, that, to a conventional eye, they might well seem like some of nature's mistakes – fragmentary, unfinished, incomplete. For this is the kaleidoscope of the new world where 'varieties of mortals blended their varieties of visage and garb. A Tartar-like picturesqueness; a sort of pagan abandonment and assurance. Here reigned the dashing and all-fusing spirit of the West, whose type is the Mississippi itself, which, uniting the streams of the most distant and opposite zones, pours them along, helter-skelter, in one cosmopolitan and confident tide.' At first that reads like a topographic and sociological description – and indeed the Mississippi setting is as important here as it is in, say, *Huckleberry Finn*. But in fact there is effectively no natural description in the novel, and it is more philosophical matters concerning 'fusion' and the 'uniting' of 'opposite zones' which gradually emerge, until the 'cosmopolitan and confident tide' finally takes on the form of the Cosmopolitan who, exactly half-way through the book, appears in his fantastic 'plumagy', many-hued and 'grotesque' dress, and announces himself as indeed the very spirit – if that is the right word – of 'fusion'. 'A cosmopolitan, a catholic man; who, being such, ties himself to no narrow tailor or teacher, but federates, in heart as in costume, something of the various gallantries of men under various suns. Oh, one roams not over the gallant globe in vain. Bred by it, is a fraternal and fusing feeling. No man is a stranger.' In an America which was showing itself to be inherently fissile and in which everyone was more or less a stranger, a figure emanating or preaching – or is it peddling? – 'federation' and the 'fusing feeling' should surely be welcome. But fusion can become confusion and have deeply ambivalent results. Like the 'tide' described at the start, the cosmopolitan is also supremely 'confident', or at least a sweet-voiced spokesman for confidence, and most certainly the ultimate confidence man. There are far-reaching problems here and none more so than those raised by the word 'confidence', which has connotations ranging from the most sacred trust, generous optimism, enabling hope, compassion and friendship, privacy and discretion; on to the darker side of the word, involving deceit, subterfuge, and trickery, leading to distrust, suspicion, and estrangement. The word and its implications are debated on almost every page of the book, and here again the reviewer was quite accurate. The book is made up almost exclusively of conversations. People talk, argue, debate, heckle, tell and re-tell stories, and then discuss them. There is no action (only one blow is struck); there are no emotional or sexual relations (indeed no women, except for two widows – perhaps one?); the boat never gets to New Orleans (and there is no discernible captain); the last named port of call is Cairo, or, more specifically and appropriately, 'a grotesque-shaped bluff' called 'the Devil's joke', terms which describe what is going on on board, and

perhaps the novel itself. The last landscape to be described, even referred to, is the 'swampy and squalid domain' which Pitch sees as he
leans over the rail, looking after the departed PIO man (who has of
course conned him) and pondering 'the mystery of human subjectivity
in general'. That – and whether there finally is any – is what the book
is pondering as well. It has no time for the mute externals of the given
world, for it is above all interested in the words men say – and write –
as they attempt to relate or exploit, to communicate or manipulate, to
enlighten or outwit, to tell the truth or insert a lie.

The negro cripple who claims to be 'werry well wordy of all you
kind ge'mmen's kind confidence' provides a felicitous pun with his
dialect pronunciation, for the actors in this book, on this boat, are
indeed 'wordy' and the connection between words and 'worth' or trustworthiness, indeed between language and value or integrity, is just
what – in suitably various guises and disguises – this masquerade of a
book is all about. And the most 'wordy' figure is the Confidence Man/
Men, who does indeed initiate a series of latter-day Platonic dialogues
with himself as an appropriately altered Socrates, metamorphosed by
the new conditions of America into a slippery (sliding and skating),
Franklinesque, shape-shifter and jack of many trades or poses –
merchant, philanthropist, speculator, healer, even philosopher (or is it
slavetrader?). Whatever else – and he receives precious little cash, and
one free haircut, for all his pains and ploys (he is not a very successful
confidence man) – he does perform a Socratic role. His various inter-
locutors are forced (or persuaded), in one way or another, to reveal
themselves, or, better, they are variously unmasked, though whether
simply to expose another mask cannot be ascertained. If much of
his talk is as bewildering as 'Greek' to the 'ordinary man' this is precisely because his aim is mystification – but his end is hardly financial.
'Was the man a trickster, it must be more for the love than the lucre.
Two or three dirty dollars the motive to so many wiles?' The motives
of the Confidence Man are unknown and undiscoverable; we have
no access to his interiority, if he has any. He has been called a satirist
and a moralist, as he has been identified as Christ and Satan. But
fixed identifications and classifications are just what this novel renders
impossible. What we can say is that he is an agent of exposure, and
many concealed qualities and aspects of people's natures are teased
or provoked into the open. Once or twice positive qualities emerge:
Mr Roberts, the merchant, is a kind man; the widow reads 1 Corinthians
13 and is indeed somewhat bemusedly charitable. But usually some

meanness, or greed, or downright inhumanity comes to light and manifests or declares itself. It may be a 'ship of fools' as one cynic shouts: it is certainly a ship of knaves. As Bruce Franklin showed, every kind of fraud and swindling is represented on board: quack-healers, herb-doctors, land agents, counterfeiters, card sharps, pseudo charity agents, transcendentalist philosophers, false clergymen (he demonstrated conclusively that the Episcopal minister is another confidence man), every variety of contemporary American operator. And a vast range of reference brings in and variously implicates many historical figures, philosophers, writers, and also mythical figures and 'gods'. The fusion/confusion starts to spread through time as well as space, and there is hardly any seeing where it will stop. For by the end all the lights are out.

Let us consider how this unusual novel begins and concludes. It starts on April the first at sunrise – hardly a subtle clue. A man in 'cream-colors' appears 'as suddenly as Manco Capac' – a founding divinity of the Inca Empire. It is stressed that he has no luggage and no friends and is 'in the extremest sense of the word, a stranger'. He wears a white 'fleecy' cap. Deaf and dumb, he writes out the Corinthian definitions of Charity on a slate. The crowd resents his 'intrusion' and regards both him and his writing as 'somehow inappropriate to the time and place'. The crowd is sceptical about him since it perceives 'no badge of authority about him'. They then revile, mock, and reject him and at the end of the chapter, looking 'gentle and jaded', he retreats or withdraws into sleep: 'his flaxen head drooped, his whole lamb-like figure relaxed'. We are almost too pointedly asked to interpret him as a Christ figure. But remember, it is April the first for the reader as well! There are two other written signs posted up on the ship. The barber's notice, 'NO TRUST', initiates a series of postures and reactions of obdurate and even violent cynicism and scepticism, distrust or disbelief which the confidence man/men meets on every appearance. And there is a placard 'offering a reward for the capture of a mysterious impostor, supposed to have arrived recently from the East; quite an original genius in his vocation, as would appear, though wherein his originality consisted was not clearly given; but what purported to be a careful description of his person followed'. The crowd has gathered round this 'announcement' as if it is 'a theatre-bill'. They are eager for amusement, for illusion; they want a performance. Now, the East may be Bethlehem, or it may be New York. We are not given the 'careful description', an occlusion which leaves it open as to whether the man in 'cream-colors', who has certainly come 'from some far country beyond the prairies', fits it or not. Or perhaps the book which follows is the 'careful description'. The Cosmopolitan will be talked about as 'QUITE AN ORIGINAL' after his performance on the ship, and it is an open question whether the man in cream-colours is the original, originary, originating impostor in the book, or whether impostors have any 'origin'. Open, because he *might* be a reincarnation of Christ, or some other God who came down to earth to help mankind. Though in retrospect we may remember the white 'fleecy' cap when we are told of the 'knotted black fleece' of the negro cripple who appears immediately after he has, perhaps, 'waked up and landed', in any case faded into 'oblivion', an indeterminable mode of departing which marks the disappearance of all the subsequent avatars or con men. White fleece and black fleece might suggest opposites, even Manichaean ones, or they might turn out to be variations on a theme – the theme of generally 'fleecing' people, whether the victims lose their money or their masks, which runs through the book. There *may* be gods around. But it *is* April the first! And the barber whose message and stance seem so antithetical to those of the man in cream-colours, turns out to be named William Cream when the Cosmopolitan persuades him, briefly, to abandon his policy of 'NO TRUST' – and cons him. This is, perhaps, a 'creamy' hint that radical opposites might turn out to share more latent similarities than we think.

A premonitory listing of some of the confidence man's subsequent roles or masks is given when the crowd, aroused to suspicion and scrutiny by the first of the crippled cynics who calls him a 'sham' and a 'white impostor', asks the negro for 'documentary proof' that he is not 'spurious'. Of course he has no such 'waloable papers'. Then the tender and innocent-looking young Episcopal clergyman ('newly arrived from another part of the boat' – *he* might be the deaf mute of chapter one) asks whether there is not someone who can 'speak a good word for you?' There are plenty of speakers of good words on this boat and the negro answers:

Oh yes, oh yes, dar is aboard here a werry nice, good ge'mann wid a weed, and a ge'mann in a gray coat and white tie, what knows all about me; and a ge'mann wid a big book, too; and a yarb-doctor; and a ge'mann in a yaller west; and a ge'mann in a wiolet robe; and a ge'mann as is a sodjer; and ever so many good, kind honest ge'mann aboard what knows me as well as dis old darkie knows hisself, God bress him!

This list has aroused much comment. Some of the descriptions certainly fit some of the figures who subsequently appear, but others seem not to. This has been seen by some critics as a sign of absent-mindedness (age and ill health are adduced) as though Melville had carelessly strayed from a fixed programme or menu of characters he started with. This is, of course, entirely to miss the point. It is both impossible and irrelevant to work out how many of the figures who subsequently appear are adumbrated here, just as it is impossible to work out how many may or may not be avatars of a single confidence man. For one thing, these are far from 'careful descriptions', more like single attributes – clothes, appurtenances, accessories – which might apply to many figures both on and off the ship (at least three figures are carrying books prominently; four are soldiers of one kind or another, and so on); secondly, Melville's own descriptions of the characters are indeterminate in the extreme. Who would care to say whether he had or had not met this figure: 'A man neither tall nor stout, neither short nor gaunt; but with a body fitted, as by measure, to the service of his mind. For the rest, one less favoured perhaps in his features than his clothes.' Hesitation, qualification, dubiety, modification, negative ascriptions along with a lot of wildly gaudy clothes – these are the mark of Melville's descriptions. And for a reason. He is demonstrating that you cannot really describe an individual, write him whole and all the way round, definitively and adequately. The signs are too elusive, approximative, partial, multivalent, promiscuously implicative. But as in his novel – which may annoy some readers – so it is in life, or at least life on board the *Fidèle*. How on earth can anyone be sure of identifying anyone – definitively, thoroughly, stably – in this 'cosmopolitan and confident tide' of 'strangers'? There are clothes, and bits and pieces – a weed, a tie, a book – and talk. It is not enough to 'identify' people in any but the most transient and superficial sense. But that is all these people have (it is all most people have in the modern urban crowd). And the negro's list concludes by invoking and thus implicating potentially everyone on board. On this ship it is simply impossible to tell who is or is not a confidence man (perhaps person, but as we noted, the passengers are overwhelmingly male) to some degree, in some way or another. And, by extension and implication, off this ship as well.

When the highly dubious Episcopal clergyman obligingly dashes off to find one of the figures (or transform himself into one of them) who will 'speak a good word' for the negro, the adversarial, crippled cynic cries out 'Wild goose chase! . . . Don't believe there's a soul of them aboard.' It is certainly a moot point whether there are any 'souls' aboard this ship or in this masquerade. But it is a 'wild goose chase' in a profounder sense. The chase is a quest for authentication, 'documentary proof', unassailably reliable testimony, infallible evidence. But in this world, where is that to be found? What would it look or sound like? There are *no* 'badges of authority' on board (the captain is an absence). Which man can speak for another? Where are guarantees to be found? The confidence men, or the avatars, at times vouch for each other (or themselves) – which is just to underline Melville's point. In a society where self-authoring is as common as self-parenting – people choose their parts then write their lines – there is no longer any source of reliable authorisation or legitimation, no captain to give guarantees, and reference, and orders. All evidence about, emanating from, other people is *potentially* suspect, synthetic, improvised. Of course from one point of view this is a problem as old as human community – the problem of trust. 'Confidence is the indispensable basis of all sorts of business transactions. Without it, commerce between man and man, as between country and country, would, like a watch, run down and stop.' This is absolutely true and of crucial importance for the State, both economic and moral, of any society. You simply cannot have a society – or indeed a life – founded on mistrust. 'But to doubt, to suspect, to prove – to have all this wearing work to be doing continually – how opposed to confidence. It is evil!' The herb-doctor this time, and whether or not it is a metaphysical evil, the habit of permanent doubt and suspicion would be terminally corrosive of community and relationship. Blind confidence, of course, has its vulnerabilities as it has its generosities. But some degree of trust is essential for any possibility of fruitful human relationship. And the request or demand for evidence and 'proof' of such impalpable qualities as honesty and authenticity is self-defeatingly dangerous. When Othello asks for 'ocular proof' that Desdemona is a whore, he is making that profoundly tragic mistake of asking for the wrong kind of evidence. As Iago says of Desdemona, with diabolical accuracy, her 'honour' is an 'essence that is not seen'. You can't see, or prove, honour, or fidelity, or trustworthiness. Iago can manufacture spurious evidence of seeming non-fidelity – nothing easier. He justs needs a few props – like a handkerchief (cf. weed or brass plate or book) – and a flow of insidiously insinuating and suggestive words, and he can do the trick. For Othello to trust that kind of 'evidence' against the admittedly ineffable and non-demonstrable 'honour' of Desdemona is, of course, his tragedy, a 'wild goose chase' of the most hideously mistaken kind. *The Confidence-Man* is not a tragedy, but Melville shows that absolutely fundamental problems, concerning trust and confidence, occur with special urgency and, perhaps, insolubility in the new world of America. Or, more largely, in the modern desacralised world which has to such a large extent lost not only its gods, but its guarantees: its sanctions and tacit assumptions, its bindings and bondings – in a word, its 'authority'. Just who and how much is to be trusted? There are no self-authenticating signs; but signs are all we have. The passengers on the *Fidèle* are perhaps only an extreme case of the now-common condition. And to *some* degree we have to trust trust, and have confidence in confidence.[18]

The 'wild goose chase' in this novel is picked up in the last chapter, in the concluding incident of the old man and the Counterfeit Detector. It is worth tracing out the final steps of the book. The Cosmopolitan goes down to the cabin to inspect a Bible, to see whether it does indeed include the cynical words of Sirach, quoted by Cream the barber: 'An enemy speaketh sweetly with his lips . . . I believed not his many words.' Professing not to believe such sceptical words can be found in the 'True Book', the Cosmopolitan approaches the old man reading the bible, asking him whether these words are there. The old man has no knowledge of them, but the Cosmopolitan finds them in Ecclesiasticus. The ensuing exchange is in some ways the most important in the book:

> 'Ah!' cried the old man, brightening up, 'now I know. Look,' turning the leaves forward and back, till all the Old Testament lay flat on one side, and all the New Testament flat on the other, while in his fingers he supported vertically the portion between, 'look, sir, all this to the right is certain truth, and all this to the left is certain truth, but all I hold in my hand here is apocrypha.'
> 'Apocrypha?'
> 'Yes, and there's the word in black and white,' pointing to it. 'And what says the word? It says as much as "not warranted"; for what do college men say of anything of that sort? They say it is apocryphal. The word itself, I've heard from the pulpit implies something of uncertain credit. So if your disturbance be raised from aught in this apocrypha,' again taking up the pages, 'in that case think no more of it, for it's apocryphal.'
> 'What's that about the Apocalypse?' here, a third time, came from the berth.

Here is the articulation of the orthodox certainty that revealed and established truth can be cleanly separated out from all which is 'of uncertain credit' and the two categories be rigidly delineated. The

Cosmopolitan purports to be relieved but adds that it is potentially misleading to have the Apocrypha inserted in the middle between the True parts of the book. 'Fact is, when all is bound up together, it's sometimes confusing. The uncanonical part should be bound distinct.' Melville's point – one which his whole work is engaged in making – is that it is not only impossible but potentially very dangerous for any man, or society, to seek to reach, ascertain, and proclaim absolute, unconditional certainty, rigid classifications of true and false, and good and bad. (It is the Ahab drive, redisplayed in this book in its purity by the Indian-hater John Moredock who sees all Indians as evil while he is a kind and good Christian with his white family and friends. It is a mark of the possible perversity to which criticism can go that this schizo-phrenic, psychopathic racist has been put forward as the hero of the novel. At least he has clear ideas and the courage of his convictions and is no con man! Such criticism simply re-enacts the real dangers of the need and quest for fixed and stable readings.) The quest for cer-tainties leads to falsifications and finally the Manichaean oppugnancy of oppositional thinking. Black and white indeed. But for Melville, life partakes of 'the *unravellable* inscrutableness of God' (*Pierre*, my italics). Man lives precisely in the universe where the Apocrypha is placed in the Book – in the middle, the zone of uncertainty, the realm of the uncanonical. That the confidence man/men can best operate in that realm, while pretending to wish to have a clear and settled distinction between the canonical, the reliable, the authoritative, and the 'not warranted', the ungrounded, the provisional, and to have the latter 'bound' and sequestered (thus travestying the 'unravelling' aspirations of traditional thought, and politics), is part of the dark irony of Melville's vision.

A voice complains at the noise of these 'two geese' gabbling and then the mysterious boy peddler enters and proceeds to sell the old man a 'traveler's patent lock' and a money-belt, thus making some-thing of a mockery of his previous claims not to distrust his fellow creatures. As a bonus, the boy – all 'roguish parody' – gives the old man a Counterfeit Detector which will lead to his final confusion. To pass the time he tries out the Detector on some bills he has recently been given. Once he starts to check the bills against the list of what the Detector says should be authenticating signs, he is reduced to a bemused bewilderment: 'I don't know, I don't know . . . there's so many marks of all sorts to go by, it makes it a kind of uncertain.' This effectively summarises the perplexed cry which comes from the heart of the book. In particular the old man cannot find the 'microscopic', indeed effectively 'unobservable', 'figure of a goose' which, says the Detector, should be there if the bill is 'good'. The Cosmopolitan maintains that he can see the goose, with a fair intimation that the only goose on view is the old man himself. Finally, he advises the old man: 'Then throw the Detector away . . . it only makes you purblind; don't you see what a wild-goose chase it has led you?' The Detector and the dollar bill are both printed items and the Detector may be as 'counterfeit' as the bills it presumes to check (as the ambiguity of the two words 'Counterfeit Detector' suggests). Neither of these groups of 'marks' can verify, or falsify, the other, and 'there are so many marks of all sort to go by'. To look for absolute guarantees of authenticity – this is indeed a wild-goose chase.

The implications of the conclusion are dark and pessimistic. Retiring for the night, the old man asks for his 'Life-preserver', which turns out to be a chair also containing a chamberpot, and there is an almost crude faecal pun in the Cosmopolitan's ironic advice to 'have confidence in that stool for a special providence', for it seems the pot has been used: 'But bless me, we are being left in the dark here. Pah! what a smell, too.' How different from the coffin-turned-life-preserver which saves Ishmael at the end of *Moby-Dick*! Here there is only the odour of excrement in the air as the Cosmopolitan extinguishes the final light and leads the old man away into the ensuing darkness. It does seem to portend some kind of terminal exhaustion, obliteration, annihilation. Hints of apocalypse, using both biblical and pagan sources, are thick in the air of the last chapter, and are too obtrusive to be missed. It is a question of what we make of them. Is this an image or adumbration of the 'promised end', or is it the final, darkly humorous, flourish of the 'roguish parody' of our brilliant, mesmerising, allusion-peddling author? The whole action of the book has taken place on April Fools' Day, related to ancient vernal celebrations of All Fool's Day; but Melville leaves it uncertain whether the last chapter takes place just before or just after midnight (the Cosmopolitan signs his Agreement with the barber at 'quarter to twelve o'clock, P.M.' and in his last conversation with the old man he alludes to this incident as being 'not a half-hour since'). Melville leaves us in teasing, and troubling, uncertainty to the last. Are we at the very end of the day of folly masquerade, in which confidence has, as it were, been carnivalised? Or is it now just over? The last chapter is indeed entitled 'The Cosmopolitan Increases in Seriousness' and so, we may feel, does the book. Certainly, by the last page, it does seem to be 'very late' and the possibility raised by the last words, that 'Something further may follow of this masquerade', might on the one hand imply that there might be a sequel, or on the other may be suggesting something more ominous. Certainly the end leaves us nothing to stand on and nothing to see by. And we still cannot be certain about the identity or significance of the Confidence Man, nor be sure of the implications and ramifications of 'His Masquerade'.

Bruce Franklin asserts, with a good deal of persuasive evidence, that 'in this universe man's Savior – Manco Capac, Vishnu, Christ, Apollo, the Buddhist's Buddha – is embodied by the Confidence Man, who is also man's Destroyer – Satan, Siva, the Hindu's Buddha. Melville's mythology converts all gods into the Confidence Man.'[19] Such a reading is certainly allowed by Melville's superabundantly allusive masquerade. We can also see more mundane and secular implications. Thomas Mann's suave confidence man, Felix Krull, while he is acting as a waiter in a luxurious hotel in Paris, often ponders a favourite idea: 'It was the idea of *interchangeability*. With a change of clothes and make-up, the servitors might often just as well have been the masters, and many of those who lounged in deep wicker chairs, smoking their cigarettes, might have played the waiter. It was pure accident that the reverse was the fact, an accident of wealth; for an aristocracy of money is an accidental and interchangeable aristocracy.'[20] This idea is peculiarly relevant to the world of *The Confidence-Man* and Melville's own vision of reversibility and 'interchangeability' – of objects, words, concepts, roles, persons, gods. And Felix Krull puts his idea into action, occasionally leaving the hotel where he is a waiter, dressing up in fine clothes, and going to another fine hotel as a patron. 'This amounted, as one can see, to a kind of dual existence, whose charm lay in the ambiguity as to which figure was the real I and which the masquerade . . . I masqueraded in both capacities and the undisguised reality behind the two appearances, the real I, could not be identified because it actually did not exist.'[21] Interchangeability is everywhere adumbrated on board the *Fidèle*, and by the same token there is a prevailing sense that it is becoming impossible to identify any 'real I', anywhere. This loss of confidence in the existence of some stable core identity increases throughout the century – thus Ibsen's Peer Gynt, *the* European confidence man of the nineteenth century, after playing so many roles and remaining so fluid, uncommitted, and opportunistic, finds that he is a series of surfaces but empty at the centre, like the onion he peels. A comparable sense of both the multiplicity and the sheer, ontological dubiety of the self is to be found in Pirandello; and an Italian critic, Guido Botta, rightly invoked his vision of man as *'un complesso di personaggi'* in connection with Melville's Confidence Man. (Anyone interested in the troubling relationship between roles and 'identity' in Pirandello should read, in particular, his novel *The Late Mattia Pascal*, and his play *Henry IV*.) The self as role-player has become something of a common-place of sociology and psychology as, for example, in Erving Goffman's *The Presentation of Self in Everyday Life*, and, arguably, we are a good deal too complacent with the notion, too mindlessly comfortable in the 'endlessly-changeable accommodations' of the Confidence Man's 'Protean easy-chair'. But Melville was a pioneer and his novel has all the powerful and unsettling originality and strangeness, and at times awkwardness, and all the ambiguous and double-edged comedy and indeterminably, interminably worrying suggestiveness, of a work explor-ing new and dangerous ground.

It certainly breaks with existing conventions of novel-writing. It is set on no ordinary boat. 'The entire ship is a riddle.' It is also a writing desk, its rooms and promenades, saloons and balconies, passages and 'out-of-the-way retreats' being described in terms of the various spaces and drawers in 'an escritoire' – and Melville keeps riddling and writ-ing, and the riddling of writing, well to the fore. His ship is Fidèle; his theme is confidence; his complaint is against those who demand 'severe fidelity to real life' in a 'work of amusement'. How does, how can, how should man keep faith with man, or an author with his readers? Melville intrudes his own voice, or holds up his own slate, in three short chapters (14, 33, and 44). He defends himself against the charge of 'inconsistency' of characterisation. It is a double defence. Surely 'to all fiction is allowed some play of invention'; but, anyway, the fact is that 'in real life, a consistent character is a *rara avis*'. What he is main-taining is that it is conventional modes of characterisation which are false. It is a crucial passage:

That fiction, where every character can, by reason of its consistency, be comprehended at a glance, either exhibits but sections of a character, making them appear for wholes, or else is very untrue to reality; while, on the other hand, that author who draws a character, even though to common view incongruous in its parts, as the flying squirrel, and, at different periods, as much at variance with itself as the caterpillar is with the butterfly into which it changes, may yet, in so doing, be not false but faithful to facts.

Melville is claiming a new kind of 'fidelity' for himself as a writer, a fidelity to the actual radical discontinuity and plurality of the self.

What may follow from this perception may hardly, perhaps, be decided. Some have seen the figure of the Confidence Man as a nihilist, cynically exploiting others; yet there is an undeniable resilience, a participatory zest in his fluent exhortations. 'Life is a picnic *en costume*; one must take a part, assume a character, stand ready in a sensible way to play the fool.' He is, of course, diabolically plausible, an abuser of trust, but the sour self-sequestration which results from habitual suspicion – 'I have confidence in distrust' says Pitch, but note that he is a bachelor – can hardly be regarded as a preferred stance, for all that its robust scepticism can find ample justification. Melville, characteristically, makes all possible positions reciprocally subversive.

In his last intervention into his own text, he discusses the possibilities of creating 'original' characters in fiction, since in modern urban conditions figures are 'novel, or singular, or striking, or captivating, or all four at once', but not 'in a thorough sense, original'. Among all the dis-originated figures in contemporary America, origin-ality is going to be a rare phenomenon, in life and in fiction. 'The original character, essentially such, is like a revolving Drummond light, raying away from itself all round it – everything is lit up by it, everything starts up to it (mark how it is with Hamlet).' We may detect a final Melvillean irony here. He specifically asserts the 'impropriety' of calling the Cosmopolitan 'quite an original', yet in many ways, as critics have decided, the Cosmopolitan's effect on those he (and his, possibly, previous avatars) meets is exactly that of the Drummond light as described by Melville. One way and another, all 'start up' and are 'lit' by him. Does this make him a sort of modern Hamlet, that figure who, more perhaps than any other, served to lay bare the problems and ambiguities in the relations between doing, acting, performing, and 'playing'? It certainly makes him a kind of Drummond light. Now, the Drummond light was used most notably by P. T. Barnum to advertise and draw people into his Museum – his Masquerade, we might say. So where does that leave the Confidence Man and Melville? Hamlets and Shakespeares? Or counterfeiters and impresarios? Perhaps – and this would be the Melville touch – there is not, finally, very much difference.

NOTES

1 Quoted in Gary Lindberg, *The Confidence Man in American Literature* (New York: Oxford University Press, 1982), p. 187.
2 Ralph Waldo Emerson, *Essays and Lectures* (New York: Library of America, 1983), p. 54.

3 Edgar Allan Poe, *The Works of Edgar Allan Poe*, 10 vols. (New York: Funk Wagnalls Co., 1904), X, 146.

4 Ibid., X, 147.

5 Ibid., X, 146.

6 Quoted in Herman Melville, *The Confidence-Man*, ed. Hershel Parker (New York: W. W. Norton & Company, Inc., 1971), p. 227.

7 Ibid., pp. 227–8.

8 Henry Adams, *History of the United States of America During the Administration of Thomas Jefferson* (New York: Library of America, 1986), p. 121.

9 Alexis de Tocqueville, *Democracy in America*, 2 vols. (New York: Vintage Books, 1990), I, 43.

10 Ibid., II, 99.

11 Ibid.

12 Adams, *History*, pp. 117–18.

13 Ibid., p. 119.

14 Lindberg, *Confidence-Man*, p. 120.

15 Ibid., p. 68.

16 See H. Bruce Franklin, *The Wake of the Gods: Melville's Mythology* (Stanford: Stanford University Press, 1963), pp. 153–87.

17 Quoted in Brian Higgins and Hershel Parker (eds.), *Herman Melville: The Contemporary Reviews* (Cambridge: Cambridge University Press, 1995), p. 491.

18 See the volume *Trust*, edited by Diego Gambetta (Oxford: Basil Blackwell, 1988), in which the necessity and difficulty of establishing some form of trust in all walks of life is discussed by writers from various disciplines. In particular see Gambetta's own concluding essay, 'Can We Trust Trust?'.

19 Franklin, *Wake of the Gods*, p. 187.

20 Thomas Mann, *Felix Krull* (London: Secker & Warburg, 1955), p. 238.

21 Ibid., p. 244.

CHAPTER 6

Henry James:
'The Story In It' – and the story without it

I have recently been engaged in assembling suitable material for an anthology of sea stories. A far from disagreeable task, though, as I read story after story, I found myself getting, at times, a little bored. Not, of course, with Conrad or Melville; or, indeed, Kipling or Crane. Rather, with something which seemed almost to inhere in the genre – something, for instance, which made many 'stories' indistinguishable from 'real-life' accounts of voyages and (of course) attendant trials and tribulations. The range of possible incidents – the source of narrative interest – is dramatic enough, but comes to seem oddly limited. There are storms, there are calms; icebergs are hit, propellers fall off, engines fail; men 'go wrong', mutinies occur or threaten; pirates may board – perhaps, even, monsters may rise from the deep. This can all be sufficiently hair-raising, no doubt; but sometimes one may be left with a faint, unformulated feeling of – is that *all*? There can be plenty of emotional states and temperaments and reactions on display – 'heroism and rascality', bravery, cowardice, panic, terror, incredulity, boredom, aggression, humour, resolve, endurance, even madness ('trust the high seas to bring out the Irrational' says Marlow in *Lord Jim*). And there *are* human relationships – of comradeship, of fear, of combat, of survival. Indeed, in *The Secret Sharer* Conrad charts one of the most extraordinary relationships between men at sea ever imagined and analysed. We may take a clue here from, what is unusual in Conrad, a confident note in a letter about it to Edward Garnett (3 November 1912):

I daresay Freya is pretty rotten. On the other hand the Secret Sharer, between you and me, is *it*. Eh? No damned tricks with girls there. Eh? Every word fits and there's not a single uncertain note.[1]

No damned tricks with girls . . . in the invariable absence of women from sea stories, sexual desire, desire itself, seems somehow to be forgotten, repressed, occluded, or otherwise left behind or put aside (male-bonding and all sorts of comradeship are, of course, both permissible and common; but in the *literature* of the sea – sea narratives – homosexual feelings, not to mention practices, are strictly taboo). For men grappling with the sea and with boats to manage, this is doubtless as it should be (sailors in port could doubtless provide a very different, and possibly not very edifying, story). Certainly, there are other things in life besides sex. But his absence, omission, excision – call it what you will – has implications when it comes to narrative. For there is a strong case to be made for saying that narration is intimately involved with desire, or what James calls 'the beautiful circuit and subterfuge of our thought and desire'. Arguably our founding western narrative – Homer's epics – start with and from the abduction of Helen – a damned trick with a girl, if ever there was one!

But let me return to dry land – exchange the parlour for the cabin, social turbulence for oceanic tempests, the domestic for the maritime. For it is here, of course, that, notoriously and inevitably, those damned tricks with girls begin.

Here is an entry in Henry James's Notebooks for 8 May 1898:

L'honnête femme n'a pas de roman – beautiful little 'literary' (?) subject to work out in a short tale. The trial, the exhibition, the proof: either it's not a '*roman*', or it's not *honnête*. When it becomes the thing it's guilty; when it doesn't become guilty it doesn't become the thing.[2]

James duly 'worked out' the subject in the short story, 'The Story In It', published in 1902. It is set in a drawing-room and concerns only three people – two women and a man. The hostess is Mrs Dyott and her friend and guest is Maud Blessingbourne. The weather is very tempestuous – there is 'trouble' and 'violence' in the climatic air. Mrs Dyott is writing letters, while Maud Blessingbourne is reading the third of the French novels ('in lemon-coloured paper') she has brought with her. Despite what we infer to be in such novels, she is finding this one rather 'mild . . . timid and tame'. Mrs Dyott doesn't know the novels. 'I knew you don't read', says Maud 'but why should you? *You* live!' 'Yes – wretchedly enough', replies Mrs Dyott. They are expecting, despite the 'wild weather', a male friend of Mrs Dyott's. This is Colonel Voyt, who has 'a reputation for gallantry', a 'dense glossy beard, that of an emir or a caliph'; he looks 'un-English' and might be taken for Jewish or Irish, though in fact he is 'only a pleasant, weather-washed, wind-battered Briton' who brings 'a certain amount of unremoved mud' into the drawing-room when he arrives, the mark of his 'struggle with the elements'. Mrs Dyott is alone to greet him, and it is clear that they are having an affair – their names, indeed, are comically similar – Dyott and Voyt, and James is not above thereby offering a tolerably broad hint that, together, they Do Yt. Maud Blessingbourne comes in and, 'round the hearth' and with tea (and cigarettes for the virile Voyt), they discuss the novels Maud likes reading. The implication is that they hardly comprise respectable reading matter for a young Englishwoman. Maud stands by her guns: 'when I read a novel I mostly read a French one . . . for I seem with it to get hold more of the real thing – to get more life for my money'. Just what 'the real thing' was, how you knew it, where you found it – was becoming an increasingly rich source of ambiguity for James. Voyt sympathises and concurs with what he takes to be Maud's dissatisfaction with the locally available, Anglo-Saxon, literature.

But if you can't read the novel of British and American manufacture, heaven knows I'm at one with you. It seems really to show our sense of life as the sense of puppies and kittens.

Maud seems rather, then, to change tack with a characteristic Jamesian double-negative. 'But what I mean . . . isn't that I don't get woefully weary of the eternal French thing. What's *their* sense of life?' Voyt defends that 'sense of life'.

Oh, but it *is* one; you can make it out . . . They do what they feel, and they feel more things than we. They strike so many more notes, and with so different a hand. When it comes to any account of a relation, say, between a man and a woman – I mean an intimate or a curious or a suggestive one – where we are compared to them? They don't exhaust the subject, no doubt . . . but we don't touch it, don't even skim it. It's as if we denied its existence, its possibility.

These sentiments exactly echo James's own recurring complaint about the 'immense omission' in Victorian fiction. Maud demurs, without giving any distinct response. Voyt surmises – 'your interest is in something different from life'; but Maud – 'Ah, not a bit! I *love* life – in art, though I hate it anywhere else. It's the poverty of the life those people show, and the awful bounders, of both sexes, that they represent.' Voyt thinks she is caught.

Oh, now we have you! . . . To me, when all's said and done, they seem to be – as near as art can come in the truth of the truth. It can only take what life gives it, though it certainly may be a pity that that isn't better. Your complaint of their monotony is a complaint of their conditions. When you say we get always the same couple what do you mean but that we get always the same passion? Of course we do!... If what you're looking for is another, that's what you won't anywhere find.

James would both agree and disagree with that last sentiment – but I'll come back to that. Maud says, modestly enough: 'I suppose I'm looking for a decent woman.' Voyt – 'Oh then, you mustn't look for her in pictures of passion. That's not her element nor her whereabouts.' 'Doesn't it depend on what you mean by passion?' Indeed it does, and Voyt reveals a limitation when he replies, 'I think one can mean only one thing: the enemy to behaviour.' Maud is more in the right of it with her rejoinder – 'Oh, I can imagine passions that are, on the contrary, friends to it.'

Returning more specifically to fiction and 'romance' she complains: 'I don't see why romance ... should be all, as the French inveterately make it, for the women who are bad.' This is easy for Voyt:

My dear lady ... their romance *is* their badness. There isn't any other. It's a hard law, if you will, and a strange, but goodness has to go without that luxury. Isn't to *be* good just exactly, all round, to go without ... one has heard your question put ... 'Why don't you, *cher monsieur*, give us the drama of virtue?' 'Because, *chère madame*, the high privilege of virtue is precisely to avoid drama.' The adventures of the honest lady? The honest lady hasn't – can't possibly have adventures.

Maud, quite correctly, rejoins that it depends on what you call 'adventures' and what you call 'romance'. Which prompts a central statement by Voyt:

Of course you may call things anything you like ... [But] [b]ehind these words we use – the adventure, the novel, the drama, the romance, the situation, in short, as we most comprehensively say – behind them all stands the same sharp fact that they all, in their different ways, represent ... The fact of a relation. The adventure's a relation; the relation's an adventure. The romance, the novel, the drama are the picture of one. The subject the novelist treats is the rise, the formation, the development, the climax, and for the most part the decline, of one. And what is the honest lady doing on that side of town?

Can't there be 'innocent' relations?

You mean that the adventures of innocence have so exactly been the material of fiction? Yes, that's exactly what the bored reader complains of. He has asked for bread and been given a stone. What is it but, with absolute directness, a question of interest, or, as people say, of the story? What's a situation undeveloped but a subject lost? If a relation stops, where's the story? If it doesn't stop, where's the innocence? It seems to me you must choose. It would be very pretty if it were otherwise, but that's how we flounder. Art is our flounderings shown.

The story is in the trajectory of the passional relation, and such relations, according to Voyt, are inseparable from 'flounderings'. Since most of such 'flounderings' will be inward and invisible, or barely perceptible, we here move into the world of metaphor, and we may note that, in his 'stories', James uses sea imagery and watery metaphors perhaps more than any other major novelist – swimming, floating, sinking, drowning, floundering/foundering, lost moorings, faulty navigation, insecure anchorage, failed ports – and so on. And whatever else that metaphorical sea, Conrad's 'destructive element', is, it is a sea of sex, or a sea of more generally diffused desire. Once launched on *that*, you are embarked on a story. There is much in James's own work to bear out Voyt's contentions.

But that is not quite the end of the story of 'the story in it'. After Voyt has gone, Maud confesses to Mrs Dyott that she does, in fact, have a 'passion', but insists that the object of it is quite unaware, and the love is unrequited. But, even if the passion is a secret, locked up inside her – she touches 'the region of her heart' – she asks: 'What more is required for a relation for *me*?' Later, Mrs Dyott tells this to Colonel Voyt, adding that she is quite sure *he* is the object of Maud's private passion – her 'evidence' is that, while Voyt was with them both, Maud was so 'charming'.

She said it in a tone that placed the matter in its right light – a light in which they appeared kindly, quite tenderly, to watch Maud wander away into space with her lovely head bent under a theory rather too big for it. Voyt's last word, however, was that there was just enough in it – in the theory – for them to allow that she had not shown herself, on the occasion of their talk, wholly bereft of sense. Her consciousness, if they left it alone – as they of course after this mercifully must – *was*, in the last analysis, a kind of shy romance. Not a romance like their own, a thing to make the fortune of any author up to the mark – one who should have the invention or who could have the courage; but a small, scared, starved, subjective satisfaction that would do her no harm and nobody else any good. Who but a duffer – he stuck to his contention – would see the shadow of a 'story' in it.

Their 'romance' is good old 'un-English' adultery (a Mrs Voyt is mentioned) – a 'subject' or 'relation' which, James himself thought, few English authors had either the requisite 'invention' or 'courage' to address. James himself, in a Notebook entry in 1887, discussed an idea for a story given to him by the French psychological novelist, Paul

Bourget. 'But to make something of it I must modify it essentially – as I can't, and besides, don't particularly want to, depict in an American magazine, a woman carrying on adulteries under her daughter's eyes. That case, I imagine, is in America so rare as to be almost abnormal.'³ Duly 'modified', this became 'A London Life'. But there was another consideration. In 1894, going over possible scenarios for what would become *The Wings of the Dove* in 1902 (the same year as 'The Story In It'), James notes: 'If I were writing for a French public the whole thing would be simple – the elder, the "other", woman would simply be the mistress of the young man, and it would be a question of his taking on the dying girl for a time – having a temporary liaison with her. But one can do so little with English adultery – it is so much less inevitable, and so much more ugly in all its hiding and lying side. It is so undermined by our immemorial tradition of original freedom of choice, and by our practically universal acceptance of divorce. At any rate, in this case, the anecdote, which I don't, by the way, at all yet *see*, is probably more dramatic, in truth, on some basis of marriage being in question, marriage with the other woman, or even with both!'⁴ European adultery was another matter – there, indeed, was a 'story' as Colonel Voyt defines it, particularly if the story is called *Madame Bovary* or *Anna Karenina* or *Effie Briest*. And when James himself made an adulterous relationship central to a major work – in *The Golden Bowl* – although the adultery takes place in England, the man involved does not only look, but *is*, 'un-English'.

But remember that Voyt concedes, or suggests, that Maud, with her passional secret silently locked up in her heart, may have her own 'small, scared, starved, subjective satisfaction' – that her 'consciousness' may, in itself, constitute a 'kind of shy romance'. Though he concludes, sceptically enough – 'Who but a duffer would see the shadow of a "story" in it?' James himself is, of course, the 'duffer', – as indeed he has just demonstrated. He certainly knew what Voyt means by a 'story', and has much sympathy with his contentions; but he also had an increasingly fine sense of the story of not having a story – at least one in Voyt's sense. He became more and more interested in the narrative possibilities of just such romances of consciousness, the stories to be found and traced in 'subjective satisfactions' – whether small and scared and starved; or ever-expanding, audacious, and gorged to repletion. 'The action of the drama is simply the girl's "subjective" adventure', he wrote of the unnamed heroine of 'In the Cage' – a young telegraphist whose imagination is as fantastically adventurous as her body is, literally, 'caged'.[5] And remember Fleda Vetch in *The Spoils of Poynton*, who flees with physical clumsiness from the encroaching possibility of physical amorousness, hides her love (or turns it into something else), and nurses her distinctive, distinguished consciousness – pursues her lonely, 'subjective adventure'. In his Preface, James rather nicely imagines a reader objecting: 'Why the deuce then Fleda Vetch, why a mere little flurried bundle of petticoats, why not Hamlet or Milton's Satan at once, if you're going in for a superior display of "mind"?'[6] I would dearly like to see James's *Hamlet*, though I fear it would have turned out to be, literally, interminable. But he rightly senses that his stories lay, one way or another, with those bundles of petticoats, more or less flurried as the case might be. Fleda adds a dimension of 'appreciation' to the story – she 'almost demonically both sees and feels, while the others but feel without seeing'. She is a 'free spirit', and though she does not get her man, or a man, she emerges as 'heroic', ironic, pathetic or whatever, and . . . ' "successful", only through having remained free'. By the time he came to write his Prefaces (and doubtless long before), James knew that part of his genius lay in telling 'stories about women', very young women, who, 'affected with a certain high lucidity, thereby become characters; in consequence of which their doings, their sufferings or whatever, take on, I assume, an importance'.[7] Laura Wing, in 'A London Life', has, like Fleda Vetch, 'acuteness and intensity, reflexion and passion, has above all a contributive and participant view of her situation'. Her 'situation' is that she is a young American girl who has come over to London to visit her married sister, only to find that sister involved in an adulterous relationship, imbroiled in what looks like a 'scandal' and generally unsavoury sexual goings-on. Laura may be as neurotic as she is naive, that is part of her story – but she is determined, as James puts it, 'to guard against personal bespattering'.[8] Pausing only to remind you of the 'unremoved mud' on Colonel Voyt as he comes in from the storm, I will go on to make my last point concerning James.

For, of course, I have been too crude, or at least failed to point an obvious and basic distinction, namely, as *Macbeth*'s Porter well knows, you can have 'desire' without 'performance'. Let me turn to *The Awkward Age*. Another tale about 'young girls', the novel centres on the problems which may arise when a young girl, presumably still virgin in mind as well as body, comes downstairs and enters the circle of adult talk round 'the liberal fireside', which, we are to assume, feels free to allude to matters pertaining to, and arising from, sexual relationships.

As James put it, ' "real" talk . . . an explicit interest in life . . . frankness and ease . . . the perfection, as it were, of intercourse, and a tone as far as possible removed from that of the nursery and the school-room'.[9] James starts from his observation of 'the difference made in certain friendly houses and for certain flourishing mothers by the sometimes dreaded, often delayed, but never fully arrested coming to the fore-front of some vague slip of a daughter . . . the "sitting downstairs", from a given datum, of the merciless maiden previously perched aloft could easily be felt as a crisis'.[10] The problem might be avoided, as it tended to be on the continent, by, as it were, erasing the difficult interval between girl-hood and wife-hood. 'A girl might be married off the day after her irruption, or better still the day before it, to remove her from the sphere of the play of mind.'[11] That, however, was the 'foreign' way – it is the way with little Aggie in the book, who is kept, supposedly, completely innocent and ignorant until her marriage, after which she *immediately* starts engaging in promiscuous, adulterous, sexual games. The old story, and, James implies, not so interesting at that. The English way, it seems, was to allow the young maiden to come 'downstairs' for the time between being a girl and becoming a wife. This way, as James sees it, was both more liberal and more risky. It is the way taken with Nanda, in the novel, and she is at once 'incorpor-ated' and 'exposed' – accepted but soiled – by her freedom of the drawing-room. The 'compromise' solution to the problem of what to do with that hovering, waiting, 'female adolescence' – let her in, but watch your talk – in the event, fatally 'compromises' her – 'the con-sequent muddle . . . representing meanwhile a great inconvenience for life, but, as I found myself feeling, an immense promise, a much greater one than on the "foreign" showing, for the painted picture of life'.[12] There are, thinks James, more narrative possibilities in the honest English 'muddle' than in the cynical 'foreign' arrangement.

Nanda has her desire – 'Nanda's fairly sick – as sick as a little cat – with her passion.' The passion is for Vanderbank, that empty 'blank' of a man who nevertheless 'gives out' 'the sacred terror'. But she will never consummate her desire, never have her man. She says at one point: 'I shall be one of the people who don't. I shall be at the end one of those who haven't.' One hardly knows if the tone is one of resigna-tion, determination, prophecy, or lament. Probably all of those, and more besides. But we must attend to the words of wise, sad Mitchy: 'Any passion so great, so complete is – satisfied or unsatisfied – a life.' He may, indirectly, be commenting on his own unrequited passion for

Nanda, as well as on Nanda's for Vanderbank, but the point holds and obtains more generally. *Un*satisfied passion can be a life – and there may be a *better* story in it.

She will never have it or do it, because the man she desires will not marry her. Vanderbank, who is having an affair with her mother, will not marry Nanda because she is 'spoilt'. In what way spoilt? Because of what she knows. And what does she know? She knows about sex, and the attendant muddles and flounderings it precipitates. And how does she know? Because of the talk she hears; because of the dirty French novels which Vanderbank leaves around the house; because 'it is in the air she breathes'. Vanderbank, who you will recognise is a real charmer, is so 'old-fashioned' that he must have a putatively ignorant, supposedly pure and unsullied little girl for a wife; meanwhile, he will continue his affair with Nanda's mother, Mrs Brook – since she is 'a married women' it doesn't matter that she is 'steeped' in the atmosphere which, apparently, is fouling Nanda's mind on account of 'her inexorable participation'. Nanda's mother refers to 'the preposterous fiction . . . of Nanda's blankness of mind', but Vanderbank requires just such a fictional maidenly blankness in any wife he may take. I suppose that if you are yourself a 'blank', you will want to marry a blank. Meanwhile and until – he can safely solace himself with Mrs Brook.

But, perversely – it is part of her story – Nanda regards *herself* as spoiled. She reproaches poor Mitchy for lacking a kind of delicacy.

'The kind that would make me painful to you. Or rather not me perhaps . . . but my situation, my exposure – all the results of them that I show. Doesn't one become a kind of little drain-pipe with everything flowing through?'
'Why don't you call it more gracefully . . . a little aeolian harp set in the drawing room window and vibrating in the breeze of conversation?'
'Oh, because the harp gives out a sound, and *we* – at least we try to – give out none.'
'What you take, you mean, you keep?'
'Well, it sticks to us. And that's what you don't mind!'
Their eyes met long on it. 'Yes – I see. I *don't* mind. I've the most extraordinary lacunae.'

We must leave poor Mitchy with, or in, his 'lacunae'. But – 'it sticks to us'. (I may note that, when it becomes clear that Van won't marry Nanda, someone says – 'He hasn't stuck.' Only whatever it is he brings into the house does.) Sticks – like the 'unremoved mud' on Colonel Voyt, perhaps. And 'drain-pipe'? This is more sewerage than mud. Voyt himself is, of course, deep in the stuff, however we care to designate it. But even to know about it – read, hear about it, makes Nanda feel that she is polluted, that she is a 'drain'. Thinking of the sexual in terms of the excremental is something associated with childhood, and here it may say something about Nanda's mind – or, but we cannot know, about James's. But we still refer to 'dirty' books, and the point is clear enough. But, is to read *about* it to be 'bespattered' *by* it? The matter, more generally, is important enough, and not only in James – to what extent may a person be defiled by a knowledge encountered and acquired 'in all innocence', as we say? Knowledge in general, if you like; but for James, knowledge of sex and matters concerning sexual behaviour is *the* quintessential knowledge. Does that make us all, most of us, drains? From one point of view, though arguably a perverse one, the answer is 'yes'. Certainly more drains than harps. A lot of Nanda's 'knowledge' comes from French (and continental) novels, brought into the house by Vanderbank, primarily for her mother. Nanda writes his name clearly on one of them, as if to designate the originating source of whatever filth in her mind he himself will find unacceptable. Zola is the only author named, though the name of Tolstoy's Anna Karenina is invoked. James, of course, admired these authors as serious writers – even if he could, while younger, deprecate their 'handling of unclean things'. Any novel purportedly about contemporary society which either ignored or denied the importance of the sexual drive in 'the great relation between men and women' was guilty of a disabling omission – James makes this opinion clear on more than one occasion. But by putting such books – books with stories in them, in Voyt's sense – in his own book, he may be suggesting that his own fiction is a more capricious one with a more complex, subtle narrative concern about someone who reads about it but doesn't do it. A kind of 'Not Madame Bovary' – not, and, perhaps, better!

It has more than once been pointed out to me that what I had to say about adultery and the novel did not particularly apply to the English classic novel. And indeed, offhand, I can only think of one Victorian novel by a major writer which makes the matter of adultery its central theme – Meredith's *One of Our Conquerors*. The preferred theme was, rather, courtship. I want to say something about this, drawing, for the next few moments, on Ruth Yeazell's admirable book, *Fictions of Modesty*.[13] She points out that by concentrating on a heroine between coming-of-age and marriage – a time of a necessary, though temporary, resistance to the clamours of the body and its desires – the

novelist could devote more time to what was going on in the heroine's
burgeoning consciousness, tell the story of *that*, and produce what Yeazell
calls 'capacious fictions of modesty'. She is particularly interesting as
she points out the sort of problems encountered by writers as they
engaged with the question of how much a young girl – marriageable
but not yet married – could, should, did; couldn't, shouldn't, didn't –
know. Know, of course, about sex. She should be modest, delicate,
pure – of course; but not 'sheepish', inanely blank, unconscious to the
point of virtual insensibility. Some writers could not decide whether
female modesty was from nature or from culture. Hume gave his
opinion that girls were trained to feel a 'preceding backwardness to
the approaches of a pleasure, to which nature has inspir'd so strong a
propensity'. Nature pushes them forward, but convention, mercifully,
pulls them backwards – at least for a time. Rousseau is, characteristically, both more vehement and more confused. He *insisted* that in
women *pudeur* is natural – he had his reasons, being not a little afraid
of female sexual aggression – but went on to bewail the fact that, in
women, voracious sexual appetite is even *more* natural. His rather desperate, and hardly tenable, position was that the Supreme Being 'while
delivering women over to unlimited desires also joins *pudeur* to those
desires in order to restrain them'.[14]

The young woman entering the marriage market (and of course
there is an important economic consideration here) was supposed not
to know anything about 'it'; but, as James indicated by calling this a
'preposterous fiction', a young woman who was remotely aware, intelligent, curious – *alive* – could hardly not know, hardly *help* knowing.
Even if, as in Nanda's case, that knowledge derives only, or mainly,
from reading and listening. And, as Yeazell demonstrates, novelists
often found their subject by exploring the temporal dimensions of
female modesty, 'sensing the narrative possibilities implicit in all the
paradoxes of anticipation and delay' – going forwards and holding
back at the same time, as it were. All of which brings Yeazell to
the fascinating subject of 'blushing'. She has read extensively in
eighteenth- and nineteenth-century tributes to, and definitions of, the
modest woman, and found that almost all of them discuss the importance of blushing. But blushing is a curiously and irreducibly ambiguous
signal. The blush is a sign of innocence, but by implication, a knowing
innocence – a sign that the woman has neither done nor thought
anything for which she ought to, well, blush. Blushing to show you
have nothing to blush about is a very odd sort of signal. True, empty-

minded innocence would surely blush at nothing. Steele, rightly, defined blushing as 'that ambiguous Suffusion which is the Livery both of Guilt and Innocence'. Milton's Eve blushes both before the Fall ('blushing like the morn') *and* after ('in her cheek distemper flushing glowed'). Wollstonecraft sensibly maintained that 'the downcast eye, the rosy blush . . . are proper in their season; but modesty . . . cannot long exist with a sensibility that is not tempered by reflection'. Since blushing was involuntary, it was felt to reliably reveal some inner truth and reality about the woman. But just what inner truth it is which suddenly glows forth – who can say? Shock, shame, indignation, anger – innocence now, but perhaps also an interest, an awareness, even an erotic promise of sexual ardour to come? Only a novelist, with privileged access to the heroine's inner workings, can tell. A blush, then, and this is Yeazell,

offers a seductive moment between, a moment in which innocent unconsciousness and erotic knowingness seem briefly to fuse, or to be confused, together . . . Extended into narrative, the moment of the blush becomes the time of the courtship novel, that period between innocence and erotic experience that marks the heroine's entrance into the world.[15]

As Yeazell amply demonstrates, there is a story in *that*, too.

In a postscript, she quotes Havelock Ellis and cites his interest in 'delay' in sexual relations – the interval that female modesty opened up for 'courtship'. (Darwin was also particularly interested in the courting habits or rituals of animals.) From Ellis: 'the passivity of women in love is the passivity of the magnet, which in its apparent immobility is drawing the iron toward it. An intense energy lies behind such passivity, an absorbed preoccupation in the end to be attained' ('The Sexual Impulse in Women'). There is a lot more plot to be engendered by that passive energy and covert desire, with its imposed obliquities or pondered deviousness or necessary indirections, than in the relatively plotless directness and initiation of male desire. The long, patient ordeal of Fanny Price; as opposed to the spasmodic, tediously repeated fornications of, say, a Ginger Man. Ellis: 'the man's part in courtship . . . is in a straight line . . . The woman's part, having to follow at the same moment two quite different impulses, is necessarily always in a zigzag or a curve.' Potentially more narrative there, on account of what he nicely calls 'the long-circuiting' of desire (a phrase I thought I had made up – there is nothing new under the sun). Ellis has much to say about the woman's blush as originating in a displaced genital flushing (he quotes an anonymous remark to the effect that 'an erection is a blushing of the penis', and I am sure Freud somewhere characterises the blush as 'a mild erection of the head').[16] More delay and long-circuiting as the blood is temporarily re-routed from the genitals to the face. And thus symbolism and narrative – the body has started to *tell*, not simply to do.

I choose two narrative blushes, or blushers, to conclude. The diarist of Kierkegaard's *Diary of a Seducer* – just to remind you – regards himself as an artist who aestheticises seduction in pursuit of 'the *interesting*' – the potentialities of the interesting must be exhausted. ('A bad conscience can still make life interesting', says the rather Kierkegaardian frame-narrator. Ordinary engagement and marriage are, of course, definitely 'not interesting'.) He is 'too intellectually inclined to be a seducer in the ordinary sense of the word'. As he writes, rather memorably, 'mere possession is not worth much' because you tend to be 'too involved in the situation to enjoy it'. Truly refined pleasure is a meta-activity – thinking *about* the process or situation and relishing it poetically. Most men, he says, 'enjoy a young girl as they do a glass of champagne in a single frothing moment' – it's alright, certainly, 'but there is more'. His story is his account of his pursuit of that 'more'. Clearly, it involved endless attenuations and nearly infinite deferral. There is to be no 'impatience or greed': having 'marked out' a suitable girl, Cordelia, she and it is to be 'enjoyed in leisurely draughts'. To this end, he stresses the importance of '*actiones in distans*' (operations directed towards a distant goal). What he enjoys – he is arguably deeply depraved – is rousing the girl until he is confident that she is completely 'in my power': and then, by making her 'introspective', introducing a permanent confusion into her being by 'developing the many-tongued reflection within her'. As he sees it, he is developing within her 'a spiritual concupiscence'. And whatever happens, he thinks 'she will save the interesting out of the shipwreck'. The frame-narrator sees him as 'perverted'. 'There is something revolting when a man directs a traveller, perplexed about his way, to the wrong road, and then leaves him alone in his error; but what is that compared with causing a [woman] to go astray inwardly?' When he does finally possess her, for one night, his story is immediately, and brusquely, ended. 'It is over now, and I hope never to see her again . . . Now all resistance is impossible, and only as long as that is present is it beautiful to love; when it is ended there is only weakness and habit.' *Finis*. But prior to that, he has had over a hundred pages of 'interesting' dalliance – art, or sadism, or both. A long-circuiting of desire.

Preferring the oblique and the 'distant', he particularly favours the subtle and suggestive potencies of the 'sidelong glance', at which he claims to be expert. With such a glance, he first makes Cordelia blush. And he is quite a connoisseur of blushes. 'There are different kinds of feminine blushes. There is the coarse brick-red blush which romantic writers always use so freely when they let their heroines blush all over.' Too crude – no thanks. But also 'there is the delicate blush; it is the blush of the spirit's dawn. In a young girl it is priceless.' It is really a blush which marks the climax of his preferred mode of seduction, the consummation of his – perverted? sublimated? – desire. 'My eyes steal over her, not with desire, in truth that would be shameless. A delicate fleeting blush passes over her, like a cloud over the meadow, rising and receding. What does this blush mean? Is it love? Is it longing, hope, fear; for is not the heart's colour red? By no means. She wonders, she is surprised – not at me, that would be too little to offer her; she is surprised, not at herself, but in herself, she is transformed within.'[17]

It was that seducer and those blushes which provided Isak Dinesen (or Karen Blixen) with the idea for her last tale – 'Ehrengard'. It is a comic-pastoral, told like a fairy story; conceived as a piece of music; with just a touch of *The Tempest* in it. It is a simple-seeming tale, set in the storybook world of the Grand Duchy of Babenhausen. The heroine is the beautiful warrior maiden Ehrengard, lady-in-waiting to the princess Ludmilla. During her secret confinement in a sylvan retreat, Ludmilla is also attended by the fascinating portrait painter Cazotte. Cazotte's ambition is to awaken the idea of the erotic in the cold and virginal Ehrengard. Cazotte sees art and seduction as interchangeable, or identical.

The whole attitude of the artist towards the Universe is that of a seducer. For what does seduction mean but the ability to make, with infinite trouble, patience and perseverance, the object upon which you concentrate your mind give forth, voluntarily and enraptured, its very core and essence . . . I have seduced an old earthenware pot and two lemons into yielding their inmost being to me, to become mine and, at the same moment, to become phenomena of overwhelming loveliness and delight.[18]

For this artist-connoisseur, mere old-fashioned, conventional seduction would 'mean nothing'. 'With regard to Ehrengard – I insist on obtaining a full surrender without any physical touch whatever.' When it is accomplished, he boasts to the friend in whom he is confiding, he will hand her over 'intact but annihilated' – still a virgin, but inwardly 'fallen, broken and lost'.[19] How will he do this; how, in what act, make

Ehrengard's nature give forth itself most exhaustively? He has his answer. 'In the blush':

You will not, I know, for a moment be thinking of the blush of offended modesty which might be called forth, from the outside, by a coarse and blunt assailant . . . To the mind of the artist the very idea is blasphemy, he turns his face away from it. You will no more be thinking of the blush of anger, the which, from the outside, I myself – preserve me – might bring about. None of the two would, in any case, be what I want . . . I shall in time be drawing my young Amazon's blood . . . upwards from the deepest, most secret wells of her being, making it cover her all over like a transparent crimson veil and making it burn her up in one single exquisite gasp of flame . . . her blood is to rise, in pride and *amour-propre*, in unconditional surrender, in the enraptured flinging over of her entire being to the powers which, till this hour, with her entire being she has rejected and denied, in full, triumphant consent to her own perdition. In this blush her past, present, and future will be thrown before my feet . . . In the high mountains . . . there exists a phenomenon of nature called *Alphen-Gluhen* . . . After the sun has set, and as the whole majestic mountain landscape is already withdrawing into itself, suddenly the row of summits, all on their own, radiate a divine fire, a celestial, deep rose flame, as if they were giving up a long kept secret. After that they disappear, nothing more dramatic can be imagined: they have betrayed their inmost substance and can now only annihilate themselves . . . what glorification. And what void afterwards.[20]

But how will he raise this blush? He chances to see Ehrengard bathing naked in the river, and decides that he will put her in a painting, naked – as Nymph or Diana. He will then show the painting at court when she is present next to him – and only she will see that it is *her* naked body. 'The figure on the canvas would remain chastely silvery before the ardent eyes of the spectators. But the maiden by his side would slowly become all aglow. Behind the shawl, silk gown, embroidered petticoats and dainty cambric, the straight, strong, pure body from heel to forehead would blush into a deep exquisite crimson, a mystical *rose person*, which no clear water of a mountain lake would ever wash away. Into that *Alphen-Gluhen* [glow] upon which night follows.' She will be blushing, 'not with indignation at an assault, but with ecstasy at a revelation, not in protest or self-defense, but in consent and surrender'.[21]

That is his plan, and he even signs one letter 'Yours in fear and trembling', so we can be sure of his role-model! But it doesn't work out as intended, and in the event the Kierkegaardian male seducer is comprehensively beaten at his own game. I'll spare you the plot, but in the climactic final recognition scene, Ehrengard astonishes everyone by claiming a baby to be her own; and on being pressed for the identity of the father, she turns and points at the utterly unprepared painter. 'Herr Cazotte is the father of my child.'

At these words Herr Cazotte's blood was drawn upwards, as from the profoundest wells of his being, till it colored him all over like a transparent crimson veil. His brow and cheeks, all on their own, radiated a divine fire, a celestial, deep rose flame, as if they were giving away a long kept secret. And it was a strange thing that he should blush. For normally an onlooker in a *fauteil d'orchestre* would grow pale at seeing the irate hero of the stage suddenly turn upon him. The actual situation held very grave possibilities to Herr Cazotte . . . Any gallant warrior, knowing Kurt von Blittersdorf's [Ehrengard's fiancé] reputation with a sword or pistol, might have gone white, even white as death.

But Herr Cazotte, who was an artist, blushed. Here ends the story of Ehrengard.[22]

Her story has contained no actual, physical sexual contact. But once again, and triumphantly, we see how there can indeed be a story without it. And for once, happily enough, the 'damned trick' is *by* a girl!

NOTES

1 See R. Frederick and D. Laurence (eds.), *The Collected Letters of Joseph Conrad, Vol. 5 1912–1916* (Cambridge: Cambridge University Press, 1996), p. 128.
2 Leon Edel and Lyall H. Powers (eds.), *The Complete Notebooks of Henry James* (New York: Oxford University Press, 1987), p. 170.
3 Ibid., p. 37.
4 Ibid., pp. 103–4.
5 Henry James, *Literary Criticism: European Writers and the Prefaces* (New York: Library of America, 1984), p. 1170.
6 Ibid., p. 1146.
7 Ibid., p. 1147.
8 Ibid., pp. 1148, 1151.
9 Ibid., p. 1123.
10 Ibid., p. 1121.
11 Ibid., p. 1124.
12 Ibid., p. 1126.
13 Ruth Bernard Yeazell, *Fictions of Modesty* (Chicago: Chicago University Press, 1991).
14 P. H. Nidditch (ed.), *David Hume: A Treatise of Human Nature* (Oxford: Clarendon Press, 1978), p. 542; Jean-Jacques Rousseau, *Emile*, tr. F. Boxley (London: Everyman, 1911), ch. 5. p. 323.

15 Yeazell, *Fictions of Modesty*, pp. 76–7.
16 Ibid., pp. 232, 233, 234.
17 See Soren Kierkegaard, 'Diary of a Seducer', *Either/Or, Vol. 1*, tr. David E. Swenson and Lillian Marvin Swenson (Princeton: Princeton University Press, 1971), pp. 299–400.
18 Isak Dinesen, *Ehrengard* (London: Michael Joseph, 1963), p. 10.
19 Ibid., p. 39.
20 Ibid., pp. 25–7.
21 Ibid., pp. 46, 46–7.
22 Ibid., pp. 71–2.

CHAPTER 7

Henry James's 'saddest story' – The Other House

In his memoir on Henry James, written in 1913, Ford Madox Ford says of James's art:

He can convey an impression, an atmosphere of what you will with literally nothing. Embarrassment, chastened happiness – for his happiness is always tinged with regret – greed, horror, social vacuity – he can give you it all with a purely blank page. His characters will talk about rain, about the opera, about the moral aspects of the selling of Old Masters to the New Republic, and those conversations will convey to your mind that the quiet talkers are living in an atmosphere of horror, of bankruptcy, of passion hopeless as the Dies Irae! That is the supreme trick of art today, since that is how we really talk about the musical glasses whilst our lives crumble to pieces around us.[1]

Ford's *The Good Soldier* is his most Jamesian novel – with its uncertainties and hesitations, its gaps and incompletions, its silences and sadnesses; the sense of accumulating horrors beneath the maintained civilities, the crumbling of lives under the cut-glass manners. It was originally entitled *The Saddest Story*, which the publishers rejected, presumably because they felt the times were already sad enough (it was published in 1915). Few people realise that this was, in fact, a quotation from James, a nod of acknowledgement, as it were, to the master. He retained it in the opening line. 'This is the saddest story I ever heard.' In *The Other House*, we read: 'Tony looked as if he were retracing the saddest story on earth.' Ford's novel, rightly, became an acknowledged modern classic. James's novel, unjustly, has suffered almost complete neglect.

An anonymous reviewer of the time recognised that the novel was something special.

The appearance of a new book by Mr Henry James is always an event to the connoisseur of letters. It cannot be stated too explicitly or published too widely that *The Other House* is an event of the first order. In a small way it is a revolution. Mr James has done something new. His name has been for long a synonym for cleverness and conscious skill, but on laying down this volume the reader is forced to confess that henceforward, if the writer so wills, it is also a synonym for power. The book has grip.[2]

The reviewer is right; the novel is – still – 'gripping'. It has a power which is, at least, different in kind from that of James's previous work. We do not measure the power of a novel by the number of violently terminated lives it contains, but it is worth remarking that this is James's one and only murder novel.

In his Notebooks, James records the moments of the novel's incubation. It offers a marvellous insight into the way his mind worked – teasing and tracing out the latent possibilities of a subject.

26 December (34 De Vere Gardens)
I have been sitting here in the firelight – on this quiet afternoon of the empty London Christmastide, trying to catch hold of the tail of an idea, of a 'subject'. Vague, dim forms of imperfect conceptions seem to brush across one's face with a blur of suggestion, a flutter of impalpable wings . . . Is there something for a tale, is there something for a play, in something that might be a little like the following. It is the *play* that I am looking for, but it is worth noting, all the same, for the *other* possibility.
    Very briefly, I imagine a young man who has lost his wife and who has a little girl, the only issue of that prematurely frustrated union. He has very solemnly, and on his honour, promised his wife, on her deathbed, that, *du vivant* of their child, he will not marry again. He has given her this absolutely sacred assurance and she has died believing him. She has had a reason, a deep motive for her demand – the overwhelming dread of a stepmother. She has had one herself – a stepmother who rendered her miserable, darkened and blighted her youth. She wishes to preserve her own little girl from such a fate. For five years all goes well – the husband doesn't think of marrying again. He delights in the child, watches over her growth and looks forward to her future. Then, inevitably, fatally he meets a girl with whom he falls deeply in love – in love as he hadn't *begun* to be with his poor dead wife. She returns his affection, his passion; but he sees the phantom of his solemn vow, his sacred promise rise terribly before him. In the presence of it he falters, and while the girl stands obviously ready to surrender herself, he hangs back, he tries to resist the current that sweeps him along. *Or*, there is another figure intensely engaged in the action – and without whom it would present no drama. This is the figure of a young woman who loves him, who has loved him from the moment she has seen him, who has seen him, known him, *du vivant* of his wife. The circumstances of this personage are all questions to determine.[3]

Initially, then, James was drawn to the narrative possibilities of the obstacles to passion thrown up by the vow, and the consequent an-guished irresoluteness of the hero. Then he sees that it will only become drama if the situation is complicated by the passion of another woman, and he begins to shift his interest to what he calls his Bad Heroine. Note that he is thinking in terms of a play.

The curtain rises on Act II, 5 years later. My hero has never married, of course – no more has my Bad Heroine. She is fearfully in love with my Hero. He meanwhile has fallen in love with my Good Heroine, who ignorantly and innocently returns his passion. My Bad Heroine is frightfully afraid the two will marry . . . Then my young lady takes a decision – she determines to poison the child – on the calculation that suspicion will fall on her rival. She does so – and on the theory of *motive* – suspicion *does* fall on the wretched girl. There are two persons to figure as the *public*, the judging, wondering, horrified world, the doctor and a convenient older woman who has been in the first act. Suspicion descends – it is *constatée* [certified] that the child is poisoned: the question is who has done it? . . . The child recovers, demanding the Good Heroine, and the attempt of the Bad Heroine is condoned and covered up by the doctor – who has aspired to her hand! – and the man who first loved her. The Hero at the '*request*' of his little daughter determines on a union with the Good Heroine; and the other woman is got off by the doctor and the 2d *amoureux*. As I so barbarously and roughly jot the story down, I seem to feel in it the stuff of a play . . .[4]

This is greatly edited, but even from what I have quoted ideas can be seen growing as James writes himself into the imagined situation. And they went on growing. The child is finally not poisoned but drowned; and instead of recovering, it dies. But the Bad Heroine, now a murderess, is still 'got off', and the conventional retributions of the law are excluded. And, at this stage, James still saw it all as making a play. Which takes us, briefly, to the matter of James and the theatre.

Between the years of 1890 and 1895, James made a concerted effort to write successfully for the theatre (for full details see the volume in Leon Edel's magisterial biography of Henry James entitled *The Treacherous Years*). He had already written six plays at the time of the above Notebook entry (only one had been produced), and he was even then working on his seventh play, *Guy Domville*. This play had a catastrophic reception when it was staged a year later. A shattered James returned to the novel, and *The Other House* is one of the first fruits of his slightly traumatised post-theatre years (the others were *The Spoils of Poynton* and *What Maisie Knew*, and all three novels have features in common – they all concern struggles for possession; of a man, of a houseful of beautiful things, of a child respectively). But if James fled from the theatre, he took a lot of theatrical experience with him; and, from the point of view of this novel, the crucial experience was his exposure to Ibsen.

In 1891 he saw Elizabeth Robbins play the heroine in Ibsen's *Hedda Gabler*, and this occasioned an important essay by James on 'Henrik Ibsen'. In describing Hedda Gabler, as acted by Elizabeth Robbins, James could be outlining the figure of Rose Armiger (described as being like an actress) in his own future novel.

It is the portrait of a nature . . . and of a state of nerves a swell as of soul, a state of temper, of health, of chagrin, of despair . . . We receive Hedda ripe for her catastrophe, and if we ask for antecedents and explanations we must simply find them in her character. Her motives are just her passions. What the four acts show us is these motives and that character – complicated, strange, irreconcilable, infernal – playing themselves out . . . The 'use' of Hedda Gabler is that she acts on others and that even her most disagreeable qualities have the privilege, thoroughly undeserved doubtless, but equally irresistible, of becoming a part of the history of others. And then one isn't so sure she is wicked, and by no means sure (especially when she is represented by an actress who makes the point ambiguous) that she is disagreeable. She is various and sinuous and graceful, complicated and natural; she suffers, she struggles, she is human, and by that fact exposed to a dozen interpretations, to the importunity of our suspense. Wrought with admirable closeness is the whole tissue of relations between the five people whom the author sets in motion and on whose behalf he asks of us so few concessions.[5]

In James's novel it will be six main characters, plus two (Doctor Ramage and Mrs Beever) who serve as what James had described as 'the judging, wondering, horrified world'. And James does not just take his ambiguous 'bad' heroine from Ibsen. In its confined, claustrophobic, inward-looking atmosphere, in what James noted in Ibsen as 'the pervasive air of small interests and standards, the signs of limited local life' and the 'parochial or suburban stamp', this whole novel is close to the Ibsenite play James undoubtedly hoped it would become. And what James admired more generally in Ibsen matched his own deepest proclivity – 'his admirable talent for producing an intensity of interest by means incorruptibly quiet, by an almost demure preservation of the appearances of the usual in which we see him juggle with difficulty and danger and which constitutes, as it were, his only coquetry'.[6] Though James does note three aspects of Ibsen's work which amount to a signal missingness – 'I mean of course the absence of humour, the absence of free imagination, and the absence of style.'[7] In his novel, James remedies the deficiencies.

James did in fact do a scenario for a three-act play to be called *The Promise*, but it was never put on and the script has not survived. Fortunately, a friend suggested he turn it into a serial for the *Illustrated London*

News, which was where the novel we have now first appeared. As a novel, *The Other House* still bears very visible marks of its theatrical incubation. It falls into three distinct parts (acts) with each part clearly organised as a series of scenes. The characters enter and leave as if on cue – as one comes in from the garden, another goes out into the hall – leading, for the most part, to a series of increasingly charged and dramatic conversations, or confrontations, between all the people involved – seemingly between every possible combination of two you can get out of eight. The accessories are minimal: the men smoke cigarettes at awkward moments (Paul eats buns); there is much play with 'the paraphernalia of tea'; there are dolls and a birthday cake for poor, doomed Effie; various pieces of furniture are mentioned; there are hats and parasols. It is invariably quiet – 'the great showy clock ticked in the scented silence'. Characters may pace restlessly, stand stupefied, sit down in confusion, rush in breathlessly (though awkward movements are rare), or just stroll amiably around. The most violent act (on stage, that is) occurs when Dennis kicks the turned up corner of a rug in frustration. During the second act, the shadows lengthen in the garden, while throughout the last act a deepening dusk seeps into the house. Each section ends at a point of drama – with the announcement that Julia is dying; the discovery of the body of young Effie; and the disappearance of Rose into the night. The tensions grow, and shocks give way to horrors until it is a 'black, bloody nightmare' not only for Dennis, but, varyingly, for everyone. But the manners remain impeccable; the civilised surface holds. 'Tony, agitated as she could see, but with complete command of his manners'. 'To look at him was to recognise the value of appearances.' Characters, even in distress, invariably find 'the right tone'. Everyone instinctively behaves so as to 'establish a superficial harmony'. There is unashamed reference to 'the necessary falsehood'. 'In this way the trick was successfully played – they found their feet.' 'It would lead to exactly nothing – that had been settled all round in advance. This was a happy, lively provision that kept everything down, made sociability a cool, public, out-of-door affair, without a secret or a mystery.' Except, of course, there are secrets and there will be mysteries. Even Rose is 'constitutionally averse to making unmeasured displays', but when her passion can no longer be 'kept down' and breaks cover, the smooth skin of the sociable surface is hideously gashed. Only briefly, however. The tear is soon healed over, though leaving what aching inner wounds we are left to surmise. These are the sort of people Ford Madox Ford was describing.

For James, the advantages of the novel over the stage are many and crucial (even if it took him some time, and a grievous disappointment, to realise it). There is, for example, the not inconsiderable matter of James's humour. Doctor Ramage (as important a figure as doctors are in Ibsen) 'had a face so candid and circular that it suggested a large white pill'. You might certainly find a pale man to play the Doctor – but you would lose that priceless pill. 'The butler retired like a conscientious Minister retiring from untenable office.' Try staging that – particularly nowadays when that is precisely what Ministers *don't* do! More generally though, what James could not put on stage was just his imagery, and so much of the important action – the humour, the imaginative play, the style – occurs precisely there. 'They faced each other over the deep waters of the accumulated and the undiscussed.' You could do the first four words on stage, but not the rest. Or again: 'They stood looking at each other like a pair who, walking on a frozen lake, suddenly have in their ears the great crack of ice.' Once more, the first six words on stage, but the vital ones which follow can only be thought. When things come to a climax and characters find themselves in 'the agony of the actual' and having to name awful facts, they speak 'with a drop, before the red real, of all vain terms'. Here, the 'real' is indeed real enough, and red enough – hopeless murderous passion, and a killed child. There are times when all the terms are vain. But, for the most part, James is lamenting 'our sad want of signs for shades and degrees', and it is his incomparably nuanced amplifying, supplementing narrative commentary which seeks to supply that want.

The amplification is everywhere. 'Mrs Beever was so "early Victorian" as to be almost prehistoric – was constructed to move amid massive mahogany and sit upon banks of Berlinwool.' It is crucial in establishing character: Tony has 'a certain quality of passive excess which was the note of the whole man and which, for an attentive eye, began with his neckties and ended with his intonations.' 'His presence was, anywhere and at any time, as much as ever the clock at the moment it strikes.' It is a vivid image, but I do not know what an actor would do with it; any more than I can see how an actress would convey the following – 'Rose stood there opposite him with a fine, rich urgency.' It is James who adds a whole extra dimension to the actual goings-on. When Tony comes downstairs after his dying wife has exacted the fatal promise – which nobody yet knows – he says 'She's there – it's all right. But ah, my dear people – !' There is a lot of James in that '– !', the always greater drama of what James calls 'the dominant unspeakable'. But here James goes on – 'And he passed his hand, with the vivid gesture of brushing away an image, over a face of which the essential radiance was visible even through perturbation.' I suppose this could just about be a stage direction; but pity the poor actor trying to juggle radiance and perturbation. As with – 'his face was a combat of mystifications'. Even more with the following, after Tony realises that both Rose (whom he does not love) and Jean (whom he does) adore him: 'He was in bliss with a great chill and in despair with a great lift, and confused and assured and alarmed.' The fact is that there are inner states so contradictory and mixed and confused that only patient, or inspired, analysis can convey them. Shakespeare can do it on the stage but his drama is unique. James needs the space of the novel.

James loved old English houses. Thus, in his journal: 'It was the old houses that fetched me – Montacute, the admirable; Barrington, that superb Ford Abbey, and several smaller ones . . . These delicious old houses, in the long August days, in the south of England air, on the soil over which so much has passed and out of which so much has come, rose before me like a series of visions.' There are many important great houses in his fiction – Gardencourt, Poynton, Fawns – and all the action of this novel takes place in two well-appointed houses – Eastmead (rather old-fashioned, as befits Mrs Beever) and Bounds (more modern – Tony Bream's taste). But they are not among James's great houses; they seem more suburban – stock-broker belt, we would now call them. This is appropriate enough since both families are in banking. They also provide that apparently secure, placid, comfortable, solidly respectable (to the point of primness) atmosphere in which Rose Armiger is to explode. For it is she, of course, who is the source of all the drama in this otherwise peaceable upper-middle-class kingdom.

When Jean first sees Rose she thinks her 'awfully plain'. Then Rose smiles, and 'the ambiguity that Mrs Beever had spoken of lighted up – an ambiguity worth all the dull prettiness in the world'. And it is that ambiguity which makes her by far the most interesting character in the book. All the others are, one feels, in their own ways, rather uncomplicatedly decent – even the 'brilliant, joking gentleman' Tony Bream. It is Rose who introduces complexity into the suburban serenity. That she is in the grip of a distinctly non-suburban passion is signalled early on. 'If there had been anyone at that moment to see her

face, such an observer would have found it strangely, tragically con-
vulsed: she had the appearance of holding in with extraordinary force
some passionate sob or cry, some smothered impulse of anguish.' Tony
does not realise what is happening, the passion he has aroused – 'the
unexpected had sprung up before him'. 'What he saw, without understanding it, was the final snap of her tremendous tension, the end of
her wonderful false calm.' It is only later that he realises what is written in her face. 'What Tony Bream saw was a circumstance of which
he had already had glimpses; but for some reason or other it was now
written with a largeness that made it resemble a printed poster on a
wall . . . This message was simply Rose Armiger's whole face, exquisite
and tragic in its appeal . . . He could meet it only with a compassion as
unreserved as itself.' Here is perhaps the central moment in the book
(it occurs almost exactly halfway):

Their eyes met, and he again felt himself in the presence of what, in them,
shortly before, had been so deep, so exquisite. It represented something that
no lapse could long quench – something that gave out the measureless white
ray of a light steadily revolving. She could sometimes turn it away, but it was
always somewhere; and now it covered him with a great cold lustre that made
everything for the moment look hard and ugly – made him also feel the chill
of a complication for which he had not allowed.

That chill settles on the book: it is at this point that things begin to
darken.

Rose shows the darkest side of her ruthless passion in two subsequent confrontations. In the first, she has the audacity to suggest to
Jean that she, Rose, is worried about what Jean might do to the child
in order that she might marry Tony. 'Jean turned again upon her
companion a face bewildered and alarmed: unguardedly stepping into
water that she had believed shallow, she found herself caught up in a
current of fast-moving depths – a cold, full tide that set straight out to
sea. "Where am I?" her scared silence seemed for the moment to ask.'
Well out of her emotional depth, as James's sustained aqueous image
makes clear.

Jean had got up before these remarks had gone far, but even though she fell
back a few steps her dismay was a force that condemned her to take them in.
'God forbid I should understand you,' she panted; 'I only make out that you
say and mean horrible things and that you're doing your best to seek a
quarrel with me from which you shall derive some advantage that, I'm happy
to feel, is beyond my conception.' Both the women were now pale as death,
and Rose was brought to her feet by the pure passion of this retort.

These are two women fighting over the same man, and, as their passions flare up, the suburbs are, briefly, on fire. Jean is left 'sick with the aftertaste of her encounter'. With her breathtakingly brazen accusation, Rose has broken all the tacit rules of civilised interchange. Instead of the usual cordial conversational potions she has poured a poisoned draught.

Perhaps even more shocking is the scene in which, playing quite shamelessly on his sturdy decency and ingrained sense of honour, she effectively forces her much abused suitor, Dennis Vidal, to lie for her, covering up the murder he knows she has committed. 'So you can't abandon me – you can't . . . You're mine!' She then takes hold of him in the most chilling embrace in the book.

He submitted, with no movement but to close his eyes before the new-born dread of her caress. Yet he took the caress when it came – the dire confession of her hard embrace, the long entreaty of her stony kiss. He might still have been a creature trapped in steel; after she had let him go he still stood at a loss how to turn.

After she has done the deed, we are told that 'Rose's mask was the mask of Medusa.' Dennis has indeed been petrified; standing by Rose and seeing her through requires that he also be a man of steel. He utters the necessary falsehood – 'He spoke with a clearness that proved the steel surface he had in a few minutes forged for his despair.' It is Dennis who, at the end, carries Rose away into the night and an imponderable future.

So why don't they hand her over to the police, since all eight of them (but no one else) know that she drowned Effie – 'She forced her in. She held her down. She left her' – and her attempts to implicate Jean are an almost immediate failure? It cannot simply be that they want to keep up the good name of the district – though I suppose that eminent banking families would particularly deprecate having a murder attached to their names. One hardly feels that the good Doctor Ramage would participate in a crude neighbourhood cover-up. It is more to do with the nature of the case, with the sad, horrible hopelessness of Rose's passion. 'Don't come near such a thing; don't touch it; don't know it!' cries Tony to Dennis, telling him that he has unwittingly intruded 'on obscure, unhappy things, on suffering and danger and death'. The knowledge cannot be eluded; though it may be, in time, frozen over, as it were. Life goes on, and, it is intimated, Tony and Jean will, some time in the post-ravage future, get married. But the 'thing', the 'unutterable horror' *is* 'obscure'. Perhaps a hopeless but insuperable passion always is: when Dennis cries out helplessly 'it's not I, it's not she, it's not you, it's not anyone', he is speaking a kind of truth. I'm not suggesting a communal guilt – Rose's is the only hand in the water – but it takes more than one person to make a situation. And how much encouragement did Tony give Rose – who must have been a good deal more interesting, at least, than dear, sweet Jean? When Jean learns that it is his – and everyone's – intention to 'let her go' – she is incredulous – 'And yet you condone the atrocity – ?' There follows a crucial exchange.

'I must tell you all,' he said once more. 'I knew it – I always knew it. And I made her come.'
'You were kind to her – as you're always kind.'
'No; I was more than that. And I should have been less.'
His face showed a rift in the blackness. 'I remember.'
She followed him in pain and at a distance. 'You mean you liked it?'
'I liked it – whilst I was safe. Then I grew afraid.'
'Afraid of what?'
'Afraid of everything. You don't know – but we're abysses. At least *I'm* one!' he groaned. He seemed to sound the depth. 'There are other things. They go back far.'
'Don't tell me all,' said Jean.

Just what the 'it' was that Tony liked, and how much more than 'kind' he was to Rose, we will never know, just as Jean will never ask. Sex is never mentioned in these high suburban households. The nearest anyone comes to it is when Dennis admits to Rose, reluctantly as one feels, 'your effect on – what shall I call it? . . . On God knows what baser, obscurer part of me!' Sexual desire is the 'obscure' thing, behind all the other things – above everything else it is *the* 'dominant unspeakable' in the Jamesian world. But, above or below everything else, it is the most powerful part of 'the red real'. Rose's 'passion' is only an extreme case; and who knows how much Tony struck the tinder and stoked the fire – wittingly or unwittingly is, after a while, beside the point. We are to feel that the unambiguous judgements of the law would be too crude to be applied to the ambiguity that is Rose, and her ambiguously engendered passion. 'Her doom will be to live.'

I have touched only on what strike me as some of the more notable features of this beautifully crafted, highly civilised novel, written when James is just about at the height of his powers. There are many other pleasures in the book – not least the exchanges between the rather officious Mrs Beever and her stolid, expressionless, bun-eating son, Paul. In truth, the whole novel is a continuous pleasure to read, as fresh today as it was a hundred years ago, even if our morals and manners have changed. Like all great artists, James, under the tea cups and the cigarettes, is dealing with matters that are unsuburban and unchanging. Late on in his life when he was working on the outline of a novel which he never finished, called *The Ivory Tower*, James suddenly writes in his Notebook – 'Oh, blest *Other House* which gives me thus at every step a precedent, a support, a divine little light to walk by.'[8] It is a light we would be foolish to deprive ourselves of.

NOTES

1 Ford Madox Hueffer [Ford], *Henry James: A Critical Study* (London: Martin Secker, 1913), p. 153.
2 Quoted in Roger Gard (ed.), *Henry James: The Critical Heritage* (London: Routledge & Kegan Paul Ltd, 1968), p. 263.
3 Henry James, *The Complete Notebooks of Henry James*, ed. Leon Edel and Lyall H. Powers (New York: Oxford University Press, 1987), pp. 80–1.
4 Ibid., pp. 81–2.
5 Henry James, *The Scenic Arts: Notes on Acting and the Drama 1872–1901*, ed. Allan Wade (London: Rupert Hart-Davis, 1949), pp. 250–2.
6 Ibid., p. 249.
7 Ibid., p. 247.
8 James, *Complete Notebooks*, p. 261.

CHAPTER 8

Henry James and Shakespeare

Speaking of an author's career in geographic terms is, at best, a game. But in the summer of 1902, James, aged sixty, was clearly at the summit of his powers. He had just finished *The Wings of the Dove*, and he was assembling some of his recent short stories for a collection. Finding himself short of material for a decently sized volume, he set about writing three more stories (all at the same time, moving from one to the other), and between July and early November he composed 'The Beast in the Jungle', 'The Papers', and 'The Birthplace' – three of his finest works. There was no time for magazine publication, and they went directly into *The Better Sort*, published in 1903. It is immensely interesting and illuminating to study the stories together, and I shall have occasion to refer to 'The Papers', but here my topic is 'The Birthplace'.

A notebook entry gives us the genesis of the story:

Lamb House, June 12th, 1901
The other day at Welcombe (May 30th or 31st) the Trevelyans, or rather Lady T., spoke of the odd case of the couple who had formerly (before the present incumbents) been for a couple of years – or a few – the people in charge of the Shakespeare house – the Birthplace – which struck me as possibly a little *donnée*. They were rather strenuous and superior people from Newcastle, who had embraced the situation with joy, thinking to find it just the thing for them and full of interest, dignity, an appeal to all their culture and refinement, etc. [They were Joseph Skipsey – a minor North Country poet – and wife; custodians from 1889–91.] But what happened was that at the end of 6 months they grew sick and desperate from finding it – finding their office – the sort of thing that I suppose it is: full of humbug, full of lies and superstition *imposed* upon them by the great body of visitors, who want the positively impressive story about every object, every feature of the house, every dubious thing – the simplified, unscrupulous, gulpable *tale*. They found themselves *too* refined, too critical for this – the public wouldn't have criticism (of legend, tradition, probability, improbability) at any price – and they ended

132

by contracting a fierce intellectual and moral disgust for the way they had to *meet* the public. That is all the anecdote *gives* – except that after a while they could stand it no longer, and threw up the position. There may be something in it – something more, I mean, than the mere facts. I seem to see them – for there is no catastrophe in a simple resignation of the post, turned somehow, by the experience, into strange sceptics, iconoclasts, positive negationists. They are forced over to the other extreme and become rank enemies not only of the legend, but of the historic *donnée* itself. Say they end by denying Shakespeare – say they do it on the spot itself – one day – in the presence of a big, gaping, admiring batch. *Then* they must go. – THAT seems to be arrangeable, workable – for 6,000 words.[1]

That it came in as something over 25,000 words is, you might say, par for the course. But the story line is all there in well-developed form, apart from the very different twist which James gave to the end. And the way James treated his *donnée* turned a potentially simple tale into one of his most profound soundings of the nature of the artist – perforce, the *great* artist.

A visit to Shakespeare's birthplace was, of course, an all too obvious pilgrimage for an American writer to make. In his travel piece 'In Warwickshire' (1877), reprinted in *Portraits of Places* (1883) and *English Hours* (1905), James makes something of a point of *not* talking about the 'sacred place'. 'Inevitably, of course, the sentimental tourist has a great deal to say to himself about this being Shakespeare's county . . . It was, however, no part of my design in these remarks to pause before so thickly besieged a shrine as this; and if I were to allude to Stratford it would not be in connection with the fact that Shakespeare planted there, to grow for ever, the torment of his unguessed riddle. It would be rather to speak of a delightful old house, near the Avon.'[2] And so James, characteristically, veers away from the obvious to attend and respond to what he calls 'the shyer and more elusive elements of the show' (we will be hearing more of 'the torment of his unguessed riddle'). You sense that, in addressing Shakespeare's birthplace directly, James felt it would be impossible to avoid or transcend clichés – clichés of awe or clichés of scepticism, or even clichés of indifference. Other American writers had already made the attempt, and James instinctively avoided the well-worn path.[3]

Before considering the tale which *does* confront – or emerge from – Shakespeare's birthplace, it is helpful to take note of what James himself said about it in the relevant Preface to the New York Edition of his collected works (1907–9). He recapitulates, in summary form, the details he had committed to his Notebook, and then adds:

For the rest I must but leave 'The Birthplace' to plead its own cause; only adding that here afresh and in the highest degree were the conditions reproduced for that mystic, that 'chemical' change wrought in the impression of life by its dedication to an aesthetic use, that I lately spoke of in connection with 'The Coxon Fund'. Beautiful on all this ground exactly, to the projector's mind, the process by which the small cluster of actualities latent in the fact reported to him was to be reconstituted and, so far as they might need, altered; the felt fermentation, ever interesting, but flagrantly so in the case before us, that enables the sense originally communicated to make fresh and possibly quite different terms for the new employment there awaiting it. It has been liberated (to repeat, I believe, my figure) after the fashion of some sound young draught-horse who may, in the great meadow, have to be recaptured and broken for the saddle.[4]

He does repeat his 'figure'. He has many images for a subject, or *donnée*, getting out of control like, for example, an untrained house-dog, and needing, somehow, to be curbed and brought to heel ('Once "out", like a house-dog of a temper above confinement, it defies the mere whistle, it roams, it hunts, it seeks out and "sees" life; it can be brought back but by hand and then only to take its futile thrashing' (preface to *What Maisie Knew*)).[5] He liked his stories, like some of his characters, to 'let go' and have their head; but the danger occurs, to radically shift metaphors, when the flowing stream of invention 'breaks bounds and gets into flood'. Here is what James was aiming for: 'To improvise with extreme freedom and yet at the same time without the possibility of a ravage, without the hint of a flood; . . . The thing was to aim at absolute singleness, clearness and roundness, and yet to depend on an imagination working freely, working (call it) with extravagance; by which law it wouldn't be thinkable except as free and wouldn't be amusing except as controlled.'[6] The generative tension between freedom and control lies at the very heart of James's aesthetic.

James's comments on 'The Birthplace' point us back to his Preface which considers 'The Coxon Fund'. This was a story triggered by a monograph on Coleridge he had read. But 'more interesting still than the man . . . is the S. T. Coleridge *type*; so what I was to do was merely to recognise the type, to borrow it, to re-embody and freshly place it; an ideal under the law of which I could but cultivate a free hand'. You can't ever truly get at the 'real person' (here Coleridge, but any actual person taken as a subject); the artist must, therefore, aim at a form of 'transplanting', 'an act essentially not mechanical, but thinkable rather – so far as thinkable at all – in chemical, almost in mystical terms'.

We can surely account for nothing in the novelist's work that hasn't passed through the crucible of his imagination, hasn't, in that perpetually simmering cauldron his intellectual *pot-au-feu*, been reduced to savoury fusion. We here figure the morsel, of course, not as boiled to nothing, but as exposed, in return for the taste it gives out, to a new and richer saturation. In this state it is in due course picked out and served, and a meagre esteem will await, a poor importance attached to it, if it doesn't speak of its late genial medium, the good, the wonderful company it has, as I hint, aesthetically kept. It has entered, in fine, into new relations, it emerges for new ones. Its final savour has been constituted, but its prime identity destroyed – which is what was to be demonstrated. Thus it has become a different and, thanks to a rare alchemy, a better thing. Therefore let us have here as little as possible about its 'being' Mr This or Mrs That.[7]

You pop in a morsel of Coleridge-eana, and after a good stew in James's imagination, it emerges as something rich and strange. And different. Thus Coleridge is nowhere named in 'The Coxon Fund'; and thus, the names of Shakespeare and, indeed, Stratford, never appear in 'The Birthplace'. Though notice that James *would* like to gain access to the 'real person', if only it were possible. But meanwhile – 'transplanting'. And let's see what happens when you pop in a morsel of *Shakespeare*.

The Gedges are not, like the couple who engendered them, 'strenuous and superior'; and they are not from Newcastle but the finely conceived Blackport-on-Dwindle. There, Morris Gedge's little private school 'dwindled to a close'; it could, one feels, do little else in a town 'so ugly with industry, so turned away from any dream, so intolerable to any taste' – so emphatically conducive, as one feels, to dwindling in general. The utterly unpractical Mr Gedge, his health, like his school, having failed, works in the grey town-library, 'all granite, fog and female fiction'. He is one of those 'poor gentlemen – too fine for their rough fate' who, in different guises, figure in the three stories James was currently writing. As far as Mrs Gedge is concerned they are 'refined' and 'cultivated', but, Mr Gedge having, as it were, *no* strings to his bow, at the beginning of the story they are 'waiting in silence'. What turns up is an invitation to take on the wardenship of a 'temple' and 'shrine' – unnamed, but hardly mistakable as, to Gedge, it figures as 'the most sacred known to the steps of man, the early home of the supreme poet, the Mecca of the English-speaking race'. The offer is made by a Mr Grant-Jackson: *he* is 'strenuous', and 'superior', at least in terms of municipal influence, 'a highly preponderant, pushing person' who has, we are told, taught the midland region in which he operates 'the size of his foot'. He embodies that real-world official power to which Gedge is such a stranger.

When the offer comes 'he felt as if a window had opened into a great green woodland, a woodland that had a name, glorious, immortal, that was peopled with vivid figures, each of them renowned' and so on – the Forest of Arden, of course, the first of a number of small allusions to Shakespeare's work with which the story is agreeably, and quite fittingly, flecked (they are easy to read and should not be seen as doing heavy intertextual duty – thus, for example, after an introductory tour of the house by the previous incumbent, Miss Putchin, Gedge 'didn't know "where to have her"', though Miss Putchin is certainly no Mistress Quickly; he also succumbs to 'the spell of silent sessions' of, no doubt, sweet thought; and he opens the door to his American visitors with 'a strange equivocation', as does the Porter in *Macbeth*. Such relatively ostentatious echoes make the 'place' doubly unmistakable while leaving Shakespeare unnamed).

In anticipation of their guardianship, the Gedges go over the awesome responsibility involved in, effectively, living with and for 'Him, *him*, HIM' (the third person pronoun is invariably capitalised, thus inevitably evoking parallels with an even more sacred birth and birthplace). Conscientiously starting to do their homework, they resolve to master all the available data – 'we must know everything', though Morris reflects that 'we don't as yet, you see, know Him tremendously well'. But the realistic and pragmatic Mrs Gedge contents herself with the consideration – 'there are the facts'. Her position is that they are well qualified for the post because:

'we know the difference between realities and shams. We hold to reality, and that gives us common sense, which the vulgar have less than anything, and which must yet be wanted there, after all, as well as anywhere else.'

To which Morris Gedge urges a supplement:

'Allow that we hold also a little to the romance. It seems to me that that's the beauty. We've missed it all our life, and now it's come. We shall be at headquarters for it. We shall have our fill of it.'

By the end, Mrs Gedge will be arguing for holding to the 'sham', while Morris comes to think there *are* no 'facts', and realises that any 'romance' will have to be his own contribution. But initially he is all confidence. 'It's absurd . . . to talk of our not "knowing". So far as we don't it's because we're donkeys. He's *in* the thing, over His ears, and the more we get into it the more we're with Him. I seem to myself at any rate . . . to see Him in it as if He were painted on the wall.' James deploys his characteristic pregnant vagueness – what is the 'it', the 'thing' *in* which He so unmistakably is? The whole place? The actual house? Or is He to be found in the Works, diffused and dispersed throughout the poetry? Questions for Gedge, and, as we shall see, questions for James. In the event, just who are the 'donkeys' becomes more problematical; Gedge comes to see 'nothing' – 'the nothing that is' in Wallace Stevens' words – clearly painted on the wall; and God alone knows where He is – if, that is, there *was* a 'He' at all.

There is one little exchange between the Gedges which is premonitory. Mrs Gedge is confident of their suitability for the job. 'We're refined. We know how to speak.' But – ' "Do we?" ' – he still, suddenly, wondered.' Just how he *is* to speak – his main task, after all, is to show 'the People' round – will become the crucial issue. The warning signals start with their arrival at the house. A table of 'instructions and admonitions' from Grant-Jackson and vague, 'official', superior authorities, together with some prescribed 'catch-penny publications' – all detailing 'the well-known facts and the full-blown legend', give Gedge 'a view as of a cage in which he should circulate and a groove in which he should slide'. (He will not be the first Jamesian protagonist to find himself 'In the Cage'.) When he 'goes round' with Miss Putchin and a squad of visitors, and watches her brisk, smoothed, automated performance, he finds that his habitual 'play of mind' deserts him, and he becomes aware of 'an agitation deep within him that vaguely threatened to grow'. Among other things, it seems that her main concern is that 'They' should be satisfied – 'They' being 'the millions who shuffled through the house'. To Gedge, this prioritising of the reactions of the 'hordes' means 'that They . . . seemed to have got into the way of crowding out Him'. He asks Miss Putchin if any of Them actually 'take an interest in Him'; his wife, scenting trouble, steps on his shoe – 'she deprecated irony', and irony, as we shall see, is to loom large as the dangerous propensity. Miss Putchin also invites him to admire how 'pretty' the whole house is, 'the way they've got it now'. 'This, Gedge saw, was a different "They"; it applied to the powers that were – the people who had appointed him, the governing, visiting Body.' Gedge is to become a man caught between the two 'Theys', each of which is possessed of dangerous, threatening power.

The next two sections of the story trace his growing distaste for, and impatience with, the 'humbug, lies, and superstition' which he is obliged to regurgitate, and which had proved too much for the original custodians. Like them, he becomes 'a sceptic, an iconoclast', and, good phrase, 'a positive negationist'. He 'prowls' around the house at night, trying to pick up some after-scent of the sacred presence, spending more and more time alone in the 'Holy of Holies . . . the sublime Chamber of Birth', which surely contains '*the* Fact itself' and must be 'the place where the spirit would most walk'. He sits there in the dark, and when his wife asks him what he sees there, his answer is – 'Nothing!' With his credulity, and thus his instinctive piety, beginning to fade, the strain of the job starts to tell. 'The point was that he was on the way to becoming two quite different persons, the public and the private, and yet that it would somehow have to be managed that these persons should live together . . . One of the halves, or perhaps even, since the split promised to be rather unequal, one of the quarters, was the keeper, the showman, the priest of the idol; the other piece was the poor unsuccessful honest man he had always been.' (This theme is wonderfully developed in 'The Private Life'.) He wonders whether his honest part 'had in reserve some supreme assertion of its identity' – a prospect which frightens him because it means that his honest part 'was just on the verge of quarrelling with its bread and butter'. His wife remains the realistic reminder of the claims of 'bread and butter', prepared to leave unconsidered what increasingly worries him, namely 'the *morality* of their position'. He rather gently urges – 'We mustn't, love, tell too many lies', and to her question 'Do you consider it's *all* a fraud?', he says 'Well, I grant you there was somebody. But the details are naught. The links are missing. The evidence . . . is *nil.*' Faced with the near-totality of her husband's scepticism, Mrs Gedge has a 'cutting' question. 'Don't you think . . . that He was born anywhere?' This should be decisive, but James himself became inclined to answer the question in the hopeless negative. Here Gedge hesitates: 'Well, we don't know. There's very little *to* know. He covered his tracks as no other human being has ever done.' It seems, however, that he will keep on 'lying', because, as his wife warns him, if he tries to 'give the place, give the story away', well, 'They wouldn't *have* it.' 'They' now means both Theys, since, to Gedge's mind, the People are effectively 'in league with the Body'. And his wife, Gedge decides, is 'no more than one of Them'. In between Them all, there is not much room for the free play of an honest, ironic mind – which has to earn its bread and butter.

This stalemate, or impasse, is broken by the late arrival one evening of 'a pair of pilgrims', rich, cultivated Americans, who precisely *don't*

have to earn their bread: 'the world was theirs; they gave [Gedge] such
a sense of the high luxury of freedom as he had never had'. Reading
'irony' in the man's smile, and sensing sympathetic spirits, Gedge
releases his long-gathering doubts and 'blasphemies'. 'He escapes us
like a thief at night, carrying off – well, carrying off everything . . .
He *isn't* here.' The intelligent woman visitor suggests: 'Why not say,
beautifully . . . that, like the wind, He's everywhere?' – an option not
taken up by Gedge, but one to which I will return. The gentleman
visitor seems instinctively to understand Gedge, and together they, as
it were, go all the way. As they are leaving, the husband says '"The
play's the thing". Let the author alone.'

Gedge, with his key on his forefinger, leaned against the doorpost, took in the
stupid little street, and was sorry to see them go – they seemed so to abandon
him. 'That's just what They won't do – not let *me* do. It's all I want – to let the
author alone. Practically' – he felt himself getting the last of his chance –
'there *is* no author; that is for us to deal with. There are all the immortal
people – *in* the work; but there's nobody else.'
   'Yes,' said the young man – 'that's what it comes to. There should really, to
clear the matter up, be no such Person.'
   'As you say,' Gedge returned, 'it's what it comes to. There *is* no such
Person.'

This visit leaves Gedge with 'a certain sweet aftertaste of
freedom . . . There were two persons in the world, at least, who felt as
he did.' There *are* 'people to whom he hadn't to talk, as he further
phrased it, rot'. It makes him become reckless:

In his reaction from that gluttony of the public for false facts which had from
the first tormented him, he fell into the habit of sailing, as he would have said,
too near the wind, or in other words – all in presence of the people – of
washing his hands of the legend. He had crossed the line – he knew it; he had
struck wild – They drove him to it . . . hurled by his fate against the bedizened
walls of the temple, quite in the way of a priest possessed to excess of the god,
or, more vulgarly, that of a blind bull in a china-shop – an animal to which he
often compared himself. *He had let himself fatally go*, in fine, just for irritation,
for rage . . . (my italics)

That was as far as James saw his story going, in his Notebook. And he
could, indeed, have ended the tale at this moment of personal crisis
when things have come to a head, and the beast, as it were, has sprung
– for he ends 'The Beast in the Jungle' at just such a moment. But now
James sees another possible turn to his story. Gedge's wife does not
go along with him: she develops, multiplies, embroiders 'the associations

of the sacred place' quite without shame, on the, in many ways un-
assailable, grounds that 'it put bread into his mouth'. Grant-Jackson,
'a banker and a patriot', duly comes round and, invoking piety and
patriotism, gives Gedge a warning. 'The words he used were that I
gave away the Show and that, from several sources, it has come round
to Them.' They 'scare' Gedge, but give him a 'second chance' (which
was what the dying writer, Dencombe, in 'The Middle Years', says
an artist, perhaps a person, never gets. 'A second chance – *that's* the
delusion. There never was to be but one'). But there is a price –
something has to go:

'my critical sense. I didn't ever know I had one – till They came and (by
putting me here) waked it up in me. Then I had somehow, don't you see? to
live with it; and I seemed to feel that, somehow or other, giving it time and in
the long run, it might, it *ought* to, come out on top of the heap. Now that's
where, he says, it simply won't do. So I must put it – I *have* put it – at the
bottom.'

His wife is relieved, just hoping that 'it doesn't struggle up again'. No
fear of that.

'I killed it just now ... There in the other place [i.e. the Birthplace] – I
strangled it, poor thing, in the dark. If you go out and see, there must be
blood. Which indeed ... on an altar of sacrifice, is all right. But the place is
forever spattered.'

He promises, in future, to 'cultivate' the art of lying. The murderous
violence of his metaphors is, of course, comic exaggeration; but 'the
critical sense', and all he made it mean, was profoundly important for
James, and to have to muffle or suppress it, for whatever exigent
reason, *was*, as far as James was concerned, a terrible deprivation and
sacrifice. It took, as it were, a dimension out of life.

The denouement of the tale is perhaps predictable. The two Americans – Mr and Mrs B. D. Hayes as we now learn – return a year later;
not, Gedge realises, for the sake of the 'shrine', but because of 'their
intelligent interest in the queer case of the priest'. Their 'tribute of
curiosity' is motivated by the unspoken question of – how, given his
confessed unbelief of a year ago, had this 'positive negationist' managed to hold his job? By way of an implicit answer, he simply treats
them to a sample of his new speech (or 'spiel', as we might say) for
visitors to the 'place':

'Across that threshold He habitually passed; through those low windows, in
childhood, He peered out into the world that He was to make so much
happier by the gift to it of His genius; over the boards of this floor – that is

over *some* of them, for we mustn't be carried away! – his little feet often pattered; and the beams of this ceiling (we must really in some places take care of *our* heads!) he endeavoured, in boyish strife, to jump up and touch. It's not often that in the early home of genius and renown the whole tenor of existence is laid so bare.'

And so on, and so on. The sort of 'rot' he had most abhorred, but played in another key and at a much higher pitch. The American visitors are 'spellbound . . . wondering, he judged, into what strange pleasantry he had been suddenly moved to break out, and yet beginning to see in him an intention beyond a joke'. That really is the nub of the matter. Is Gedge being even more subtly subversive of the stale pieties by travesty and exaggeration – or is there something more to it? Mrs Gedge is worried – 'she wondered if he had not simply embraced another, a different perversity. There would be more than one fashion of giving away the show, and wasn't *this* perhaps a question of giving it away by excess? He could dish them by too much romance as well as by too little . . . It was a way like another, at any rate, of reducing the place to the absurd; which reduction, if he didn't look out, would reduce *them* again to the street, and this time surely without an appeal.'

But the Americans can see a genuine art in how Gedge has transformed the obligatory reverent paean – 'with the staleness so disguised, the interest so renewed, and the clerical function, demanded by the priestly character, so successfully distilled'. When he has finished, Mrs Hayes says 'You're really a genius', with what one feels to be unironic admiration. Lyrical rhapsody, or mocking parody? Perhaps both, for in art such a double voice is possible. 'Whether or no he had . . . found a new perversity, he had found a vocation much older, evidently, than he had at first been prepared to recognise.' Cunning as ever, James omits to say just what that vocation is. Oratory, perhaps? Rhetoric – the art of pleasing and persuading, disregardful of the truth? It is best left undesignated, thus sustaining the ambivalence. Gedge perhaps does 'overdo' it, but he has discovered that, with Them (both of Them), you simply *can't* overdo it – the unspoken implication is that there is no limit to the tosh They will take. His wife is, again, worried. '"Don't they want then *any* truth – none even for the mere look of it?" "The look of it," said Morris Gedge, "is what I give!"' And perhaps, in the circumstances, that is enough. Certainly, Morris Gedge *now* knows 'how to speak'.

In any case, with his new mode of address 'these were golden days – the show had never so flourished'. The final bit of drama in the tale is provided by a second visit from the always potentially threatening

Grant-Jackson, emissary from those vague 'powers' above Gedge. After a little obligatory suspense – during which the Americans promise Mrs Gedge to 'set you up' if they are fired – Morris returns from the dreaded interview to announce that 'They' have doubled his stipend in recognition of his immense success, measurable by notably increased 'receipts'. '*They* at least' – Gedge and Hayes share a joke – 'speak the truth.' And – 'there you are'. Gedge happily concludes the tale with an appropriate terminal ambiguity.

I mentioned similarities with 'The Papers'. The Papers are the popular press, 'the dreadful nasty vulgar papers', and the story concerns two journalists, Maude and Bight, with the second, as you might guess from his name, seemingly the more ruthless and successful one; 'his mastery of the horrid art' is referred to. They often discuss the ethics of pandering to 'the Organ of Public Opinion', and they know that in trying to manipulate the 'terrific forces of publicity' they are riding a tiger. They also recognise that they have to produce 'rot' for their 'bread and butter'. Bight can write 'a column concocted of nothing'; and sometimes they build up a story when it is questionable whether there are 'any authentic facts to give'. The people who read the papers are 'dunderheads', and it is somehow disgusting to have to please them. So far, the similarities, or comparabilities, with 'The Birthplace' are obvious enough. (There is one enjoyable echo-plus-comment: 'There you are', says the semi-scrutable Bight to Maude. 'Well he might say that, "There you are", as often as he liked without, at the pass they had come to, making her in the least see where she was.' A reaction, I fancy, we sometimes have to the Master himself!) The stories end differently. Gedge makes his ambiguous peace; but Maude and Bight determine on 'getting out' – they 'chuck them'. 'Damn the Papers.' Still, they are to get married, so it is another sort-of happy ending. And one meditation expresses a vital concern, central to both tales. It appears (wrongly as it transpires) that some of Bight's journalism might have contributed to a man's suicide. Maude ponders the implications of this:

Bight, of course, rare youth, had *meant* no harm; but what was precisely queerer, what, when you came to judge, less human, than to be formed for offence, for injury, by the mere inherent play of the spirit of observation, of criticism, by the inextinguishable flame, in fine, of the ironic passion? The ironic passion, in such a world as surrounded one, might assert itself as half the dignity, half the decency of life; yet, none the less, in cases where one had seen it prove gruesomely fatal (and not to one's self, which was nothing, but to others, even the stupid and the vulgar) one was plainly admonished to – well, stand off and think a little.

You will hardly come closer to James himself in any other paragraph of his work. The 'ironic passion', comprising observation, criticism, and the free play of an honest mind – so valued by Gedge and Bight, and exercised by them, if at all, under difficulties in alien and anti-pathetic conditions – *did*, for James, 'assert itself as half the dignity, half the decency, of life' – or so I think. And while Bight's irony proves *not* to have been 'gruesomely fatal', James also recognised that irony was, latently, a dangerous weapon, and that there were times when, for very considerateness, kindness, or tact, one had to – well, stand off a little and think.

Violet Hunt was an occasional writer who lived a rather bohemian life, whom James had known since she was a girl. He occasionally invited her to Lamb House to listen to what Leon Edel calls 'her sex-charged gossip'. James called her his 'Purple Patch'. After a visit there in the summer of 1903, she wrote to him, obviously including some comments on Shakespeare; for in his reply of 11 August 1903, James writes:

Your comparison of genius to the passenger on the 'liner' with his cabin and his 'hold' luggage is very brilliant and I should quite agree with you – and *do*. Only I make this difference. Genius gets at its *own* luggage, in the hold, perfectly (while common mortality is reduced to a box under the berth); but it doesn't get at the Captain's and the First Mate's, in *their* mysterious retreats. Now William of Stratford (it seems to me) *had* no luggage, could have had none, in any part of the ship, corresponding to much of the wardrobe sported in the plays.[8]

She clearly sent him a book advancing the pointless 'theory' that Bacon wrote Shakespeare's plays, which elicited the following rather remarkable response, in a letter of 26 August of the same year:

I am 'sort of' haunted by the conviction that the divine William is the biggest and most successful fraud ever practised on a patient world. The more I turn him round and round the more he so affects me. But that is all – I am not pretending to treat the question or to carry it further. It bristles with difficulties, and I can only express my general sense by saying that I find it *almost* as impossible to conceive that Bacon wrote the plays as to conceive that the man from Stratford, as we know the man from Stratford, did.[9]

Clearly, he gave Morris Gedge all his 'positive negationist' doubts.

In 1907, a young Boston printer, William Dean Alcott, invited James to write an introduction to *The Tempest*, and James replied with un-usual alacrity. 'I will challenge this artist – the master and magician of a thousand masks, and make him drop them, if only for an interval.'[10]

It is an extraordinary essay. The play, as play, scarcely concerns him. 'The "story" in *The Tempest* is a thing of naught, for any story will provide a remote island, a shipwreck and a coincidence.'[11] So much for that, then. He is still exercised, even obsessed, by the man and 'the torment of his unguessed riddle'.

The man himself, in the Plays, we directly touch, to my consciousness, positively nowhere: we are dealing too perpetually with the artist, the monster and magician of a thousand masks, not one of which we feel him drop long enough to gratify with the breath of the interval that strained attention in us which would be yet, so quickened, ready to become deeper still.[12]

You feel he almost wants to call Shakespeare a spoil-sport, or, as my mother used to say, 'a mouldy bit'. Couldn't he have just shown us a *bit*, the rotter?

The man everywhere, in Shakespeare's work, is so effectually locked up and imprisoned in the artist that we but hover at the base of thick walls for a sense of him; while, in addition, the artist is so steeped in the abysmal objectivity of his characters and situations that the great billows of the medium itself play with him, to our vision, very much as, over a ship's side, in certain waters, we catch, through transparent tides, the flash of strange sea-creatures. What we are present at in this fashion is a series of incalculable plunges – the series of those that have taken effect, I mean, after the great primary plunge, made once for all, of the man into the artist . . .[13]

Shakespeare's work primarily offers 'high testimony to this independent, absolute value of Style'. James is hardly interested in separating out themes, ideas, motives in the plays for specific consideration. What he points to, and shakes his incredulous head before, is Shakespeare's gift of Expression, or 'power of constituted speech', which was

something that was to make of our poor world a great flat table for receiving the glitter and clink of outpoured treasure. The idea and the motive are more often than not so smothered in it that they scarce know themselves, and the resources of such a style, the provision of images, emblems, energies of every sort, laid up in advance, affects us as the storehouse of a kind before a famine or a siege – which not only, by its scale, braves depletion or exhaustion, but bursts, through mere excess of quantity of presence, out of all doors and windows. It renders the poverties and obscurities of our world, as I say, in the dazzling terms of a richer and better.[14]

But – we are left 'in gross darkness about the man'. Why, after *The Tempest*, with 'its refinement of power . . . and distinction unequalled, on the whole . . . in any predecessor', did he, He, suddenly 'shut down the lid . . . on the most potent aptitude for vivid reflection ever lodged in a human frame'? It makes no kind of sense, and it is simply 'imposed on our bewildered credulity' and accepted 'only in stupefaction'. (James himself, one feels, would have been happy to go on writing even *after* he was dead.) But, there it is; 'and it puts into a nutshell the eternal mystery, the most insoluble that ever was, the complete rupture, for our understanding, between the Poet and the Man'.[15]

Why not let it alone – why suffer 'our imaginations to meddle with the Man at all'? Does it not, perhaps, testify to 'a morbid and monstrous curiosity'? But James can't quite rest with the ' "The play's the thing" – let the author alone' attitude. What the genius produced must have *some* connection with how the man behaved – 'the elements of character melt into each other':

> where does one of these provinces end and the other begin? We may take the genius first or the behaviour first, but we inevitably proceed from the one to the other; we inevitably encamp, as it were, on the high central table-land they have in common. How are we to arrive at a relation with the object to be penetrated if we are thus forever met by a locked door flanked with a sentinel who merely invites us to take it for edifying? We take it ourselves for attaching – which is the very essence of mysteries – and profess ourselves doomed forever to hang yearningly about it.[16]

Since Shakespeare was 'the human character the most magnificently endowed, in all time, with the sense of the life of man', it is a bit hard to take that we know nothing about how he acquired 'the apparatus for recording it'. What sort of life did he have that he was '*able* to write Lear and Othello'? But, 'no bricks without straw' – and there's no straw. We must let the man go. 'He slunk past us in life: that was good enough for him, the contention appears to be. Why therefore should he not slink past in immortality? One's reply can indeed only be that he evidently must.'[17]

And yet, and yet.

The secret that baffles us being the secret of the Man, we know, as I have granted, that we shall never touch the Man *directly* in the Artist. We stake our hopes thus on indirectness, which may contain possibilities; we take that very truth for our counsel of despair, try to look at it as helpful for the Criticism of the future. That of the past had been too often infantile; one has asked one's self how it *could*, on such lines, get at him. The figured tapestry, the long arras that hides him, is always there, with its immensity of surface and its proportionate underside. May it not then be but a question, for the fullness of time, of the finer weapon, the sharper point, the stronger arm, the more extended lunge?[18]

James, seemingly, has not given up all hope of a final piercing, penetrating, all-exposing thrust: 'Dead for a ducat, dead!'[19]

When Gedge said that Shakespeare was 'not here', and Mrs Hayes suggests that he is 'everywhere', I described this as an available option, not pursued by Gedge, or James either, it would seem. Yet, he might have; and, in effect, Borges did. In 'Everything and Nothing' he tells of a man who found there was no one and nothing inside him. But he found that he had a prodigious gift of simulating that he was someone, anyone, and so he became a great actor. 'No one has ever been so many men as this man who like the Egyptian Proteus could exhaust all the guises of reality.' But one day he is 'suddenly gripped by the tedium and the terror of being so many kings who die by the sword and so many suffering lovers who converge, diverge and melodiously expire'. He gives it all up, sells his theatre, and goes back to his native village for a quiet life – and death.

History adds that before or after dying he found himself in the presence of God and told Him: 'I who have been so many men in vain want to be one and myself.' The voice of the Lord answered him from a whirlwind: 'Neither am I anyone; I have dreamt the world as you dreamt your work, my Shakespeare, and among the forms in my dream are you, who like myself are many and no one.'[20]

NOTES

1 Henry James, *The Complete Notebooks of Henry James*, ed. Leon Edel and Lyall H. Powers (New York: Oxford University Press, 1987), p. 195.

2 Henry James, *English Hours*, ed. Alma Louise Lowe (London: Heinemann, 1960), pp. 133–4.

3 I might mention two previous American 'pilgrims'. In *The Sketch Book of Geoffrey Crayon, Gent* (1819–20) Washington Irving included a sketch of 'Stratford-on-Avon' in which he tackles Shakespeare's house head-on. 'The most favourite object of curiosity, however, is Shakespeare's chair. It stands in the chimney nook of a small gloomy chamber, just behind what was his father's shop. Here he may many a time have sat when a boy, watching the slowly revolving spit with all the ponging of an urchin' – *may* – Irving knows, or at least suspects, that the 'garrulous old lady' who shows him round, with her 'inexhaustible collection of relics' – Shakespeare's this, Shakespeare's that – is telling him a series of what Huckleberry Finn calls 'stretchers', but, amiably, he goes along with it. 'I am always of easy faith in such matters, and am ever willing to be deceived, where the deceit is pleasant, and costs nothing. I am therefore a ready believer in relics, legends, and local anecdotes of goblins and great men; and would advise

all travellers who travel for their gratification to be the same. What is it to us whether these stories be true or false, so long as we can persuade ourselves into the belief of them, and enjoy all the charm of the reality?' And the church in which Shakespeare is buried – the Deathplace – gives Irving what he is sure is the real thing. 'The feelings, no longer checked and thwarted by doubt, here indulge in perfect confidence: other traces of him may be false or dubious, but here is palpable evidence and absolute certainty. As I trod the sounding pavement, there was something intense and thrilling in the idea, that, in very truth, the remains of Shakespeare were mouldering beneath my feet' (New York: Library of America, 1983), pp. 984, 985, 988–9. This is the kind of response that James sedulously eschews.

Nathaniel Hawthorne, being Hawthorne, goes for the negative reaction. Having described the supposed house of Shakespeare's birth in harsh, rather belittling details, he adds: 'I should consider it unfair to quit Shakespeare's house without the frank acknowledgement that I was conscious of not the slightest emotion while viewing it, nor any quickening of the imagination' (*Our Old Home: A Series of English Sketches* (1863; rpt. Columbus: Ohio State University Press, 1970), p. 99). I am sure Hawthorne was being no less than honest; but this kind of non-response is in line with an habitual refusal of a number of American writers to be awed by the sacred places of the Old World. Thus Mark Twain on Christ's supposed birthplace: 'I touch, with reverent finger, the actual spot where the infant Jesus lay, but I think – nothing' (*Innocents Abroad* (1869; rpt. New York: Airmont Publishing Co., Inc., 1967), p. 407). This was hardly James's way, either.

4 Henry James, *Literary Criticism: European Writers and the Prefaces* (New York: Library of America, 1984), p. 1252.

5 Ibid., pp. 1159–60.

6 Ibid., p. 1184.

7 Ibid., pp. 1236–7.

8 Henry James, *Henry James Letters*, ed. Leon Edel, 4 vols. (Cambridge: Harvard University Press, 1984), IV, 281.

9 Henry James, *The Letters of Henry James*, ed. Percy Lubbock, 2 vols. (London: Macmillan and Co., Ltd. 1920), I, 432.

10 For details of this invitation, see William T. Stafford, 'James Examines Shakespeare', *PMLA*, LXXIII (March 1958), pp. 123–8.

11 Henry James, *Literary Criticism: Essays on Literature, American Writers, English Writers* (New York: Library of America, 1984), p. 1213.

12 Ibid., p. 1209.

13 Ibid.

14 Ibid., p. 1211.

15 Ibid., pp. 1214, 1215.

16 Ibid., p. 1217.

17 Ibid., p. 1219.

18 Ibid., p. 1220.

19 James himself was notoriously ambivalent about attempts to get at, and into, the private lives of writers. He deprecated, indeed loathed, such attempts. Yet, he defended what he rather euphemistically called 'the ideal biographical curiosity', and was himself, for example, avid to insatiability when it came to reading every available scrap about George Sand's very private, very sexual life (I have written a little about this ambivalence in *Venice Desired* and will not repeat myself). When it came to the possibility of posthumous revelations about his own life, it was, of course, a very different matter. He wrote to his nephew, Henry, in 1914 – 'I have long thought of launching, by a provision in my will, a curse not less explicit than Shakespeare's own on any such as try to move my bones' (*Letters*, IV, 806). What's sauce for the goose, is very much *not* sauce for the gander – not this gander.

20 Jorge Luis Borges, *Labyrinths* (London: Penguin Books, 1970), pp. 284–5.

CHAPTER 9

'Feelings of middle life':
William Dean Howells's Indian Summer

'*Make me young, make me young, make me young*', pleads one of the fictional characters to the author at the end of Kurt Vonnegut's *Breakfast of Champions*. When Mark Twain had finished reading the second instalment of *Indian Summer*, he wrote to his old friend Howells:

You are really my only author; I am restricted to you; I wouldn't give a damn for the rest . . . I have just read Part II of Indian Summer, & to my mind there isn't a waste-line in it, or one that could be improved. I read it yesterday, ending with that opinion; & read it again to-day, ending with the same opinion emphasized . . . It is a beautiful story, & makes a body laugh all the time, & cry inside, & feel so old & so forlorn; & gives him gracious glimpses of his lost youth that fill him with a measureless regret, & build up in him a cloudy sense of his having been a prince, once, in some enchanted far-off land, & of being in exile now, & desolate – & lord, no chance to ever get back there again! That is the thing that hurts. Well, you have done it with marvelous facility – & you make all the motives & feelings perfectly clear without analyzing the guts out of them, the way George Eliot does.[1]

This intensely wistful and even rather sentimental effusion was written long before Mark Twain would have reached one of the last conversations in the book, between Colville and Mrs Bowen, which explicitly articulates the theme, the mood, the regret which is constantly adumbrated and sounded in different tones and registers throughout the novel:

'I heard just such singing before I fell asleep the night after that party at Madame Uccelli's, and it filled me with fury.'
'Why should it do that?'
'I don't know. It seemed like voices from our youth – Lina.'
She had no resentment of his use of her name in the tone with which she asked: 'Did you hate that so much?'
'No; the loss of it.'
They both fetched a deep breath.

149

It is doubtless a theme as universal as it is ancient, but the idealising, one might even say the fetishising, of youth and the attendant resistances to, and exaggerated horror at, the signs of age are proclivities and dispositions experienced or indulged with quite peculiar intensity in America. How much this has to do with the privileging of the child in American culture, or with the mythology of Adamic innocence, new-ness, new beginnings, inextricably intertwined with the nurturing and flaunting of the young republic in the New World, is perhaps idle to speculate. But more than any other national literature, the literature of America has celebrated, mythologised, idolised, cherished, worshipped, recalled, re-created, relived youth – or mourned and lamented the loss of what so many writers imagine it, or want it, or perhaps un-consciously will it, to have been. Needless to say, this inclination or obsession can produce writing of very different degrees of richness and subtlety, with sentimentality an ever-present danger, and lachrymosity not far behind. But it is possible for the obsession or tendency to be submitted to some kind of critical or ironic examination – put in larger and longer perspectives than it itself furnishes or allows – and then you can have a literature of wit, sophistication, even, if one may say it, wisdom. *Indian Summer* is such a work.

Howells was perfectly clear about the organising intent of the novel, writing to Edmund Gosse in December 1883 that he was 'far into the heart of a new story, the idea of which pleases me greatly. It is that of a man whose youth was broken sharp off in Florence twenty years ago, and who after a busy newspaper life in our West, fancies that he can renew his youth by going back to Italy. There he falls in love with a girl young enough to be his daughter. It is largely a study of the feelings of middle-life in contrast with those of earlier years.' A study of the 'feelings of middle-life' it certainly is, as the opening words of the novel tactfully suggest by positioning Colville 'lounging' – indecisive, suspended, isolated, vague – 'Midway of the Ponte Vecchio'. He is in the middle of life's journey and he has indeed lost his way, or rather not found or formed one. What is to happen to him is rather more complicated than Howells suggests in his outline since he only thinks he has fallen in love with Imogene, or, more subtly, thinks he has fallen in love with the idea that she has thought herself into the appro-priateness of being in love with him. Imogene is well into the romance of noble self-sacrifice and reparation. 'I want you to feel that *I* am your youth – the youth you were robbed of – given back to you', she cries to Colville. He is not deluded but he feebly capitulates to a situation, in the making of which he has at least culpably colluded, and which he, arguably, irresponsibly provoked and promoted. He complains or confesses to Mr Waters: 'I have lived my life, such as it is. But the child is full of fancies about me that can't be fulfilled. She dreams of restoring my youth somehow, of retrieving the past for me . . . Sometimes I think that the kindest – the least cruel – thing I could do would be to break with her, to leave her. But I know that I shall do nothing of the kind; I shall drift.' There is something hapless about his extreme passivity, and Howells has to enlist a wild horse to trample him into unconsciousness and out of responsibility for a decision which is clearly beyond his capacity. It is Imogene who comes to her senses while he is, appropriately, out of his.

It is a peculiar feature of this state of 'mid-wayness' – this mid-life crisis, perhaps – that life seems definitively elsewhere, while the present seems to be a site of loss, emptiness, formless futility – Carlyle's 'centre of indifference'. Colville comes to Italy from America in quest of renewal, 'drained and feeble', and finds himself in a state of dazed disorientation attendant on unemployment, for his occupation is very decidedly gone. Feeling that 'an objectless life was disgraceful to a man' he nevertheless fails to find any real 'object', any point or project to awaken and sustain motivation and direction. In his state of suspended vacillation he is a man waiting for a motive. He seems to have no volition. He continually contrives to get others to take his decisions for him – most notably and, really, shamefully leaving it to Imogene to decide whether they are formally engaged or not. In what is effectively their last conversation, when she asks him, with some understandable exasperation, 'what do you intend to do?', she has chosen just the right word. Colville has lost all relationship with intentionality. When he limply offers to defer entirely to her wishes, her response again goes to the heart, or heartlessness, of the man: 'Do *you* wish nothing?' He might rationalise his paralysis by maintaining that he is still trying to do the most honourable – the least dishonourable – thing, but what Howells is diagnosing and depicting is a crippling weakness of will, the death of desire. Having decided to leave Florence he allows himself to talk himself out of it. 'Better stay, then, something said to him; and when he answered "I will", something else reminded him that this also was not willing but unwilling.' Colville, corpulent, indolent, finding it difficult to stay awake, and to struggle up out of chairs; fussing about his rheumatism and the room temperature; yawning, bored, and looking at his watch; consuming endless cups of tea in an endless series of rooms, is an American Superfluous Man, with a touch of Oblomov and perhaps a hint of Baudelairean ennui. He is, not surprisingly, particularly happy as a convalescent, easily reconciled to 'a life of inaction and oblivion'. Howells conveys very well Colville's sense of himself 'crumbling away' in random momentary impulses, dissolving 'in one abortive intent and another', trying somehow to clasp and comprehend 'the secret of his failure in life'. It is in this light, I think, that we should see his endless 'banter', his 'tone of persiflage' which Imogene finds, briefly, 'intoxicating', his compulsive facetiousness which so delights little Effie, and which indeed delighted Henry James. 'Theodore Colville, in *Indian Summer*, is so irrepressibly and happily facetious as to make one wonder whether the author is not prompting him a little, and whether he could be quite so amusing without help from outside.'[2] Curiously, I think James has missed a point. Colville's constant recourse to banter is perhaps a mark of some degree of urbanity and sophistication; but it is also self-protective, defensive, anxious, even desperate. Banter is what Colville tries to employ to fill up the gaps and vacancies of feeling, motive, and desire. His 'bantering talk' is, as Howells exactly formulates it, 'a respite from the formless future pressing close upon him'. It is his only occupation. Even Imogene, who feels herself seduced by Colville's mechanical banter, at last cries out against it. 'Oh, don't joke about it! This perpetual joking, I believe it's that that's wearing me out.' The jesting indeed becomes 'dreary' to all concerned, including, particularly, Colville. It is a symptom, not a relief; a sickness, not a grace. It could be seen as an indication of a more profound impotence.

Howells is fastidious to the point of prudishness about sexual matters (despite having written about a squalid divorce case in his previous novel, *A Modern Instance*), and there is a minimum amount of physicality in this novel. The turning-point in Colville's relationship with Imogene occurs when he simply lays his hand on hers. In this world of avoided or denied bodily contacts, this is tantamount to a plea or a proposition. Consider, then, this description of Colville's reaction to a small degree of physical initiative from Imogene, some time after he has, in his evasive non-committal way, 'committed' himself to her, and she to him. 'She pulled him to the sofa, and put his arm about her waist, with a simple fearlessness and matter-of-course promptness that made him shudder . . . She took hold of his hand and drew his lax arm taut.' Howells, I am sure, meant no more than he wrote, but the spectacle of a beautiful young female trying to arouse this prematurely aged man to some sort of appropriate masculine 'tautness' surely suggests some deeper 'laxness' or laxity in Colville, a positive fear of all the energies and entanglements of the erotic. It is his *verbal* power over Imogene which gives him gratification: 'he felt the witchery of his power to make this young, radiant, and beautiful creature hang flattered and bewildered on his talk'. He is, indeed, playing with Imogene, 'amused at her seriousness', but he uses talk as much to avoid feelings as to articulate them, just as he had addressed his young love 'in words and phrases that, taken in themselves, had no meaning – that neither committed him nor claimed her'. This indeed is neutered speech, or talking to neuter, and Colville's pleasure in the oral (not just banter, for at the dance we see him 'cramming himself with all the solids and fluids in sight' – his one hundred and eighty-five pounds are not surprising!) is surely a compensation and cover for a profound fear of the sexual. We may think that the lady who rejected him in his youth and thus saved him from the disturbing intensities of sexual intimacy was putting it mildly when she called him 'too much of a mixture'. When Imogene described him as making you feel 'that he has exhausted all feeling', it provokes one to wonder just how much feeling there was to exhaust.

One particular aspect or result of the onset of the 'feelings of middle life' is the sense of being no longer young but not yet ready to accept the classification of 'old' – however old *old* may be – with all that it is felt to apply. This period of hesitation between generational identity, in which a man 'stands at pause', so to speak, is given an added twist for an American in Europe since America is youth and Europe is, of course, old, old, old. Colville is thus in a paradoxical position. He is an American who, finding life in America dull and insipid (people never go out, there is no real society, etc.), has come to Europe for rejuvenation. To compound the irony it is the benign, Emersonian Mr Waters, happily expatriated in Florence (and, among other things, this novel is an early and subtle study of the various modes and manners of American expatriation), who acts as both a counsellor and a warning to Colville. It is he who utters what must be taken as the wisdom of the book in his paean to the felicities of the age of forty at the middle of the book (in chapter XI): 'We are in a sort of quiet in which we peacefully enjoy. We have enlarged our perspective sufficiently to perceive things in their true proportion and relation . . . we have got into the habit of life . . . it is a beautiful age.' It is this amiable scourge of the absurdities of puritanism who effectively points Colville in the appropriate direction of Mrs Bowen. But it is also the sight of Mr Waters, immersed and content in his studies, placidly resigned to the solace offered by 'the magic of the book', which provokes a crucial moment of resistance in Colville, just exactly the critical moment.

Colville stared after him; he did not wish to come to just that yet, either. Life, active life, life of his own day, called to him; he had been one of its busiest children: could he turn his back upon it for any charm or use that was in the past? Again that unnerving doubt, that paralysing distrust, beset him, and tempted him to curse the day in which he had returned to this outworn Old World. Idler on its modern surface, or delver in its deep-hearted past, could he reconcile himself to it? What did he care for the Italians of to-day, or the history of the Florentines as expressed in their architectural monuments? It was the problems of the vast, tumultuous American life, which he had turned his back on, that really concerned him. Later he might take up the study that fascinated yonder old man, but for the present it was intolerable.

He was no longer young, that was true; but with an ache of old regret he felt that he had not yet lived his life, that his was a baffled destiny, an arrested fate.

This is the epiphanic moment of uncertainty which always awaits the figure of the American expatriate and Howells shows real insight and originality in his depiction of it.

Howells generously conceded to Henry James the distinction of having first discerned the potentialities of 'the international theme' – Americans in Europe and the effects they have on each other. In fact, his own first international novel, *A Foregone Conclusion*, is exactly contemporaneous with James's, *Roderick Hudson* – both appearing in 1875. However, there is no point in discussing primacy. The important thing to remember is that Howells produced pioneering and important 'international' novels of his own, including of course *Indian Summer*. In connection with the concluding words of the last long extract, it is particularly interesting and apt that Henry James's *The Ambassadors* owes its origin to a very Colvillean sort of remark made by Howells to a young man in Paris, which provided the inaugural germ. Howells told the young Jonathan Sturges to 'live all you can', adding that for himself it was too late, he was too old, but that Sturges was young and should 'Live!'. Sturges told James and James conceived of Lambert Strether, who also tells a young man in Paris to 'Live all you can. It's a shame not to.' Of course the problem is thus posed, what exactly is it to 'live'? James, bolder and more probing than Howells, could see that matters concerning sexual pleasure and fulfilment were both involved and implied. Howells, always more reticent, and perhaps more simply frightened by sexual matters, hardly confronts – indeed conspicuously avoids naming and entering – the zone of the sexual; yet the gentle polemics given to Mr Waters against the damaging effects of the 'hysterical excess of Puritanism' on America suggests that he was well aware of the sexual impoverishment – if not impotence – implied by the pervading sense of loss, unsatisfaction, unnamable frustration, and inarticulate regret experienced by Colville – and the extreme mechanisms of repression which must somewhere lie behind his gasping sense of unfulfilment. And it is perfectly appropriate to see James's Strether as another version of the Colville type, only older and thus perhaps more plausibly disinclined to consider – indeed ruling as out of the question – sexual relationships, up to and including marriage by the end. Colville, to be sure, ends by marrying Mrs Bowen and to that extent is notionally admitted into the sexual order. But she is a firm American puritan and we can hardly imagine her so determinedly drawing his 'lax arm taut' like the boisterously adolescent Imogene in her one doomed attempt to arouse him!

As well as a study of the vacillations, hesitations, and temporisings of an expatriate consciousness, the novel is also, of course, a love story. Even, we might say, three love stories, for Colville effectively seeks to enchant Effie with his humour, impress Imogene with his suffering and melancholy maturity, and win Mrs Bowen with his sophistication and gallantry. There is one amusing moment when Colville, by now 'engaged' to, or at least formally involved with, Imogene, finds himself effectively making up to Mrs Bowen and saying words that sound improperly ingratiating, indeed using very much the language of courtship. He stares after his own words in surprise and embarrassment, and Howells comments, with that confident aphoristic tone which is a mark of his style, that Colville was 'struggling stupidly with a confusion of desires which every man but no woman will understand. After eighteen hundred years the man is still imperfectly monogamous.' This is almost brave on Howells's part since he is effectively stating that a man can be sexually attracted to more than one woman at the same time, indeed that, at least momentarily, any woman may arouse an interest, an instinct to woo, in a man. It is a mark of his somewhat ponderous gentility that he, as it were, de-eroticises the declaration by muffling it in the sombre polysyllabicism of 'imperfectly monogamous'. We may take it as a sign of his patriarchal times that he so confidently excludes the possibility that the same truth might obtain in the case of the woman! This possibility of the multiplicity or repetition of desire and attraction across women of different generations was perhaps most remarkably explored in that novel of Thomas Hardy's so admired by Proust, *The Well-Beloved*, in which a man falls successively in love with a woman, her daughter, and her grand-daughter. But Howells gives some intimations of it from the start, when Colville finds Effie and her mother 'bewitchingly alike' and at the conclusion of his first meeting with them 'was rewarded with two pretty smiles, just alike, from mother and her daughter'.

From the start, Howells had made a speciality of studying and scrutinising American women in a non-romantic light. In this, as in so much else, he was innovative in American fiction, with Henry James, as so often, following in his own unique way. The studies, or portraits, of the witty Kitty Ellison in *A Chance Acquaintance*, the independent Lydia Blood, who is *The Lady of the Aroostock* who sails to Venice unchaperoned, the temperamental Florida Vervain in *A Foregone Conclusion*, the theatrical *femme fatale* Mrs Farrell in *Private Theatricals*, the economically lost Helen Harkness in *A Woman's Reason*, the professional Grace Breen, who gives up medicine for love in *Dr. Breen's Practice*, and, most notably, Marcia Gaylord, the new American 'Medea', in *A Modern Instance*, all these are indicative of and products of Howells's concern with the position and role – and plight and fate – of woman in American society as they were developing after the Civil War. Some of his attitudes to women may now seem somewhat patronising and deeply bound in convention, but he had precious little to build on in previous American fiction, in which women tend to be angels or allegories or clichés. Contemporary fiction was, to Howells's eye, intolerably and dangerously romantic and sentimental, particularly in its treatment of women, and it was a real achievement on his part to create a series of sympathetic, critical, plausible, and astute portraits of individuated women of authentic contemporary American pedigree. There was a very real social need for this kind of work. As one contemporary admirer of Howells put it, Howells was concerned with the 'emotional anarchy' in America in which 'an emotion is so sacred a thing that not only no outsider but not even its possessor may presume to undertake its regulation', thus leaving America 'a society without an emotional code'.

It is in the light of this attempt to begin to outline some kind of emotional code that we should appreciate Howells's gentle but firm critique of what he saw as the related temptations and vices of perverse 'self-sacrifice' and myopic egotism. Thus in a note for the novel, Howells stresses that 'Imogene shd typify the fatuous egotism of youth. She never imagines Mrs. B. in love.' And the ending of the novel, over which he took great care, while 'happy' in a conventional sense, in fact includes, or concludes, what has been a subtle but incisive – and fairly devastating – ironic critique of Mrs Bowen. As Edwin Cady noted, she is, in large measure, responsible for the errors of Imogene and even those of Colville, since she knows exactly what is going on and how self-deceived or self-deceiving the other two are, yet out of a perverse pride will do nothing to stop it – indeed does much to promote it. Cady's words are apt: 'The truth is that she has been infected with grand illusions, with an almost monstrous romantic *hubris* . . . she dramatizes herself as the blameless matron, the perfect duenna, antiseptically mounted above the reach of the human emotions to which the girl in charge is subject and from which she must be protected.'³ At the end, when she initially rejects Colville's proposal with a dramatic 'Never!', she embarks on a discourse of extreme moral outrage, invoking 'self-respect' and complaining histrionically of her 'humiliation', 'degradation' – 'you made me violate every principle that was dear to me'. Striking a pose of high-mindedly sacrificing her love for her dignity, it seems she will let Colville retreat with his tail where it usually is – between his legs. It is only the direct cry of Effie which resolves the perverse and sterile impasse which Mrs Bowen threatens to impose. And the last sentence, describing her reluctant capitulation, shows Howells's irony at its most effective. ' "Oh, you must stay!" said Lina, in the self-contemptuous voice of a woman who falls below her ideal of herself.' Howells spent a good deal of his life campaigning against misplaced and mischievous notions of 'the ideal' – both in art and in life – and his portrait of Mrs Bowen is one of his most subtle, and powerful, demonstrations of how pride and distorted egotism may be masked by intense and often self-mystifying invocations of ideals of 'self-sacrifice' which, both in her case and Imogene's, would in fact have involved self-mutilation. It is not an unsympathetic portrait, however, and indeed his first description of Mrs Bowen shows Howells at his most delicate, civilised, and urbane.

Lady-like was the word for Mrs. Bowen throughout – for the turn of her head, the management of her arm from the elbow, the curve of her hand from the wrist to finger-tips, the smile, subdued, but sufficiently sweet, playing about her little mouth, which was yet not too little, and the refined and indefinite perfume which exhaled from the ensemble of her silks, her laces, and her gloves, like an odorous version of that otherwise impalpable quality which women call style. She had, with all her flexibility, a certain charming stiffness, like the stiffness of a very tall feather.

The tone and touch are alike impeccable, courteous; and the concluding simile shows Howells's style at its most felicitous.

The atmosphere of the book is autumnal, wistful, as befits an Indian summer, and there is much in the book that has the quality of a late-afternoon idyll with the shadows just beginning to lengthen. This, and its Florentine setting, contribute greatly to the very real charm and quiet pleasures of the novel, which remained Howells's personal favourite. It was to have been called 'September and May' and there are many references to the seasons, the climate, the temperature indoors and out (and, by implication, inside the characters – the fire in the hotel dining-room of which 'the warmth was potential rather than actual' may be said to shed a flickering light on the varying capacity for emotional heat of the characters). The action takes place in winter moving forward into spring – or is it backwards? By the end Mrs Bowen looks 'younger and prettier'. Perhaps she, at least, has drunk of the fountain of youth in the Boboli Gardens, which Colville sadly recalls. 'The slow, orderly advance of the Italian spring' is compared to 'the rush of the American spring' and there is some consideration of the joys of the flowers of spring as compared with 'the pleasant little fire on the hearth' which winter ordains. Indeed, there is an unusually large number of references to indoor fires and more than one chapter concludes with a description of just such a fire flaring up or fading to embers – unobtrusively keeping alive the central question of to what extent the fires of youthful intensity of appreciation and desire can be rekindled. The Italian background also glows and fades alternately as Howells fills out the settings with somewhat dogged detailing – there is none of the sheer magic of Henry James's 'sense of place' here. In some ways this is appropriate, since for Colville 'some charm' has gone out of the 'operatic spectacle of Florence' – somewhat wearily inventoried by Howells. Instead of his youthful 'rapture' his response is now 'faint and thin'. There was a straight autobiographical basis for this, as there often is in Howells's fiction.

Howells had first gone to Italy in 1861 when he was twenty-four. He had been awarded the consulate at Venice as a reward for his campaign biography of Lincoln and he did not return to America until 1865 (thus missing the Civil War – something about which he always felt guilty). He immersed himself in Venice and Italian culture (the consular duties were notably unexacting), and if his response was somewhat lower-keyed than Henry James's, it was nevertheless a period of revelation and excitement, of expansion and growth, for the young Howells, who at that time still aspired to be a poet. (His careful, scrupulous documentations of his impressions gathered in this period were

published in *Venetian Life* and *Italian Journeys*.) On his return to America
he worked for the *Atlantic Monthly*, finally, from 1871 to 1881, as editor.
The immeasurable importance of that editorship for American literature, indeed for American culture (encouraging new young writers
such as Mark Twain and Henry James, introducing America to the
great writers of Europe – Flaubert, Tolstoy, Turgenev, and literally
hundreds of others then almost unknown in America), is deservedly a
well-known story. In 1881 he became perhaps the first true American
man of letters, making his living solely by his pen. He was working
on *A Modern Instance* at the time and finishing it left him in a state of
exhaustion. His daughter Winifred was also ill, so in 1882 he decided to
take his family back to Italy – to rejuvenate himself, rather like Colville.
He was disappointed with Venice: 'the poor old place is forlorner and
shabbier than ever. I don't think I began to see the misery of it when
I lived here', he wrote to Mark Twain.[4] And to Thomas Sergeant
Perry: 'I have been . . . putting myself in rapport with Italy again. But
I'm not sure that it pays. After all, *we* have the country of the present
and the future.'[5] How much of Colville's disillusion is Howells's own may
thus be guessed. His age, like his weight, is roughly Howells's own!
Howells spent the winter and spring in Florence, gathering material
for another travel book, *Tuscan Cities*, but he was very glad to return
to America in July of 1883. We may consider *Indian Summer*, with its
modulated regrets and nostalgia, the mellow fruit of that return visit.
In a way it was Howells's fond valedictory to Italy – and youth.

The tone and timbre of Howells's writing are quite distinctive and
represent the sounding of a new note in American literature. 'Describe
closely and realistically, keep the tone low', he once wrote to his sister.
It has been rather more usual for American writers to keep the tone
markedly high, aspiring to new reaches of thought and expression,
moving towards the frontiers and edges of experiential possibilities
seeking out the further, more remote areas of life and feeling, going –
in short – to extremes. In his own way, Howells sought to civilise
American writing, to rein in its wildness, chastise and chasten its appetite for romance, educate it out of its deplorable tendency to opt for sentimentality (what he called 'effectism'), open it to the tempered maturity
of writers such as Flaubert and Turgenev. That, in his efforts along
these lines, he was in danger of making American writing bourgeois,
genteel, tame, even of emasculating it, later writers, feeling somehow
hampered under the benign hegemony of his immense authority, would

predictably – and perhaps understandably – claim. Yet he was absolutely indispensable for American literature, indeed for the bringing of America – the knowable, meetable, measurable, tangible, unavoidable, contemporary America – into literature.

In his first novel, which characteristically was basically autobiography and travelogue, Howells tried simply to see the American scene. *Their Wedding Journey* (1871) opens with Howells self-deprecatingly 'distrusting my fitness for a sustained or involved narration' and promising only 'to talk of some ordinary traits of American life . . . to speak a little of well-known and easily accessible places, to present now a bit of landscape and now a sketch of character'. He is going to keep the tone low. It is while describing some desultory conversation between a young man and woman on a Hudson River boat that he makes a declaration which would become famous. 'Ah! poor Real Life, which I love, can I make others share the delight I find in thy foolish and insipid face?' Such an avuncular and cosy – and patronising – attitude to 'Real Life' will hardly seem a very exciting prescription for fiction, indeed for any kind of writing, and the degree of blandness and complacency that we hear in the words is always a possible danger in Howells's writing; but we should bear in mind just how little of 'Real' American life was finding its way into fiction at that time. Another incident and comment perhaps indicate more clearly what Howells was attempting to bring about. The couple – Basil and Isabel March (the slightest of fictional covers for William Dean and Elinor Mead Howells) – visit the Genesee Falls at Rochester. The Falls are sublimely beautiful. Basil points out a rock from which one, Sam Patch, had made a celebrated and fatal leap. Isabel rejects the association: 'Patch! What a name to be linked in our thoughts with this superb cataract.' This allows Basil to launch into a Howells manifesto.

Well, Isabel, I think you are very unjust. It's as good a name as Leander, to my thinking, and it was immortalized in support of a great idea – the feasibility of all things; while Leander's has come down to us as that of a weak victim of passion. We shall never have a poetry of our own till we get over this absurd reluctance from facts, till we make the ideal embrace and include the real, till we consent to face the music in our common names, and put Smith into a lyric and Jones into a tragedy.

There is, perhaps, something a little naïve in the formulation, but it is heartfelt and, quite as sincerely as Whitman, Howells worked and wrote for the true democratisation of literature – though Whitman included facts, from which Howells had a particular reluctance. (In an early – 1860 – essay on Whitman, Howells showed his disquiet, or disgust: 'He has told too much . . . the secrets of the body should be decently hid . . . [Whitman] goes through his book, like one in an ill-conditioned dream, perfectly nude, with his clothes over his arm.')[6]

It is, however, a mark of Howells's realism that he aimed to keep the tone *particularly* low. When the Marches are enjoying 'A Day's Railroading', Howells makes this comment.

It was in all respects an ordinary carful of human beings, and it was perhaps the more worthy to be studied on that account. As in literature the true artist will shun the use even of real events if they are of an improbable character, so the sincere observer of man will not desire to look upon his heroic or occasional phases, but will seek him in his habitual moods of vacancy and tiresomeness . . . I never perceive him to be so much a man and brother as when I feel the pressure of his vast, natural, unaffected dulness.

Such a realism is not only low; it is potentially lowering. In seeking to avoid and eradicate the worst excesses of romantic literature, Howells is in danger of narrowing the spectrum of legitimate fictional concerns quite impossibly. But, again, this must be seen as polemical, a redressing of the balance, an insistence on looking at the usually unlooked-at.

Over the years, Howells's concept of realism matured and broadened and deepened (though never, really, to include the sexual). It must be remembered that there was very little coherent theory of fiction available at that time, in America or indeed in England. In his ongoing discussions of realism, Howells was working to formulate the new possibilities and responsibilities of fiction.

In this connection it is worth mentioning an important article by Howells on Henry James which was published in 1882 (while he was on his return trip to Europe) and which is thus from the period just before he started writing *Indian Summer* (published in 1886). In it he made a statement which seems unexceptionable now, but which caused outrage and fury in England at the time.

The art of fiction, has, in fact, become a finer art in our day than it was with Dickens and Thackeray. We would not suffer the confidential attitude of the latter now, nor the mannerism of the former, any more than we could endure the prolixity of a Richardson or the coarseness of Fielding . . . The new school . . . studies human nature much more in its wonted aspects, and finds its ethical and dramatic examples in the operation of lighter but not really less vital motives. The moving accident is certainly not its trade; and it prefers to avoid all manner of dire catastrophes. It is largely influenced by French fiction in form . . . This school, which is so largely of the future as well as the present, finds its chief exemplar in Mr. James . . . Will the reader be content to accept a novel which is an analytic study rather than a story, which is apt to leave him arbiter of the author's creations?[7]

Now 'analyst' was something of a dirty word when it came to discussing novelists around this time. If a novelist was an 'analyst' it usually meant that his work would offer a 'dissection of some moral cancer' and 'a show of stolid indifference to high ideals and "imaginative lift"' (this from Maurice Thompson in 1886 who, we may note, goes on to exonerate Howells from the charge of being a real 'analyst' because he is so 'clean . . . so sane in his imaginings' and has 'one of the finest and sweetest imaginations that America has had'). Though a champion of 'analysts' and analytic fiction, Howells was not really an 'analyst' nor did he regard himself as one. Nevertheless he was criticised because his characters seemed 'clinically studied' and later his own work would be attacked for his air of almost scientific detachment, indeed for being too 'analytic'. It is necessary to remember the resistance to even Howells's 'clean' realism, the antagonism it aroused, to realise what he was up against. An American Catholic reviewer of *The Rise of Silas Lapham*, for instance, saw Howells's realism as being a form of Darwinism, and that was simply 'the descent to dirt'.[8] More articulately and temperately, a critic named Hamilton Wright Mabie, also reviewing *Silas Lapham* (which, incidentally, was written largely concurrently with *Indian Summer* and in fact published one year earlier) made the case against realism in a way which enables us to understand what was perceived to be at stake.

But modern realism knows nothing of any revelation in human life; of any spiritual facts of which its facts are significant; of any spiritual laws to which they conform in the unbroken order of the Universe. It does more than ignore these things; it denies them. Under the conditions which it imposes art can see nothing but the isolated physical fact before it; there is no infinite blue heaven over it. It forms no part of a universal order; it discovers no common law; it can never be a type of a great class. It is, in a word, practical atheism applied to art. It not only empties the world of the Ideal, but, as Zola frankly says, it denies 'the good God'; it dismisses the old heaven of aspiration and possible fulfillment as an idle dream; it destroys the significance of life and the interpretative quality of art.[9]

Howells kept his distance from Zola, but he certainly wanted to empty the world of all cant about 'the Ideal'. For the rest, he thought that the significance of life would speak for itself, if life was truly and scrupulously represented, and as for interpretation, that should be left to the reader. We now find matters connected with respresentation and 'the real' a good deal more problematic than Howells seems to have done. But he was pointing fiction towards the modern world.

Writing of Howells in 1886, Henry James singled out for praise 'his unerring sentiment of the American character'. 'Other persons have considered and discoursed upon American life, but no one, surely, has *felt* it as completely as he. I will not say that Mr Howells feels it all equally, for are we not perpetually conscious of how vast and deep it is? – but he is an authority upon many of those parts of it which are most representative.'[10] He adds that 'his work is of a kind of which it is good that there should be much to-day – work of observation, of patient and definite notation'.[11] And he goes on to provide a fair and generous assessment of Howells's virtues and predilections and attitudes which can hardly be bettered.

He is animated by a love of the common, the immediate, the familiar and vulgar elements of life, and holds that in proportion as we move into the rare and strange we become vague and arbitrary; that truth of representation, in a word, can be achieved only so long as it is in our power to test and measure it. He thinks scarcely anything too paltry to be interesting, that the small and the vulgar have been terribly neglected, and would rather see an exact account of a sentiment or a character he stumbles against every day than a brilliant evocation of a passion or a type he has never seen and does not even particularly believe in. He adores the real, the colloquial, the moderate, the optimistic, the domestic, and the democratic; looking askance at exceptions and perversities and superiorities, at surprising and incongruous phenomena in general. One must have seen a great deal before one concludes; the world is very large, and life is a mixture of many things; she by no means eschews the strange, and often risks combinations and effects that make one rub one's eyes. Nevertheless, Mr Howells's stand-point is an excellent one for seeing a large part of the truth, and if it were less advantageous, there would be a great deal to admire in the firmness with which he has planted himself.[12]

The good-natured delicacy of the stricture does not conceal James's sense of the limitations, and possible defects, in Howells's prescriptions for fiction. He touches on another notable absence or exclusion a shade more firmly – though quite as good-naturedly. 'If American life is on the whole, as I make no doubt whatever, more innocent than that of any other country, nowhere is the fact more patent than in Mr Howells's novels, which exhibit so constant a study of the actual and so small a perception of evil.'[13] It is perhaps amusing that in *Indian Summer* the cheerful confidence of Mr Waters as to the innocence of the carnival and masquerade – with all the sexual licence and intoxication which they permit (a very little of which Howells allows into his book, well diluted and laundered) – prompts Colville to remember 'reading once in a passage from Swedenborg, that the most celestial angels had scarcely any power of perceiving evil'. Whether in Howells's own case it was an inability or a disinclination is necessarily a moot point, but although his outlook on life darkened as he got older, and tensions, corruptions, violence, and widespread economic distress appeared on the surface of American society, James is right – Howells has no real vision of evil. He can see, and conscientiously transcribe, injustice, inequality, squalor, cruelty, hardship, and pain, even murder and slaughter. But there is no sense of *evil* – the real Iago thing. It is why his novels lack an ultimate tension, urgency, force. They are just a little slack, just a shade too at-ease and comfortable with themselves. This effect is compounded by one other tendency which James gently rebuked. 'I should also venture to express a certain regret that Mr. Howells . . . should appear increasingly to hold composition too cheap – by which I mean, should neglect the effect that comes from alternation, distribution, relief.'[14] It would have to be admitted that Howells's theory of fiction and ideas about the art of the novel are crude indeed beside James's.

But none of this matters in connection with *Indian Summer*. The tone is comic, ironic, and elegiac, and corrigible folly rather than irremediable evil is the order of the day. And it is – I think – the most subtly, carefully, and felicitously composed of his novels. It is, thus, perhaps more appropriate to conclude with the appreciative words which Henry James's brother, William, sent to Howells after he finished reading the novel: 'it has given me about as exquisite a kind of delight as anything I ever read in my life, in the line to which it belongs. How you tread the narrow line of nature's truth so infallibly is more than I can understand. Then the profanity, the humor, the humanity, the morality – the everything! In short, 'tis cubical, and set it up any way you please, 't will stand.'[15]

NOTES

1 *Mark Twain–Howells Letters*, ed. Henry Nash Smith and William M. Gibson, 2 vols. (Cambridge: Harvard University Press, 1960), II, 533–4.
2 Henry James, *Literary Criticism: Essays on Literature, American Writers, English Writers* (New York: Library of America, 1984), p. 505.
3 Edwin H. Cady, *The Road to Realism: The Early Years of William Dean Howells* (Syracuse: Syracuse University Press, 1956), p. 227.
4 *Twain–Howells Letters*, I, 430.

5 *Life in Letters of William Dean Howells*, ed. Mildred Howells, 2 vols. (New York: Doubleday, Doran and Company, Inc., 1929), I, 338.

6 Quoted in Cady, *The Road to Realism*, p. 86.

7 William Dean Howells, *Representative Selections*, ed. Clara Marburg Kirk and Rudolf Kirk (New York: Hill and Wang, 1961), p. 353.

8 Quoted in Edwin H. Cady and Norma W. Cady (eds.), *Critical Essays on W. D. Howells, 1866–1920* (Boston: G. K. Hall & Co., 1983), p. 45.

9 Ibid., p. 54.

10 James, *Literary Criticism*, p. 500.

11 Ibid., p. 502.

12 Ibid., pp. 502–3.

13 Ibid., p. 504.

14 Ibid., p. 505.

15 William James, *The Letters of William James*, ed. Henry James III, 2 vols. (London: Longmans, Green, and Co., 1920), I, 253.

CHAPTER 10

'*The story of the moon that never rose*':
F. Scott Fitzgerald's The Great Gatsby

It was not always to be called *The Great Gatsby*. In a letter to Maxwell Perkins Fitzgerald wrote: 'I have now decided to stick to the title I put on the book. *Trimalchio in West Egg*' (*circa* 7 November 1924).[1] Trimalchio is, of course, the vulgar social upstart of immense wealth in the *Satyricon* of Petronius – a master of sexual and gastronomic revels who gives a banquet of unimaginable luxury in which, unlike Gatsby who is a non-drinking, self-isolating spectator at his own parties, he most decidedly participates. He is a most literal glutton, while Gatsby stands at a curious distance from all he owns and displays, just as at times he seems to stand back from his own words and consider them appraisingly, as he would the words of another, just as he will display shirts he has never worn, books he has never read, and extend invitations to swim in the pool he has never used.

If Fitzgerald thought of Gatsby as some sort of American Trimalchio thrown up by the riotous licence of the Twenties, he certainly subjected him to some remarkable metamorphoses. (He is called Trimalchio just once in the novel.) But there are some distinct genealogical traces of Gatsby's ancient ancestor. In the *Satyricon* Trimalchio is first mentioned in the conversation of two friends discussing where that night's feast is to be held: 'Do you not know at whose house it is today? Trimalchio, a very rich man, who has a clock and a uniformed trumpeter in his dining-room, to keep telling him how much of his life is lost and gone.'[2] Gatsby's concern with time – its arrestability, recuperability, repeatability – is equally obsessive (as was Fitzgerald's – he seemed to write surrounded by clocks and calendars, said Malcolm Cowley). One of the 'punctilious' Gatsby's few clumsy physical movements nearly results in the breaking of a clock. No doubt in some corner of his being he would like to break them all. The obsession is partly the Trimalchian fear of transience – there is always too little time left: more grandly (if more foolishly), it comes from some deep

166

refusal to accept the linear irreversibility of history. 'Banish the uni-formed trumpeter!' would be Gatsby's cry: 'I will not hear his flourish.'

When Gatsby's illustrious forebear Trimalchio is first seen he is 'busily engaged with a green ball. He never picked it up if it touched the ground.'[3] Gatsby comes to orient his life in relation to not a green ball but a green light. 'You always have a green light that burns all night at the end of your dock', he says to Daisy. Seen from across the water – and everything else – that separates him from Daisy, the green light offers Gatsby a suitably inaccessible focus for his yearning, some-thing to give definition to desire while indefinitely deferring consumma-tion, something to stretch his arms towards, as he does, rather than circle his arms around, as he tries to. The fragile magic of the game depends on keeping the green light at a distance or, we might say, on keeping the green ball in the air. The green ball fallen to the ground would be too much of a reminder of that ineluctable gravity that pulls all things back to the earth, balls and dreams alike. Likewise with the annulment of distance: lights too closely approached may well lose their supernal lustre and revert to unarousing ordinariness. You can wish only on the star you can't reach.

Daisy put her arm through his abruptly, but he seemed absorbed in what he had just said. Possibly it had occurred to him that the colossal significance of that light had now vanished forever. Compared to the great distance that had separated him from Daisy it had seemed as close as a star to the moon. Now it was again a green light on a dock. His count of enchanted objects had diminished by one.

Possibly – and possibly not. Or possibly something different. Cer-tainly in this book there is abroad a hunger for 'enchanted objects', a taste for the 'colossal' and a concern to try to establish and differentiate those times – moments, configurations – when a light might be a star of 'colossal significance' as opposed to just another dock light. This is Nick Carraway's version, and we may wonder whether, in retrospect, the green light didn't shine more brightly for him even than, possibly, for Gatsby.

Of the many exotic courses served at Trimalchio's banquet I want to single out one:

a tray was brought in with a basket on it, in which there was a hen made of wood, spreading out her wings as they do when they are sitting. The music grew loud: two slaves came up and at once began to hunt in the straw . . . Peahen's eggs were pulled out and handed to the guests . . . we took our spoons and hammered at the eggs, which were balls of fine meal. I was on the point of throwing away my portion. I thought a peachick had already formed. But hearing a practised diner say, 'What treasure have we here?' I poked through the shell with my finger and found a fat baccafacio rolled up in spiced yoke of egg.[4]

In October 1922 the Fitzgeralds moved to a house in Great Neck, Long Island, on a peninsula at the foot of Manhasset Bay. Their house was a relatively modest one compared with the opulent summer homes of the seriously rich old American families – the Guggenheims, the Astors, the Van Nostrands, the Pulitzers – on another peninsula across the bay. This, of course, provided Fitzgerald with the basic topography for his novel: new-money Gatsby and no-money Nick on one side of the bay and 'old-money' (but what is 'old' money in America?) Buchanans on the other. In the course of being transposed into the novel the 'Necks' became 'Eggs'.

Twenty miles from the city a pair of enormous eggs, identical in contour and separated only by a courtesy bay, jut out into the most domesticated body of salt water in the Western hemisphere, the great wet barnyard of Long Island Sound. They are not perfect ovals – like the egg in the Columbus story, they are both crushed flat at the contact end – but their physical resemblance must be a source of perpetual wonder to the gulls that fly overhead. To the wingless a more interesting phenomenon is their dissimilarity in every particular except shape and size.

A deep, generating question behind the whole book is just this. As a result of the 'domestication' of the great wild continent discovered by Columbus, what has been hatched from it? What will you find if you take your spoon to the great egg – or is it eggs? – of America? A disgusting, aborted, stunted and still-born thing, fit only to be thrown away? Or a treasure, something special (baccafacio, a small bird, was considered a great delicacy) and marvellous and rare? Are the true products of America as 'dissimilar' as the two Eggs might suggest, with the East Egg Buchanans representing and embodying the sort of devouring, self-pleasuring and hypocritical materialism that the stupendous and ruthless success of nineteenth-century capitalism fostered and enabled, and the West Egg alliance of Nick and Gatsby holding out for the possibility, the necessity, of that something else, something more, which materialism can never satisfy – a nostalgic yearning for some sort of ideal that refuses to concede any absolute dominion to the merely accidental triumphs of the matter and matters of the day? From this point of view, if you went back far enough into American history, then, archetypally, Benjamin Franklin was the driving genius of East Egg, while Jonathan Edwards would be the tutelary spirit of West Egg. This is a comprehensible and justifiable reading of the striking 'dissimilarity' of two of the more striking types hatched by America – Nick himself speaks of 'the bizarre and not a little sinister contrast' between the two Eggs. But, in his own terms, this is the perspective of the 'wingless'. Seen from a sufficiently soaring height, it is their 'resemblance' that is a source of 'perpetual wonder'. This novel will indeed concern itself with dissimilarities and resemblances, and there is no disputing the differing aspirations and fates of the necessarily wingless protagonists. But near the end Nick makes a summarising statement: 'I see now that this has been a story of the West, after all – Tom and Gatsby, Daisy and Jordan and I, were all Westerners, and perhaps we possessed some deficiency in common which made us subtly unadaptable to Eastern life.' Is there a Buchanan egg and a Gatsby egg? This one an abortion, that one a treasure? Or, allowing for mutations and variations, does the barnyard produce only one animal? It depends, perhaps, on how high you fly, how far away you stand – which points to a crucial matter raised by the book: what is and is not 'distorted' vision? What mixture of proximity and distance affords the best, the most appropriate, perception? How should Nick look at what he has seen?

In 'Winter Dreams', a story Fitzgerald wrote in 1922, Dexter Green is the son of a grocery-store owner in Minnesota, a quick, alert Midwestern lad who is 'unconsciously dictated to by his winter dreams'. The winters are characteristically 'dismal'; the dreams, reactively, turn towards intimations of the 'gorgeous'.

But do not get the impression, because his winter dreams happened to be concerned at first with musings on the rich, that there was anything merely snobbish in the boy. He wanted not association with glittering things and glittering people – he wanted the glittering things themselves. Often he reached out for the best without knowing why he wanted it – and sometimes he ran up against the mysterious denials and prohibitions in which life indulges . . . He made money. It was rather amazing.

Dexter Green is an embryonic Gatsby, and we may note a rather curious distinction on which the narrator insists – 'not association with glittering things and glittering people [but] the glittering things themselves': not association but *possession*. But what would, or could, or might it be to possess a glittering thing or a glittering person? Can the attempt to go beyond association into appropriation ever *not* encounter 'denials and prohibitions'? These are tacit questions that will haunt the later novel.

Like many aspiring children of immigrant parents, Dexter cannot afford to be natural and spontaneous, for that might betray something of his 'peasant' origin. He assembles himself, as he assembles his wardrobe, with care. 'He recognized the value to him of such a mannerism and he had adopted it.' This is to build the self from the outside, as it were. The result is successful – 'He made money. It was amazing' – but vulnerable and precarious. The more he gets, the less he has. On one level he simply allows himself to be ensnared and enthralled – and used and abandoned – by a heedless, capricious, whimsical, dizzy, shallow rich girl, Judy Jones, who announces and reveals herself in her smile, 'radiant, blatantly artificial – convincing' (like Gatsby's smile). But she is perhaps no more artificial, self-constructed, than Dexter himself, and we might think of it as a matter of artifice reaching out and responding to artifice. We might, a little, think of Gatsby and Daisy that way too. For Dexter it is simply immaterial whether Judy is sincere or acting when she again takes him up before she again lets him down: 'No illusion as to the world in which she had grown up could cure his illusion as to her desirability.' It might seem as though Judy is the glittering thing-person of his winter dreams, but in a curious way she is a rather incidental figure, almost a function around which he can assemble and indulge a personal lexicon of ineffable glitteringness – 'beautiful', 'romantic', 'gorgeous', 'ecstasy', 'magic of nights', 'fire and loveliness'. His relationship is with these words more than with her. Early in their relationship he says to her: 'I'm nobody . . . My career is largely a matter of futures.' But – and this is the other, more important, level of his relationship with her – his future is largely a matter of pasts.

As a boy Dexter was a caddy. Now a wealthy young man, he can afford caddies of his own when he goes golfing. But he keeps glancing at them, 'trying to catch a gleam or gesture that would remind him of himself, that would lessen the gap which lay between his present and his past'. The greatest intensity of feeling comes not from possession but from intimation of imminent or actual loss. Fairer through fading, writes Emily Dickinson: glittering because going, Fitzgerald implies ('It was a mood of intense appreciation, a sense that, for once, he was magnificently attuned to life and that everything about him was radiating a brightness and a glamour he might never know again'), glittering because the radiance is about to dim. And when it has dimmed and the world seems definitively deglamorised, then emotionally the only future that matters really *is* the past.

The story concludes with an incident that occurs many years after Dexter has resigned himself to the fact that Judy has disappeared from his life. From a chance encounter Dexter learns that Judy has married a boor who 'drinks and runs around' – shades, or rather intimations, of Tom Buchanan – that she probably loves him and that her looks have gone: squalor and degradation all round, in other words. And now Dexter feels a further loss:

The dream was gone. Something had been taken from him. In a sort of panic he pushed the palms of his hands into his eyes and tried to bring up a picture of the waters lapping on Sherry Island and the moonlit veranda, and gingham on the golf-links and the dry sun and the gold color of her neck's soft down. And her mouth damp to his kisses and her eyes plaintive with melancholy and her freshness like new fine linen in the morning. Why, these things were no longer in the world! They had existed and they existed no longer.

For the first time in years the tears were streaming down his face. But they were for himself now. He did not care about mouth and eyes and moving hands. He wanted to care, and he could not care. For he had gone away and he could never go back any more. The gates were closed, the sun was gone down, and there was no beauty but the grey beauty of steel that withstands all time. Even the grief he could have borne was left behind in the country of illusion, of youth, of the richness of life, where his winter dreams had flourished.

'Long ago,' he said, 'long ago, there was something in me, but now that thing is gone. Now that thing is gone, that thing is gone. I cannot cry. I cannot care. That thing will come back no more.'

This is a very young man's prose, and such a plangent lament for not only loss but also the loss of the sense of loss comes across as barely post-adolescent. I quote the passage at length partly to suggest how much Fitzgerald had to excise or, let us say, otherwisely to absorb before he could achieve the perfect tonal command of *The Great Gatsby*. One feels here, as so often with Fitzgerald's earlier writing, that the author has very imperfectly distanced himself from the emotional turbulence of his own autobiography. He needed to put something, someone, between himself and his writing if he was to avoid ending up in a sentimental cul-de-sac. The passage also reveals, in inchoate form, an insight that I believe is absolutely central to Fitzgerald's work; namely, that the American Dream – whatever one takes that phrase to mean – is not an index of aspiration but a function of deprivation. But, as Gatsby shows, there can be another turn to the screw. Dexter sinks rather wallowingly into his sense that his future is largely a matter of the past. Gatsby too recognises this, but he will not let the issue rest there, for he insists that the past can be turned into the matter of the future by someone who has made so much, including himself. And begone the uniformed trumpeter!

'It might interest you to know that a story of mine, called "Absolution" . . . was intended to be a picture of Gatsby's early life, but that I cut it because I preferred to preserve the sense of mystery' (to John Jamieson, 15 April 1934).[5] How much the stature of *The Great Gatsby* depends on what Fitzgerald cut out is a matter to which I will return. Here we might consider what he had initially decided to write in as a crucial episode in Gatsby's childhood.

Eleven-year-old Rudolph Miller – young Gatsby – has rebelled against his 'ineffectual' father and been forced to attend confession, during the course of which he lies. He has come to tell his story to Father Schwartz, to whom he admits that he is guilty of 'not believing I was the son of my parents' (a fantasy Fitzgerald himself owned to – 'that I wasn't the son of my parents, but a son of a king, a king who ruled the whole world' – exactly Freud's 'Family Romance'). For the dismalness of being Rudolph Miller he substitutes the gorgeousness of imagining himself to be Blatchford Sarmenington. 'When he became Blatchford Sarmenington a suave nobility flowed from him. Blatchford Sarmenington lived in great sweeping triumphs.' But he keeps the lie in the confessional to himself; indeed, the secret lie, like the secret fantasy, comes to constitute his essential self.

An invisible line had been crossed, and he had become aware of his isolation – aware that it applied not only to those moments when he was Blatchford Sarmenington but that it applied to all his inner life. Hitherto such phenomena as 'crazy' ambitions and petty shames and fears had been but private reservations, unacknowledged before the throne of his official soul. Now he realized unconsciously that his private reservations were himself – and all the rest a garnished front and a conventional flag. The pressure of his environment had driven him into the lonely secret world of adolescence.

Effectively, the boy is rejecting his biological father and rebelling against his spiritual father, as if to say: most importantly, essentially, I *am* my 'private reservations' – my refusals, my repudiations, my fantasies, and, yes, my guilty lies. If you want *me*, don't ask for Rudolph Miller. Ask for Blatchford Sarmenington. Ask for Jay Gatsby.

But the most interesting aspect of the story is the curiously disturbed state of Father Schwartz. (I am not concerned here speculatively to relate this figure to such people as Father Sigourney Webster Fay, who undoubtedly had an important influence on Catholic Fitzgerald. André le Vot has done this well in his biography, *F. Scott Fitzgerald* (1983).) At the start the Father is clearly disturbed by 'the hot madness of four o'clock' – a 'terrible dissonance' made up of the rustle of Swedish girls, yellow lights, sweet smells, and the Dakota wheat that is 'terrible to look on'. After he has listened to the boy's story the Father breaks into a trembling, monologue, which is distracted, if not deranged.

'When a lot of people get together in the best places things go glimmering . . . The thing is to have a lot of people in the centre of the world, wherever that happens to be. Then . . . things go glimmering . . . my theory is that when a whole lot of people get together in the best places things go glimmering all the time . . . Did you ever see an amusement park? . . . It's a thing like a fair, only much more glittering. Go to one at night and stand a little way off from it in a dark place – under dark trees. You'll see a big wheel made of lights turning in the air, and a long slide shooting boats down into the water. A band playing somewhere, and a smell of peanuts – and everything will twinkle. But it won't remind you of anything, you see. It will all just hang out there in the night like a colored balloon – like a big yellow lantern on a pole . . . But don't get up close . . . because if you do you'll only feel the heat and the sweat and the life.'

These are, in fact, the dying words of the Father, and we may take them as expressing his delirious regret for all the sexuality and glamour, the heat and light, that, as a celibate priest, he has repressed and kept his distance from. But as the expression of an eager, tremulous excitement aroused by the thought, the sense, the apprehension, of some kind of glittering glimmeringness – sexual and immaterial, incandescent and transcendent – generated by a forgathering of the beautiful and the blessed (or damned), the glamorous and the gorgeous, at a mythical, unreachable 'centre' – a heavenly amusement park – these words testify to a confused and inarticulate longing – for what? The light that never was on land or sea? – that is somewhere at the heart of Fitzgerald's work, to be indulged or dealt with as the case may be. It is a sort of uninstructed neo-Platonism gone somewhat berserk amid the endless wheat, the untouchable girls and the occasional brilliances of an otherwise dreary and dismal Middle West.

But there is a crucial difference between Dexter Green's desire to possess the glittering things and Father Schwartz's advice to stand back from the glimmering light, and it lies precisely in the latter's apprehension that getting too close might be dangerous, ruinous to the vision of earthly (and heavenly?) delights. Rudolph Sarmenington

Gatsby is partly Green and partly Schwartz (and André le Vot has shown how careful Fitzgerald was with his colour ascriptions – of which more later). He thinks he can possess – repossess – the glittering girl. Indeed, he attempts to make his house into a glimmering, glamorous centre to attract her: 'Your place looks like the World's Fair', says Nick to him, seeing his house 'lit from tower to cellar'. We know that as a boy Fitzgerald was very struck by the brilliance of the Pan-American Exposition in Buffalo in 1901, where there was 'a Goddess of Light whose glow could be seen as far away as Niagara Falls',[6] and Gatsby also uses the magic of electricity (he is after all a dedicated reader of Benjamin Franklin) to signal what he hopes and believes is a more than electrical glimmering. But for all the dedication of his quest for repossession, re-enactment, he can enjoy, indeed experience, his desire and his dreams better at a distance. He is not really at home in the light he has himself turned on and is more usually to be found, as the good Father advised, standing 'a little way off from it in a dark place'. When he does 'get up close' and encounters 'the heat and the sweat and the life' – particularly in the form of Tom Buchanan, the crude but confident snobbery of his discourse, the class-supported brashness of his hypocrisy, the brutality of his 'cruel body' – Gatsby is indeed destroyed. The Green is gone: all is Schwar(t)z.

Fitzgerald planned *The Great Gatsby* during the summer of 1922 but wrote it during the summer of 1924 while living on the Riviera (he – crucially – revised the proofs in Rome during January and February of the following year). This is just when Nick Carraway is writing *his* book about his summer with Gatsby of two years earlier – but he is back in the Midwest. Fitzgerald has introduced a narrator between himself and his omniscient indulgences. Fitzgerald's book is Nick's book, but Nick is not Fitzgerald, however many refracted biographical fragments we may imagine we can discern. Nick is a character, of confessedly limited literary abilities (he has written only 'a series of very solemn and obvious editorials for the Yale News'), and while Nick is trying to write Gatsby, we are also reading Nick.

Among writers he admired Fitzgerald had plenty of precedents for the introduction of a narrator. Henry James, discussing how a writer can extract maximum significance from his material, stresses the value of sometimes choosing a particular kind of narrator: 'By so much as the affair matters *for* some such individual, by so much do we get the best there is of it.' He points out the need for 'a reflecting and colouring medium' and adds:

We want it clear, goodness knows, but we also want it thick, and we get the thickness in the human consciousness that entertains and records, that amplifies and interprets it . . . prodigies, when they come straight, come with an effect imperilled; they keep all their character, on the other hand, by looming through some other history – the indispensable history of somebody's *normal* relation to something.[7]

Gatsby is a self-styled, self-styling 'prodigy' of some sort – prodigiously criminal, prodigiously romantic – and Nick is, or so he would insist, nothing if not 'normal', though he would add, 'abnormally honest'. Gatsby certainly looms – looms and fades, looms and fades – through Nick's 'history', and Nick certainly 'amplifies and interprets' – amplifies, we might come to think, quite inordinately.

Joseph Conrad made some of his most important innovations in the art of fiction through the introduction and deployment of his sailor-narrator Marlow, particularly as Marlow tries to put together a narrative that will somehow make sense of Lord Jim. Was Jim a coward or an idealist? Coward *and* idealist? What is the significance, what are the implications, for 'us' – us sailors, us British, us decent and reliable white Westerners – of his aspirations and failures, his dreams and defections? Marlow has a lot invested in Jim, and in his attempts at narrative recuperation and evaluation. For surely Jim was 'one of us'. And yet . . . *Mutatis mutandis*, much of this is paralleled in the relationship of the bondsman-narrator Nick with the enigmatic Gatsby. Is Gatsby criminal or romantic? Criminal *and* romantic? What are the implications for us Americans of his grandiose plans and their dubious grounding? Of his glamorous dreams and the 'foul dust' that, inevitably, 'floated in the wake of his dreams' and in his wretched waking from them? Nick has a lot – a *lot* – invested in Gatsby and in his own written attempt at the retrieval and, indeed, elegiac celebration of the man. 'They're a rotten crowd . . . You're worth the whole damn bunch put together.' So they are, and so – Nick can make us feel – he is. For surely America can produce something better than Buchanans, more splendid than Carraways. And yet . . .

The extent to which the book *is* Nick's version can hardly be overstressed. To be sure, he assembles his material from different sources. In addition to his own memory, there are documents, like the youthful Gatsby's copy of *Hopalong Cassidy* with its Franklinesque 'SCHEDULE' on the flyleaf and Nick's own infinitely suggestive list of Gatsby's guests of the summer of 1922, which is now 'disintegrating at its folds', suggesting perhaps the inevitable disintegration of other depositories of time – including the memory of the narrator. Then there is the long

oral account of the first phase of the relationship between Gatsby and
Daisy, given to him by Jordan Baker, and the accounts of Gatsby's
early life, Dan Cody and the war years given to him by Gatsby himself
during the doomed and hopeless vigil after the night of the fatal road
accident. But it is Nick who transcribes these accounts; how much he
may be requoting his sources and how much translating them – transforming, embellishing, amplifying, *re*wording – we can never know. By
the conventions of fictional narrative, if a narrator gives the words
of another character in quotation marks, then these were indeed the
very words: he is allowed a (slightly implausible) perfect recall. Now,
by my admittedly rough count, about four per cent of the book is in
Gatsby's own words, and it is revealing to discover that Fitzgerald
considerably *reduced* the amount of direct speech given to Gatsby in the
draft of the novel. For example: ' "Jay Gatsby!" he cried suddenly in a
ringing voice. "There goes the great Jay Gatsby. That's what people
are going to say – wait and see." ' With such outbursts Gatsby would
too crudely and unequivocally have announced and revealed himself.
By systematic deletion Fitzgerald makes Gatsby a far more shadowy,
less knowable, more ultimately elusive figure. Instead we get more of
Nick's hypothesising, speculating, imagining – and perhaps suppressing, recasting, fantasising.

His account is constantly marked by such words and phrases as
the following: 'I suppose', 'I suspect', 'I think'; 'possibly', 'probably',
'perhaps'; 'I've heard it said', 'he seemed to say', 'there must have been',
'I have an idea that', 'I always had the impression'. 'As though' and 'as
if' (used over sixty times) constantly introduce his own transforming
similies and metamorphosing metaphors into the account. 'Possibly it
occurred to him' – and possibly it didn't. We can never know. What
we do know is that it occurs to Nick. However we assess or respond to
'Gatsby' – 'the man who gives his name to this book', as Nick rather
interestingly scruples to spell out – we should always remember that
we are responding to what Nick has made of him. From Gatsby's first
appearance ('a man of about my own age') to the moment after Gatsby's
death, when Nick is mistaken for Gatsby by a telephone caller and he
subsequently experiences 'a feeling of defiance, of scornful solidarity
between Gatsby and me against them all', we are aware of a strong
tendency on Nick's part to identify with Gatsby as well as to make him
a hero. This is why it is so important for him to be able to feel that the
account Gatsby gives of his life is 'all true', why he is glad to have 'one
of those renewals of complete faith in him that I'd experienced before'.

Outside business hours, when he is mainly moving around the money that money makes, Nick invests everything in Gatsby – *his* Gatsby.

Nick reveals, or portrays, himself as the very antithesis of Gatsby, as one of Fitzgerald's 'Sad Young Men'. (There is some resemblance here to the emotionally timid Lockwood putting together his narrative account of the passionate Heathcliff in *Wuthering Heights*.)

I knew the other clerks and young bond-salesmen by their first names, and lunched with them in dark, crowded restaurants on little pig sausages and mashed potatoes and coffee. I even had a short affair with a girl who lived in Jersey City and worked in the accounting department, but her brother began throwing mean looks in my direction, so when she went on her vacation in July I let it blow quietly away.

When it comes to emotional or sexual involvements, what he doesn't let blow quietly away he blows away himself – as he did an earlier 'engagement', as he does Jordan Baker. He is a self-isolating voyeur (characteristically, at one point: 'I was conscious of wanting to look squarely at everyone, and yet to avoid all eyes.' In this he is like the sexually anxious Isabel Archer in Henry James's *Portrait of a Lady*, who wants 'to see but not to feel'). When it comes to the erotic, life in fantasy is safer than real life.

I liked to walk up Fifth Avenue and pick out romantic women from the crowd and imagine that in a few minutes I was going to enter into their lives, and no one would ever know or disapprove. Sometimes, in my mind, I followed them to their apartments on the corners of hidden streets, and they turned and smiled back at me before they faded through a door into warm darkness. At the enchanted metropolitan twilight I felt a haunting loneliness sometimes, and felt it in others – poor young clerks who loitered in front of windows waiting until it was time for a solitary restaurant dinner – young clerks in the dusk, wasting the most poignant moments of night and life.

As against this – and this is surely 'dismal' – it is perhaps not surprising that Nick looks hungrily for signs of the 'gorgeous' – one of his favoured words – in the life and style of Jay Gatsby. He, he implies, is everything that Gatsby is not. 'Thirty – the promise of a decade of loneliness, a thinning list of single men to know, a thinning brief-case of enthusiasm, thinning hair' – thinning everything. As opposed to, and perhaps to compensate for, these gathering attenuations and impoverishments, Gatsby surely embodies more flourishing and fecund, less emotionally etiolated and self-retractive, possibilities and potentialities.

Nick is a spectator in search of a performer. He sees Gatsby in gestural terms: 'If personality is an unbroken series of successful gestures, then there was something gorgeous about him, some heightened sensit-ivity to the promises of life.' No little pig sausages and mashed potatoes for Gatsby, not anyway in Nick's version. His own preferred position, on the other hand, observational and non-gestural, is at the margins. At the first party in New York his instinct is to 'get out', but he keeps getting 'entangled' and 'pulled back'. 'Yet high over the city our line of yellow windows must have contributed their share of human secrecy to the casual watcher in the darkening streets, and I saw him too, looking up and wondering. I was within and without, simultaneously enchanted and repelled by the inexhaustible variety of life.' Whether he knows it or not, he is quoting Whitman almost verbatim ('in and out of the game, watching and wondering at it'), and 'wonder' – the instinct, the need, the capacity for it – is as important for Nick as it has been for so many American writers. Wondering *at* often involves and requires distance and betokens a disinclination, if not an incapacity, for parti-cipation – a distaste for, if not a fear of, all that sweat and heat and life, and one senses that Nick, for all his regrets, somehow prefers the role of 'casual watcher in the darkening streets'. A difference from Whitman is his almost equal capacity for 'repulsion'. When Nick is not enchanted, he is likely to be starting to feel disgusted. For all the seeming reason-ableness and the proffered impartiality of his tone, his Gatsby book is generated by a tendency to move between these extremes. It is a very American oscillation.

At the start Nick puts himself forward, fairly explicitly, as someone with an above-average 'sense of the fundamental decencies' which now manifests itself as a wish for 'the world to be in uniform and at a sort of moral attention forever'. Could it be that he is briefly attracted to Jordan Baker because, with her male-like ('slender and small-breasted') body and 'erect carriage', she looks like 'a young cadet'? Be that as it may, he clearly has something of an authoritarian character with a developed instinct for discipline, hygiene, and tidiness, as he readily admits (it is part of his engagingness as a narrator). At times he is, I won't say priggish, but a touch prim. He prefers life in some sort of uniform. Indeed, on one occasion, at a peculiarly embarrassing moment at the Buchanans', he admits, 'my own instinct was to phone immediately for the police'. When he decides to make a clean break with Jordan Baker, he explains in housekeeping terms: 'I wanted to leave things in order and not just trust that obliging and indifferent sea to sweep my refuse away.' (We may note, however, that he didn't mind some unidentified element blowing an earlier involvement away.)

Nick's manifest dislike of 'refuse', a slightly obsessive compulsion to clean things up, reveals itself on a number of occasions, of which I will mention two.

At the first, drunken, party in New York, as things are disintegrating into increasingly messy incoherence, even though this is one of the two times in his life Nick has allowed himself to get drunk, his fastidious instincts do not fail him: 'Mr McKee was asleep on a chair with his fists clenched in his lap, like a photograph of a man of action. Taking out my handkerchief I wiped from his cheek the spot of dried lather that had worried me all the afternoon.' Shortly after this Tom Buchanan breaks Myrtle's nose, and the party collapses into terminal chaos. But that's the Buchanans for you. 'They were careless people . . . they smashed up things and creatures and then retreated back into their money or their vast carelessness, or whatever it was that kept them together, and let other people clear up the mess they had made.' Tom brutally spills blood; Nick meticulously wipes off a speck of shaving lather, a tiny fragment of that matter-out-of-place which we call dirt. As well as having a politely controlled instinct to be society's moral policeman, Nick also has it in him to be one of its janitors.

The most graphic example of this is what is effectively the last gesture he makes before leaving the East for good. He returns for one more look at Gatsby's 'huge incoherent failure of a house': 'On the white steps an obscene word, scrawled by some boy with a piece of brick, stood out clearly in the moonlight, and I erased it, drawing my shoe raspingly along the stone.' Part of his 'fundamental decency' no doubt, and one can readily share and approve of his instinctive distaste for disrespectful defacement and profanation. But this gesture of 'erasure' has a farther-reaching aptness and suggestiveness. While it might be too much to say that Gatsby's actual career (we'll set aside his dreams for the moment) is itself an 'obscenity', his career, money, and identity are clearly grounded in a series of more or less dirty, more or less criminal activities. There are signs that he more than once tries to signal as much to Nick and make him confront and recognise this fact. Nick always refuses: he prefers to 'erase' whatever might be the 'dirty' side of the story, either by omission, denial, over-writing, reinterpretation, or by transformation, though, of course – it is part of the brilliance of the book – we keep getting glimpses and intimations of what he is trying to keep, and write, out. (For instance, he makes of the early relationship of Gatsby and Daisy a romantic, poetic affair, and it is only subsequently he learns that he took her 'ravenously and

unscrupulously'.) For the purposes of his book, Nick prefers to concentrate on the figure of the hopeful, hapless dreamer in the pink suit.
At one point he informs us that he is putting down what he has subsequently learned about Gatsby's early life – Dan Cody and so on – 'to
clear this set of misconceptions away', these being the wild and silly rumours that circulated around the enigmatic Gatsby. He certainly clears
these away, but it is possible that he clears away – cleans up – much
more as well. We take what he tells us about Dan Cody as faithfully
transcribed. But what about this as a compressed account of Gatsby's
adolescence?

But his heart was in a constant, turbulent riot. The most grotesque and
fantastic conceits haunted him in his bed at night. A universe of ineffable
gaudiness spun itself out in his brain while the clock ticked on the washstand
and the moon soaked with wet light his tangled clothes upon the floor. Each
night he added to his fancies . . . these reveries provided an outlet for his
imagination; they were a satisfactory hint of the unreality of reality, a promise
that the rock of the world was founded on a fairy's wing.

Who is this? Gatsby? Or Nick? Or should we by now simply say
Nick Gatsby? Gatsby tries to use the light of the moon (dream, imagination) to defeat the tick of the clock (history, irreversibility), but Nick
also favours moonlight, and he tries to prevent its being fouled and
contaminated by the inscribed obscenities of the real. Gatsby provides
Nick with an outlet for *his* imagination – he is Nick's reverie of 'gaudiness' – and seems to offer him a satisfactory, or almost satisfactory,
hint of 'the unreality of reality'. The 'rock of the world' is hard and
breaks fragile, vulnerable things, as do Tom Buchanan's fists and words;
Nick prefers to imagine Gatsby imagining the world's rock impossibly
taking second place to the fairy's wing – as if anything could be *founded*
on fairy, grounded in gossamer, as we might say. The more general
point is that it is invariably impossible to know when Nick is adding or
subtracting, to establish when he is amplifying or erasing, to guess
when he is simply fantasising or, more imaginatively, empathetically
eliding. On page one he tells us that, perhaps because of his perceived
inclination to 'reserve all judgements' (he unreserves them in this book),
he has often been the recipient of 'intimate revelations of young men'
and that he has noted that the terms in which they express these 'are
usually plagiaristic and marred by obvious suppressions'. We may thus
be alerted early to the possibility that his own 'intimate revelations' –
perhaps *all* such revelations – will also and inevitably be marked by
these characteristics as well. Nick may be one of the few honest people

he has ever known, but Jordan Baker may not be all wrong when, by way of farewell, she tells him that, in his way, he is 'another bad driver'.

Let me put it another way. When Nick first drives out to Wilson's garage in the valley of ashes, this is his response: 'The interior was unprosperous and bare; the only car visible was the dust-covered wreck of a Ford which crouched in a dim garage. It had occurred to me that this shadow of a garage must be a blind, and that sumptuous and romantic apartments were concealed overhead.' Nick cannot tolerate the thought of confronting a reality that is *merely* poor and bare, dust-covered and wrecked. There *must* be more than that, a whole hidden dimension of sumptuousness and romance for which the manifest impoverishment and degradation of the apparitional, the given, are simply a misleading 'blind', a deceptive mask. But the untranscended bareness of the garage in the valley of ashes is real enough and con-ceals nothing except a squalid affair. In the valley of ashes what you see is what you get. The phantasmal 'sumptuous and romantic apart-ments' are provided by the more generous architecture of his imagina-tion, a function at once of his deprivation and desire. So that rather than thinking of repression and plagiarism, we might more accurately speak of erasure and supplementation provided by his imagination, and of course his writing.

I want to focus on three examples of the 'supplementation' evident in some of the key lines and passages of the book. One of the many master-strokes in Fitzgerald's almost uncannily sure-handed, almost inspired, deletions and additions to the galley proofs of the novel was the insertion of Gatsby's famous comment, 'Her voice is full of money.' Nick's comment and gloss are remarkable and remarkably revealing: 'That was it. I'd never understood before. It was full of money – that was the inexhaustible charm that rose and fell in it, the jingle of it, the cymbal's song of it . . . High in a white palace the king's daughter, the golden girl.' Nick is off on a reverie of unsyntactical free association. But one might legitimately feel that that is not it at all, and jingles and symbols and king's daughters are not at all to the point. Gatsby is more probably intimating that Daisy is a very expensive product, that it takes a great deal of money to make and maintain such a product, that she veritably *breathes* money, and signalling his awareness of this. Nick prefers to pass over the material base, 'the rock of the world', and take wing into fairyland. Whatever Gatsby meant by his fine, enig-matic statement, it is Nick who, confessedly, from the first finds Daisy's voice 'thrilling', full of not money but 'excitement' and 'promise'. When he speculates – 'I think that voice held him most, with its fluctuating, feverish warmth, because it couldn't be over-dreamed' – we may per-haps be more certain that it was the voice that held *Nick* most because it certainly can be over-dreamed, as he later shows (in the passage quoted above). As well as being something of a disenchanted moralist, Nick reveals himself to be quite a committed 'over-dreamer'. It is by no means a wholly unsympathetic characteristic.

At one point, when Nick has entirely taken over Gatsby's story, which he is telling in confident third-person indirect discourse, he indulges himself with this lyrical account:

Out of the corner of his eye Gatsby saw that the blocks of the sidewalks really formed a ladder and mounted to a secret place above the trees – he could climb to it *if he climbed alone,* and once there he could suck on the pap of life, gulp down the incomparable milk of wonder.

His heart beat faster as Daisy's white face came up to his own. He knew that when he kissed this girl, and forever wed his unutterable visions to her perishable breath, his mind would never *romp again like the mind of God.* So he waited, listening for a moment longer to *the tuning fork that had been struck upon a star.* Then he kissed her. At his lips' touch she blossomed for him like a flower and the incarnation was complete.

Through all he said, even through his appalling sentimentality, I was reminded of something – an elusive rhythm, a fragment of lost words, that I had heard somewhere a long time ago. For a moment a phrase tried to take shape in my mouth and my lips parted like a dumb man's, as though there was more struggling upon them than a wisp of startled air. But they made no sound, and what I had almost remembered was uncommunicable forever. (my italics)

Perhaps the first question to ask is: *whose* appalling sentimentality? Gatsby, we learn, took Daisy 'unscrupulously and ravenously' and perhaps did not have much about 'unutterable visions' and 'perishable breath' on his mind. Tuning forks on stars are the stuff of a hundred popular songs, and not the best ones at that, and they must be humming in Nick's mind. It is surely the confirmed bachelor Nick who feels that for maximum gratification it is better to climb alone, just as there is surely something regressive about the thought of climbing to a secret place to suck wondermilk from the pap of life. (There will be more to say about paps of life and milk of wonder.) This hint of nostalgia for the pleasures of childhood is extended by the use of the word 'romp', and to compare the anarchic and egotistical freedoms and indulgences of the nursery with the mind of God is an audacious attempt to give a religious slant to these regressive yearnings. Whatever Gatsby was thinking when he was courting Daisy, he surely wasn't thinking all this, was he?

The question gains force once we discover that at one stage Fitzgerald added to the galley proofs six pages that made it very clear that the 'appalling sentimentality' *was* centrally Gatsby's. There is a dialogue between the two men in which, for instance, when Nick sympathetically says that Daisy is 'a pretty satisfactory incarnation of anything', Gatsby says, with far too much clear-eyed resignation: 'She is . . . but it's a little like loving a place where you've once been happy.' Even more ruinous would have been the insertion, or retention, of this self-analytical confession from Gatsby: ' "But the truth is I'm empty and I guess people feel it . . . Daisy's all I've got left from a world that was so wonderful that when I think of it I feel sick all over." He looked round with wild regret. "Let me sing you a song – I want to sing you a song . . . the sound of it makes me happy. But I don't sing it often because I'm afraid I'll use it up." ' The song, something he wrote when he was fourteen – fourteen! This man's future really is the past – is quoted in full and amply justifies Nick's comment on his 'appalling sentimentality'. All this disastrous, self-reducing explicitness was, unerringly as ever, cut. Fitzgerald left in only the last paragraph of the passage quoted above. The deletions increase the unknowability of Gatsby, while the retained paragraph suggests that whatever chord of nostalgia, memory and desire the figure of Gatsby might touch, it remains irrecoverable, uncommunicable, inarticulable – lost (like, indeed, the American Dream). And it is no longer clear where the sentimentality, and the regressive impulses, are coming from. We sense only that they are in the air – in the air of the writing. And the writing is Nick's.

Perhaps the following is the most famous paragraph of the book.

I suppose he'd had the name ready for a long time, even then. His parents were shiftless and unsuccessful farm people – his imagination had never really accepted them as his parents at all. The truth was that Jay Gatsby of West Egg, Long Island, sprang from his Platonic conception of himself. He was a son of God – a phrase which, if it means anything, means just that – and he must be about His Father's business, the service of a vast, vulgar, and meretricious beauty. So he invented just the sort of Jay Gatsby that a seventeen-year-old boy would be likely to invent, and to this conception he was faithful to the end.

He supposes – but goes on to declare 'the truth'. This 'truth' that he asserts about Gatsby – and that audaciously, if not blasphemously, invokes the authority of both Plato and God – springs from the fact that Gatsby never accepted his parents as his parents. Like Rudolph Miller, like Fitzgerald himself, and like many another self-parenting figure in the history of America, life and literature. The reasons for this deter- mination or instinct to reject or deny the parents – more specifically it is mainly a repudiation of the authority, prescriptive and proscriptive, of fathers, biological or Founding – range from the practical (slough off your immigrant identity) to the ideological (throw off the coercive, restrictive, predetermining weight of the past). I am not so foolish as to suggest that the instinct to deny parents is peculiarly American – after all, Freud's 'Family Romance' would suggest that it is more or less uni- versal; but there is no doubt that it is felt with special force in America. Moreover, it receives specific cultural endorsement and support. Indeed, it is embedded in American literature as something of an obligation and a prerequisite for the achievement of an 'American' identity. 'Our age is retrospective. It builds the sepulchres of the fathers.' So starts Emerson's first work, the enormously influential 1836 essay 'Nature'. Building sepulchres to the fathers is just exactly what Americans should not be doing, as far as Emerson was concerned: fathers (and fathering countries, like England) are to be forgotten. 'Why should not we also enjoy an original relation to the universe? . . . The sun shines today also . . . There are new lands, new men, new thoughts.'[8] Emerson, and many writers who followed him, stressed self-reliance, self-sculpting, self- architecturing, self-inventing – the metaphors are many. The American 'self-made man' had a prestigious legitimation and encouragement. Jay Gatsby is a very American young man.

But what about God and Plato? Here I must bring together a few passages to point up a particular characteristic of Nick's vocabulary. Near the end, after summarising the legal and logistical business that followed the shooting of Gatsby, Nick writes: 'But all this part of it seemed remote and unessential.' Even nearer the end he refers to the 'inessential houses' melting away as the moon rises. Between 'un–' and 'in–', as prefixes expressing negation, there is not much difference: either way, not essential, not of the essence. When Nick imagines Gatsby's state of mind as he awaits a phone call from Daisy, and instead receives a visit from Wilson, he becomes quite metaphysical.

I have an idea that Gatsby himself didn't believe it would come, and perhaps he no longer cared. If that was true he must have felt that he had lost the old warm world, paid a high price for living too long with a single dream. He must have looked up at an unfamiliar sky through frightening leaves and shivered as he found what a grotesque thing a rose is and how raw the sunlight was upon the scarcely created grass. A new world, material without being real, where poor ghosts, breathing dreams like air, drifted fortuitously about . . . like that ashen, fantastic figure gliding toward him through the amorphous trees.

'Material without being real' is a straightforward neo-Platonic distinction (the really Real is to be found, or sought, in the realm of unchanging Ideas or Forms). But Nick is transcribing something more like a moment of existential panic, such as is described by Sartre in *La Nausée* when Roquentin, staring at a tree, experiences a terrible sense of the sheer, absurd, horrible gratuitousness of things – a negative epiphany in which matter without meaning turns monstrous, 'frightening', 'grotesque'. To Gatsby, thinks Nick, this is how the world empty and bereft of his dream of Daisy must have appeared: to Nick, perhaps, this is how the world without Gatsby, and thus without Gatsby's tenacious but doomed dreaming, is beginning to look.

This passage is followed by Nick's description of what he saw when they hurried down to the pool in which Gatsby had been shot. 'There was a faint, barely perceptible movement of the water as the fresh flow from one end urged its way towards the drain at the other. With little ripples that were hardly the shadows of waves, the laden mattress moved irregularly down the pool. A small gust of wind that scarcely corrugated the surface was enough to disturb its *accidental* course with its *accidental* burden' (my italics). In a book in which there is much bad driving and so many accidents, including the fatal one that precipitates the catastrophic conclusion, the italicised word is highly appropriate. But the deliberate repetition serves to remind us of the more general, philosophical meaning of the word – exactly, not essential. Nick tells us that when Gatsby met Daisy he found himself in her house by a 'colossal accident': wittingly or not, he has chosen an ominously apt phrase, for their relationship also ends with and by a 'colossal accident' of a more horribly literal kind. Was it all an 'accidental' matter, from beginning to end? Now that Gatsby is dead, it would seem that Nick feels he is confronting a wholly contingent world. Inessential. Unessential. When Tom Buchanan, confident that he has exposed Gatsby as a common criminal, contemptuously dismisses Gatsby and Daisy to drive back together, Nick writes: 'They were gone, without a word, snapped out, made accidental.' In a world dominated by Buchanans, pure contingency reigns: frightening, grotesque.

During the reunion of Gatsby and Daisy, recounted at the very centre of the book, according to Nick Gatsby sometimes 'stared around at his possessions in a dazed way, as though in her actual and astounding presence none of it was any longer real'. More filtered neo-Platonism with the higher 'actual' (ideal) displacing and devaluing, indeed effectively dematerialising, the merely materially real. No wonder that Gatsby feels momentarily ontologically all at sea. 'Once he nearly toppled down a flight of stairs.' Where Gatsby is concerned, just what is 'real', and where it is to be found, becomes problematical, surprising. There is a marvellous scene in which the slightly drunk guest with the owl-eyed spectacles, whom Nick and Jordan come across in Gatsby's library, begins to eulogise admiringly.

'What do you think about that?' he demanded impetuously.
  'About what?'
He waved his hand toward the book-shelves.
  'About that. As a matter of fact you needn't bother to ascertain. I ascertained. They're real.'
  'The books?'
He nodded.
  'Absolutely real – have pages and everything. I thought they'd be a nice durable cardboard. Matter of fact, they're absolutely real. Pages and – Here! Lemme show you.'
Taking our scepticism for granted, he rushed to the bookcases and returned with Volume One of the *Stoddard Lectures*.
  'See!' he cried triumphantly. 'It's a bona-fide piece of printed matter. It fooled me. This fella's a regular Belasco. It's a triumph. What thoroughness! What realism! Knew when to stop, too – didn't cut the pages, But what do you want? What do you expect?'

David Belasco was a Broadway producer famous for the realism of his sets. Gatsby theatricalises himself and his surroundings, and it is often difficult to know which parts of the show – how much of what he shows – is 'real'. It can happen that just where you expect, or suspect, the most obvious artifice and artificiality – in the books in his library, say, or in his embarrassingly clichéd account of his life, which does not so much challenge credulity as defy it – you find you have stumbled into authenticity: 'They're real . . . Absolutely real', 'Then it was all true.' Perhaps, then, we should look for the 'real' where we might least expect it, ready in the case of Gatsby (perhaps in the case of America) to discern merit in meretriciousness, value in the vulgar.

It is worth pausing briefly on the word 'absolutely'. It is the first word Jordan Baker says in the opening scene, so seemingly *à propos* of nothing it makes Nick jump; she is also, she says, 'absolutely in training'. 'Is this absolutely where you live, my dearest one?' Daisy gaily asks Nick as they approach Gatsby's house; and on another occasion she indeed calls Nick 'an absolute rose' – a less appropriate description of the somewhat prim and shrinking wallflower, Nick, it would be hard to imagine. Clearly, 'absolutely' has here become one of those empty words that make up part of the bantering argot of a particular social set, or indeed period, and is conceptually meaningless. So we should not lean too heavily on the word, nor hear too much in it, when the man in the owl-eyed spectacles remarks in some amazement on the absolute reality of Gatsby's books. But clearly there is in Nick's narrative discourse a hunger for something absolute, something essential, something that is Real in a more than contingent, material, 'accidental' way. There is a theological and metaphysical yearning – confused and vestigial though it may be – mixed up with Nick's desire to believe in some form or figure of gorgeousness to offset the dismalness with which he is all too, and now increasingly, familiar, which is why he deliberately and daringly invokes God and Plato in his celebratory elegy of the sentimental American criminal in the pink rag of a suit. At the end of Thomas Pynchon's *The Crying of Lot 49* the heroine, Oedipa Maas, has come to a personal crisis that also involves no less than the meaning of America itself.

Another mode of meaning behind the obvious, or none. Either Oedipa in the orbiting ecstasy of a true paranoia, or a real Tristero. For there either was some Tristero beyond the appearance of legacy America, or there was just America and if there was just America then it seemed the only way she could continue, and manage to be at all relevant to it, was as an alien, unfurrowed, assumed full circle into some paranoia.[9]

Nick is no Oedipa, and Gatsby is not the Tristero (an ambiguous secret society operating beyond or beneath the reach of the official established power structures). But there is a similarity in the stance, and the need, and the perceived alternatives, that is recognisable and may be found throughout American literature. From the time of the Puritans, the idea that it might be 'just America' has been felt to be intolerable and unacceptable. There *must* be 'another mode of meaning behind the obvious'. You may discover and assert it the Puritan way (God) or the Transcendentalist way (Plato), but one way or another the urge to do so, or fear of being unable to do so, is recurrent. It drives and worries Nick, as it does Oedipa Maas, and while Nick gives no indication of having recourse to Oedipa's alternative of paranoia, it could be argued that he finds a refuge in writing and fantasy to console himself in a post-Gatsby world. He catches glimpses of some of

the uglier and more sordid social, sexual, and economic realities of the
story he has to tell, but he refuses to let them dominate his narrative as
they do life – if they did, there would be 'just America'. Consequently,
writes Richard Godden, 'whenever the contradictions within his subject
become too disquieting, he turns social aspiration into "dream", sexual
politics into "romance", and translates class conflict as "tragedy"'.[10]

When Nick is introducing himself to us, he speaks about his family
with such casual, disarming honesty that it is easy to overlook the
implications of what he reveals.

My family have been prominent, well-to-do people in this Middle Western
city for three generations. The Carraways are something of a clan, and we
have a tradition that we're descended from the Dukes of Buccleuch, but the
actual founder of my line was my grandfather's brother, who came here in
fifty-one, sent a substitute to the Civil War, and started the wholesale hard-
ware business that my father carries on today.

Underneath the cosmetic vocabulary of 'clan', 'tradition', 'Dukes', etc.,
this 'actual' is a pretty inglorious, cowardly, materially opportunistic
affair. Towards the end of *The American Scene* Henry James, having
visited the old town of St Augustine in Florida, recalls how the magazine illustrators had contrived, or conspired, to give the town an
intensely 'romantic character', investing it, quite falsely, with all sorts of
vistas and attributes of 'Spanish antiquity'. This sets James musing:

The guardians of real values struck me as, up and down, far to seek. The
whole matter indeed would seem to come back, interestingly enough, to the
general truth of the aesthetic need, in the country, for much greater values, of
certain sorts, than the country and its manners, its aspects and arrangements,
its past and present, and perhaps even future, really supply; whereby, as the
aesthetic need is also intermixed with a patriotic yearning, a supply has somehow to be extemporized, by any pardonable form of pictorial 'hankey-pankey'
– has to be, as the expression goes, cleverly 'faked' . . . the novelists improvise,
with the aid of the historians, a romantic local past of costume and compli-
ment and sword-play and gallantry and passion; the dramatists build up, of a
thousand pieces, the airy fiction that the life of the people among whom the
elements of clash and contrast are simplest and most superficial abounds in
the subjects and situations and effects of the theatre; while the genealogists
touch up the picture with their pleasant hint of the number, over the land, of
families of royal blood . . . It is the public these appearances collectively refer
us to that becomes thus again the more attaching subject; the public so
placidly uncritical that the whitest thread of the deceptive stitch never makes
it blink, and sentimental at once with such inveteracy and such simplicity
that, finding everything everywhere perfectly splendid, it fairly goes upon its
knees to be humbuggingly hum-bugged.[11]

Nick certainly doesn't find 'everything everywhere perfectly splendid', and I would never for a moment suggest that even in the most
metaphorical way he ever goes upon his knees before Gatsby to be
'humbuggingly humbugged'. But there is about him just a touch of the
novelist and dramatist James describes, and once or twice he makes a
point of *not* blinking at the white threads of some fairly visible deceptive stitches. And if he himself refuses to go along with the sort of
genealogical 'hankey-pankey' that apparently prevails in his family –
rather, indeed, blowing the whistle on it, albeit in passing – he nevertheless reveals, or conjures up, a society tolerably permeated with
'hankey-pankey', not to say misrepresentation and fakery, of many
kinds.

There is certainly a lot of visible architectural hankey-pankey, starting with Gatsby's own mansion, which is 'a factual imitation of some
Hôtel de Ville in Normandy'. In the ambiguous atmosphere in which
Gatsby moves and operates factual imitations cannot easily be distinguished from imitation facts. (If you fix the World Series, you have
created an imitation fact. Gatsby knows the man who did it: that is
part of the company he keeps.) The mansion has a tower that is, as
Nick's often entirely unhumbugged eye notes, 'spanking new under a
thin beard of raw ivy'. This perfectly exemplifies the practice of 'misrepresentation', the hankey-pankey and fakery that earned James's
strictures: the crude superimposition of a false veneer of antiquity (the
thin beard of raw ivy) on the 'spanking newness' of – well, of America,
James would say. This desire to affix a prestigious patina of pastness to
a less obviously distinguished present can spring from many sources.
Gatsby didn't build his phoney French mansion. It was commissioned
a decade earlier by a brewer who took his passion to reimpose an alien
pastness on the new American landscape to extreme lengths: 'there
was a story that he'd agreed to pay five years' taxes on all the neigh-
bouring cottages if the owners would have their roofs thatched with
straw'. They wouldn't, and he died. Crazy indeed; but Gatsby also, in
his own way, seeks to 'repeat the past' – ' "Why, of course you can!" '
Things aren't so different over on more fashionable East Egg. The
Buchanans live in a 'red-and-white Georgian Colonial mansion' with
an 'Italian garden'. Tom certainly has the worst kind of 'colonizing'
mentality – all others exist only to satisfy his needs and appetites – but
he is no more grounded in, or significantly related to, ancient American history than Gatsby. This house originally belonged to 'Demaine,
the oil man', and one can see how deftly yet unobtrusively Fitzgerald

makes his points. A brewer and an oil man: the money that could afford
to erect these grandiose architectural masks, drawing on Europe and
history for façades at once to cover and dignify the origins of their
wealth, is derived from alcohol and oil, two of the basic raw materials
that indeed serve to fuel much of American society, moving both the
economy and the people in different and dangerous ways: think how
much of this novel is taken up with drinking and driving – and drunken
driving. Later in the novel Tom boasts that, while you often hear of
people making a garage out of a stable, he is the first man to make a
stable out of a garage. It is a suggestive conversion: once you have made
enough money – let's say in oil – you can 'thatch' it over with your
preferred pastoral fakery. Of course, there are many, many American
garages that are doomed to remain always and only garages – unprofit-
able, unconvertible, irredeemable. Ask Wilson in the valley of ashes.

There is more decorative hankey-pankey in the book – the tapes-
tried furniture covered with 'scenes of ladies swinging in the gardens of
Versailles' in Myrtle's apartment, for example – but enough has been
noted to indicate that Fitzgerald gives us glimpses of a country where
the past is pretty thin on the ground and of a society in which people,
once they can afford to, reach out eclectically for all kinds of imported
façades (exotic, historic) to cover not just the naked facts of how they
make or made their money (which is not unique to them – Victorian
England did that too) but also their 'spanking newness'. There is a nice
moment recorded by Nick, who, shortly after arriving in West Egg is
feeling alone and new when a stranger asks him the way to the village.
'I told him. And as I walked on I was lonely no longer. I was a guide,
a pathfinder, an original settler.' This is Nick's tone at its most sympathetic, a kind of tasteful exaggeration that contrives to be at once
playful and modest. But in the lightest of ways he is touching on a
matter of great import. His instant transformation from lonely new-
comer to 'original settler' is a comic version of something that has
concerned Americans in various ways since the first settlements. As the
inhabitants of America (once the Indians had been effectively erased)
have all been, in a sense, displaced newcomers, they have always wanted
to 'originate' themselves somehow in America; they have conducted a
search, let us call it, for modes of more or less instant racination. In
their agonistic confrontation, Tom derides Gatsby as 'Mr Nobody
from Nowhere'. He is talking defensive 'gibberish' at the time, as Nick
notes, but the phrase does pose an implicit question: can *anybody* in this
book be said to be Mr, or Ms, Somebody from Somewhere? They are

all restless nomads from the Midwest, simply with more or less money: restlessness is the predominant mood of the novel, and the word and its variants occur frequently. 'There is no there there', said Gertrude Stein of Oakland: one might, not unfairly, extend the remark to cover the America of this book. 'I didn't want you to think I was just some nobody', says Gatsby to Nick in their first real conversation, explaining why he has ventured to tell him his life story to date. And if any of these nobodies, driving from nowhere to nowhere, does become Some-body, then, by the grace of Nick's text, it is Gatsby – the *great* Gatsby.

But how and why 'great'? And how much of Gatsby is 'hankey-pankey'? Does Nick to any extent allow himself to be 'humbuggingly humbugged'? There is a most revealing exchange between the two men at the start of their first conversation and Gatsby's life story.

'I'll tell you God's truth.' His right hand suddenly ordered divine retribution to stand by. 'I am the son of some wealthy people in the Middle West – all dead now. I was brought up in America but educated at Oxford, because all my ancestors have been educated there for many years. It is a family tradition.'

He looked at me sideways – and I knew why Jordan Baker had believed he was lying. He hurried the phrase 'educated at Oxford', or swallowed it, or choked on it, as though it had bothered him before. And with this doubt, his whole statement fell to pieces, and I wondered if there wasn't something a little sinister about him, after all.

'What part of the Middle West?' I inquired casually.

'San Francisco.'

'I see.'

'My family all died and I came into a good deal of money.'

His voice was solemn, as if the memory of that sudden extinction of a clan still haunted him. For a moment I suspected that he was pulling my leg, but a glance at him convinced me otherwise.

Incurably dishonest herself, we may perhaps expect Jordan Baker to know a liar when she hears one, and indeed most of this part of Gatsby's story is pure hankey-pankey, even if the Armistice did give him five not-in-the-ancestral-family-tradition months at Oxford. The question is, how much does he expect to be believed? The invoking of God and the theatrical gesture with the right hand, followed by the sideways look . . . Of course his statement falls to pieces. But some-thing odder follows. When he puts San Francisco in the Middle West – rather as if, in Britain, someone told you he came from Glasgow in the Midlands – Nick simply says, 'I see.' Now at this point Gatsby is surely showing Nick the white thread of the deceptive stitch, and Nick chooses not to see it, or rather not to acknowledge or draw attention to it. There is a way of saying 'I see' (it is probably Nick's) that tacitly states: 'I know you're lying, and I know *you* know I know you're lying, but for my own reasons, perhaps politeness, perhaps embarrassment at such brazen mendacity, perhaps something more inscrutable, I choose not to challenge your statement.' It is exactly what Nick says again when Gatsby suddenly and inexplicably dismisses his former staff and fills his house with a bunch of deliberately rude and villainous-looking thugs. Gatsby 'explains': 'They're all brothers and sisters. They used to run a small hotel.' This, surely, is another exposure of the deceptive white thread. I think Richard Godden is absolutely right to suggest that with this sudden and crude termination of his lavish, star-studded, hyper-elegant, conspicuously consuming summer parties Gatsby is deliberately showing Nick (and perhaps, indirectly, Daisy) his *real* milieu, his 'actual' criminal grounding – really rubbing his nose in it, as it were. Nick 'sees' but chooses not to see or, rather, chooses to concentrate on seeing something else.

As Nick has revealed, he knows a thing or two about families inventing ancestors and traditions, and he even extends to Gatsby's relatives his preferred and rather pretentious word 'clan', a more inappropriate appellation, surely, for Gatsby's 'shiftless and unsuccessful farm people' even than for the war-dodging Carraways. It is as if a part of him at least is prepared to participate in Gatsby's hankey-pankey – it runs in the family, we might say. Another part of him knows very well that he is having his leg pulled – Gatsby could hardly have tipped him a more visible wink – but he is extraordinarily quick to be 'convinced otherwise'. We may see this as eager credulity or engaging trust. Constant suspicion and a wary determination never to be taken in are not the most attractive of characteristics, and there is something sympathetic in Nick's tremendous keenness to give Gatsby the benefit of the doubt. How much this is generosity prompted by attraction to the man (and revulsion from the others) and how much is collusion, the willing suspension of disbelief, motivated by a desire for the 'gorgeous', would be impossible to determine. What is clear is that, faced with the Buchanans of this world, Nick will go along with Gatsby's hankey-pankey, will, indeed, justify, amplify and celebrate it in his writing. He is certainly loyal to him to the end, taking charge of his exequies at that sad funeral to which an ungrateful and forgetful 'Nobody' comes except for a few servants, his pathetic father who 'et like a hog' and the man in owl-shaped spectacles who wondered at the absolute reality of

Gatsby's books and who pronounces one of his epitaphs, 'The poor son-of-a-bitch.' Nick will write a more encomiastic commemoration.

While waiting for proofs in Rome, Fitzgerald wrote to Maxwell Perkins: 'Strange to say, my notion of Gatsby's vagueness was O.K. . . . *I myself didn't know what Gatsby looked like or was engaged in* . . . Anyhow after careful searching of the files (of a man's mind here) . . . I know Gatsby better than I know my own child. My first instinct was to let him go and have Tom Buchanan dominate the book . . . but Gatsby sticks in my heart. I had him for a while, then lost him, and now I know I have him again' (*circa* 20 December 1924).[12] And in a letter to John Peale Bishop a little later: 'You are right about Gatsby being blurred and patchy. I never at any one time saw him clear myself' (9 August 1925).[13] This is all exactly right. Nick has Gatsby, loses him, then has him again in a different way. More generally, now you see Gatsby, now you don't. On more than one occasion Nick looks for Gatsby, only to find him 'not there', and, of course, he does not even appear until chapter three (a quarter of the way into the book) and disappears before the end. In a way Tom *does* dominate the book; he dominates everyone and every thing, and Nick drinks with him before he meets Gatsby and shakes his hand after Gatsby's death. Buchanans, as a type, go on for ever, survive everything. Gatsby, for all his 'connections', is frailer and more vulnerable. And, in a more general epistemological sense he is and remains (for us the readers too) vague as to what he is and what he does. As we have seen, Fitzgerald deliberately contributed to his vagueness by cutting out too explicit dialogue, and this was not a matter of, as it were, withholding information in the interests of mystification; that strange hint of ontological insubstantiality about him is absolutely crucial. Of a look that passes over Gatsby's face while Tom is insulting him Nick states that it was 'definitely unfamiliar and vaguely recognizable'. Notice the perfection, for suggestivity, of the apparent oxymorons: the recognisability is vague, but the unfamiliarity is definite. Gatsby looms and fades, sharpens and blurs. Now you see him, you think; and now you don't, you are almost sure. This wonderfully maintained 'vagueness' is better than 'O.K.': it is an essential part of the magic of the book. For, after even the harshest scrutiny of the figure of Gatsby – which might reduce him to a sentimental roughneck, a criminal with a soppy dream, a ruthless social climber determined to buy himself a very classy piece of female goods – Gatsby does, somehow, stick in the heart.

At times, when he does appear, he reminds people of a popular journal or an advertisement. 'My incredulity was submerged in fascination now; it was like skimming hastily through a dozen magazines,' writes Nick of his response to Gatsby's life story. 'You resemble the advertisement of the man . . . You know the advertisement of the man – '. Daisy doesn't finish her sentence. Presumably he looks like the man in any number of advertisements. (Jordan Baker is said to look like a 'good illustration': the effects are everywhere.) In today's parlance we might say that he sometimes strikes people as being all 'simulacra'. Advertising was booming in the America of the Twenties. Gatsby is very much a child of his culture and equips and surrounds himself with all the most fashionable and flamboyant commodities, from shirts to cars. The 'formal note' with the signature in a 'majestic hand' with which he first announces himself to Nick is the first sign of his careful self-fashioning (and observe how quick Nick is to pick up hints of regality in this democratic republic). In a way his ostentatious house and expensive parties are an elaborate advertising display designed to impress Daisy. His certainty that he can repeat the past, his confidence that he can 'fix everything just the way it was', owes a lot to this advertising culture. (In the book I have referred to Richard Godden details how Henry Ford, in 1922, recreated his old home exactly as it had been sixty years earlier. 'In the marketplace, time is reversible,' Godden comments.)[14] In reality, of course, his dream founders on his impossible insistence that time can be not only reversed but erased. He has lost Daisy (and dream) from the moment he tries to make her tell Tom that she had never loved him, 'and it's all wiped out forever'. You can wipe away graffiti and stray shaving soap but not time; time is the one thing Gatsby cannot 'fix'. He cannot even handle it very well: in the central chapter of the book (five), when he meets Daisy again, he very nearly knocks over a clock. This clock happens to be 'defunct', which perhaps makes it a fitting adjunct and material witness to the attempt he is making to stop time, but elsewhere the clocks are ticking like mad. (There is an unusually large number of time words in the novel – over four hundred.) It is no wonder that he looks at Daisy's child with surprise: 'I don't think he had ever really believed in its existence before.' And Tom has only to cite the times and places of his sexual possession of Daisy, and Gatsby is pretty well done for. I should say 'Gatsby' – '"Jay Gatsby" had broken up like glass against Tom's hard malice, and the long secret extravaganza was played out.' His constructed identity, the simulacrum, which has been buoyed up and motivated by the cherished notion of a recapturable, repurchasable, Daisy *and* an erasable time, is in ruins. Daisy stays bought.

So is 'great' an irony or a wishful hyperbole that recoils on itself? Is the whole work the self-consoling hankey-pankey of a miserable failure of a bachelor, who invents a 'gorgeous' figure to compensate for the 'dismal' Middle West to which he has retreated – Nick's fakery of Gatsby's fakery? This cannot be all there is to it, although I believe there are those who think so. To the extent that it *is* this, we know it from Nick himself. Just as Gatsby occasionally shows him the white thread of the deceptive stitch, so Nick does to the attentive reader. There is more to Gatsby than the shivered glass of his custom-made identity after his shattering encounter with Tom's 'rock' at its most obdurate, something that in the end he inadequately articulates and imperfectly incarnates but is indeed part of the 'essence' of that self-inventing, self-parented nation of which he is at once so remarkable and so representative a product. We may call it, with Nick, 'an extraordinary gift for hope, a romantic readiness', an adherence to, or gesturing towards, a conviction or a feeling that there must be something more to life than the 'corruption' that surrounds and attends Gatsby, the appetitive, self-gratifying, sheer, mere materiality in which the Buchanans are so heedlessly at home. That this hope takes the form of a romantic dream or impossible obsession, which is at once doomed and unrealisable, does not necessarily invalidate the need or desire that nourished it. If 'the colossal vitality of his illusion' does finally go 'beyond everything', and thus must perforce be disappointed and come to naught, it does not mean that the devitalising lifelessness that may result from determined disillusion necessarily offers the better way. It does mean that there is a special kind of sadness to the book. For there is pathos (as well as, if you like, puerility) about Gatsby – his aura of loneliness and isolation, the emptiness that seems to flow from his house, his piles of 'beautiful shirts', his always unappreciated generosity (no thanks for covering for Daisy, which costs him his life), his mean death and unattended funeral. And to the extent that Gatsby – 'Gatsby' – is excessive, foolish and foredoomed, so, the whole book suggests, is America.

Not long after the novel was published Fitzgerald wrote to Marya Mannes: 'America's greatest promise is that something is going to happen, and after a while you get tired of waiting because nothing happens to people except that they grow old, and nothing happens to American art because America is the story of the moon that never rose' (October 1925).[15] When the moon famously *does* rise at the end of

The Great Gatsby, it prompts one of the most famous paragraphs in American literature:

the inessential houses began to melt away until gradually I became aware of the old island here that flowered once for Dutch sailors' eyes – a fresh, green breast of the new world. Its vanished trees, the trees that had made way for Gatsby's house, had once pandered in whispers to the last and greatest of human dreams; for a transitory enchanted moment man must have held his breath in the presence of this continent, compelled into *an aesthetic contemplation he neither understood nor desired*, face to face for the last time in history with something commensurate to his capacity for wonder. (my italics)

This passage was originally at the end of chapter one until, with another of those unerring corrections, Fitzgerald moved it to the end, the dusk of the narrative where its crepuscular tone is so fitting. The original early positioning indicates that the book was always going to be an elegy, pervaded with a sense of something muffed, something lost – a chance missed, a dream doomed. The 'green breast of the new world', the pap of a possible new life, might have offered an inexhaustible supply of the 'milk of wonder'. But whatever the sailors came for – all the sailors, from Puritans to pirates – they came not to wonder at America but rather, in various ways, to 'rape' it, to use William Carlos Williams's metaphor for the various and multiple spoliations of the American land. The green breast of the new world has given way, as an image, to the shocking spectacle of Myrtle's left breast, 'swinging loose like a flap' after the road accident. Fitzgerald was very insistent about retaining this spectacle: 'I *want* Myrtle Wilson's breast ripped off – it's exactly the thing, I think' (to Maxwell Perkins, 24 January 1925).[16] Fitzgerald knows, of course, exactly what he is doing. He *wants* to show America desecrated, mutilated, violated. Whatever the might-have-beens of the new world – and the incoherent, hopeful yet hopeless reachings out of a Gatsby perhaps offer a vague, vestigial and distorted hint of a kind of gladly accepted 'capacity for wonder', desired if not fully understood, that might have made something better out of the great last chance that was America – America has contrived to make itself utterly accidental and accident-prone. Of what might have been a Wonderland (a theme endemic to American literature suggests) we have made a wasteland.

Fitzgerald knew T. S. Eliot's poem of that name pretty much by heart, and of course he created his own wasteland in the valley of ashes (indeed, one title he considered for the novel was *Among the Ash Heaps and Millionaires*): 'a fantastic farm where ashes grow like wheat into ridges and hills and grotesque gardens; where ashes take the forms of houses and chimneys and, finally, with a transcendent effort, of ash-grey men, who move dimly and already crumbling through the powdery air. Occasionally a line of grey cars crawls along an invisible track, gives out a ghastly creak, and comes to rest.' 'Transcendent' is a peculiarly loaded word in America, and it is used here with dark irony. This is negative transcendence, a travesty, the very reverse of what Emerson and his friends had hoped for America, with the land actually producing, *growing*, ashes. Fitzgerald was neither the first nor the last American writer to have an entropic vision of America – the great agrarian continent turning itself into some sort of terminal rubbish heap or wasteland, where, with ultimate perversity, the only thing that grows is death.

Fitzgerald was canny enough to associate this process with the exponential spread of the automobile. As already noted, the book is full of cars, bad driving and accidents, and together they conspire to kill not only people but the land itself. Bad driver Jordan Baker's very name is composed of the brand names of two automobiles. Aptly, Fitzgerald places the garage – Wilson's garage, but let us say the generic garage – at the heart of the valley of ashes that it is producing. Henry Adams, who was the first American writer to employ the word 'entropy' to describe the future he foresaw, related this predicted accelerating entropy to the rapid increase of new discoveries of sources of energy and power, coupled with a decrease in the human ability to control it. In his *Education* he wrote:

Power leaped from every atom, and enough of it to supply the stellar universe showed itself running to waste at every pore of matter. Man could no longer hold it off. Forces grasped his wrists and flung him about as though he had hold of a live wire or a runaway automobile; which was very nearly the exact truth for the purposes of an elderly and timid single gentleman in Paris, who never drove down the Champs Elysées without expecting an accident and commonly witnessing one; or found himself in the neighbourhood of an official without calculating the chances of a bomb. So long as the rates of progress held good, these bombs would double in number and force every ten years.[17]

Fitzgerald chose to double up on the automobile accidents. A contemporary writer might prefer to go for bombs.

Overlooking, though not overseeing, the valley of ashes are, of course, the eyes of Doctor T. J. Eckleburg.

The eyes of Doctor T. J. Eckleburg are blue and gigantic – their retinas are one yard high. They look out of no face, but, instead, from a pair of enormous yellow spectacles which pass over a non-existent nose. Evidently some wild wag of an oculist set them there to fatten his practice in the borough of Queens, and then sank down himself into eternal blindness, or forgot them and moved away. But his eyes, dimmed a little by many paintless days, under sun and rain, brood on over the solemn dumping ground.

André le Vot has most sensitively traced the various subtle ways in which Fitzgerald deploys colours, above all blue and yellow. As le Vot points out, blue is water, the sky, twilight, cool, restful, inviting. Yellow is wheat, sunshine and fertility but also whisky, gold (lucre) and dead, combustible straw, and is thus ambiguous, for what seems attractive and warm may turn combustible, violent, too hot. (Tom is 'straw-haired'.) Ideally the two colours, and all they evoke, should be in harmony with each other, as in Nick's odd but suggestive phrase 'the blue honey of the Mediterranean'. But in this book they seem to drift apart and tend to opposition. Misleadingly, perhaps, Gatsby's car is yellow (though it is part of the dubiety that surrounds him that people disagree about the colour: one describes it as cream-coloured, another light green – like its owner, it appears differently in different lights), while Tom's convertible is blue. But, appropriately, they exchange cars, at Tom's insistence, when their struggle over Daisy heads for climax and show-down.

To return to Doctor T. J. Eckleburg, to the extent that his blue eyes are fading and 'dimming a little' while the yellow spectacles persist untarnished, this may intimate, as le Vot suggests, 'a withering of spiritual power and a corresponding increase in materialism'.[18] Spectacles are designed to help you to see better. But see what? See how? For Nick, after Gatsby's death, 'the East was haunted . . . distorted beyond my eyes' power of correction', so he retreats (one might be tempted to say 'regresses') back home which at the start of his narrative seemed like 'the ragged edge of the universe' but is now again, perhaps, 'the warm centre of the world'. The 'wild wag oculist' whom Nick posits and who has also absented himself from the area, may be an allusion to a God who should oversee the world but who has become a *deus absconditus*, or who no longer cares to turn his eyes on man in the wasteland he has made, or who may simply be dead, having left behind what man hath made – an advertisement. After the accident Michaelis is shocked to see that while Wilson is invoking God, he is looking at the eyes of Doctor T. J. Eckleburg. ' "God sees everything," repeated Wilson. "That's an advertisement," Michaelis assured him.'

Whatever may have been the religious intentions and aspirations of the original Puritan settlers, the landscape is now dominated entirely by commercial and material considerations. As we have seen, Gatsby lives in and through an advertising world and is something of a composite advertisement himself. The question, perhaps, is whether his 'gestures', which result from and express, thinks Nick, 'some heightened sensitivity to the promises of life', are indicative of an inchoate form of a 'piety' all his own.

When Nick says that the East is 'haunted for me like that, distorted beyond my eyes' power of correction', 'that' refers to 'a night scene by El Greco'. El Greco is famous for his elongations and what some might call his feverish exaggerations. Since by Nick's own confession his vision of what happened is uncorrected and uncorrectable, we should perhaps take the hint, intended or not, that he has given us an El Greco-ish version – heightened, enlarged, excitably glorified – of Gatsby and what surrounded him. But El Greco, like Vermeer, whom we may regard as much less inclined to distortion than El Greco (indeed, as painting with as miraculously a correct vision as is possible to attain) is an artist, and all art involves distortion – selection, interpretation, amplification. It could be argued that distortion is inseparable from representation. Whatever the motivation for Nick's writing, even if it was simply a 'winter dream' to occupy and console him in the dismal fastnesses of the Middle West, he has still delivered a work of art; and there can never be any unravelling of the motives that lie behind the making of a work of art.

It is Fitzgerald's book, of course, and in showing us Nick working on the problems and pitfalls involved in 'seeing' his material, working out his way of 'writing' Gatsby, both faking and fêting him, Fitzgerald added a whole new dimension to his work. Henry James once wrote: 'There is the story of one's hero, and then, thanks to the intimate connexion of things, the story of one's story itself.'[19] In giving us not only the story of Gatsby but the story of Nick trying to write that story, Fitzgerald confronts no less a problem than what might be involved, what might be at stake, in trying to see, and *write*, America itself. The result is short (those inspired excisions), deceptively simple, with something of the lean yet pregnant economy of a parable (for a book so explicitly rooted in the Twenties, it contains surprisingly little in the way of sociological or anthropological data). It is word-perfect and inexhaustible. *The Great Gatsby* is, I believe, the most perfectly crafted work of fiction to have come out of America.

When Nick attends his first party at Gatsby's mansion he is 'on guard against its spectroscopic gaiety': he finds some things 'graceless', others 'vacuous'. After two glasses of champagne 'the scene had changed before my eyes into something significant, elemental, and profound'. There is a touch of self-mockery in the knowing exaggeration (if that's all it takes . . .). A critic such as Richard Godden might say that the champagne is pretty flat (his chapter on the novel is entitled 'Glamour on the Turn'), but this, I think, is to miss something of the undoubted magic of the book and its irreducible polyvalency. Call it undecidability. Some days the car is yellow; on others it looks light green. At times Gatsby may stick in your throat as well as your heart. Perhaps he is like the books in his library: 'absolutely real' where you most expect him to be fake, but finally absolutely unreadable because his inner pages are uncut.

But what do you want?

What do you expect?

NOTES

1 F. Scott Fitzgerald, *The Letters of F. Scott Fitzgerald*, ed. Andrew Turnbull (London: The Bodley Head, 1964), p. 169.
2 *Petronius*, tr. Michael Heseltine (London: William Heinemann Ltd, 1956), p. 39.
3 Ibid.
4. Ibid., pp. 49–50.
5 Fitzgerald, *Letters*, p. 509.
6 André Le Vot, *F. Scott Fitzgerald: A Biography* (London: Allen Lane, 1983), p. 27.
7 Henry James, *Literary Criticism: European Writers and the Prefaces* (New York: Library of America, 1984), p. 1259.
8 Ralph Waldo Emerson, *Essays and Lectures* (New York: Library of America, 1983), p. 7.
9 Thomas Pynchon, *The Crying of Lot 49* (London: Picador, 1979), p. 126.
10 Richard Godden, *Fictions of Capital: The American Novel from James to Mailer* (Cambridge: Cambridge University Press, 1990), p. 92.
11 Henry James, *The American Scene* (London: Penguin Books, 1994), p. 336.
12 Fitzgerald, *Letters*, pp. 172–3.
13 Ibid., p. 358.
14 Godden, *Fictions of Capital*, p. 89.
15 Fitzgerald, *Letters*, p. 488.
16 Ibid., p. 175.
17 Henry Adams, *The Education of Henry Adams* (London: Penguin Books, 1995), p. 467.
18 Le Vot, *F. Scott Fitzgerald*, p. 156.
19 James, *Literary Criticism*, p. 1309.

CHAPTER 11

Don DeLillo and 'the American mystery':
Underworld

The true underground is where the power flows. That's the best-kept secret of our time . . . The presidents and prime ministers are the ones who make the underground deals and speak the true underground idiom. The corporations. The military. The banks. This is the underground network. This is where it happens. Power flows under the surface, far beneath the level you and I live on. This is where the laws are broken, way down under, far beneath the speed freaks and cutters of smack.

DeLillo, *Great Jones Street*

'All plots tend to move deathward. This is the nature of plots. Political plots, terrorist plots, lovers' plots, narrative plots, plots that are part of children's games. We edge nearer death every time we plot. It is like a contract that all must sign, the plotters as well as those who are the targets of the plot.'
   Is this true? Why did I say it? What does it mean?

DeLillo, *White Noise*

> 'You think the stories are true?'
> 'No,' Eric said.
> 'Then why do you spread them?'
> 'For the tone of course.'
> 'For the edge.'
> 'For the edge. The bite. The existential burn.'

DeLillo, *Underworld*

Some years ago – it must be about a dozen – I was sitting in an airport, flipping through *Time* magazine, and I came across a brief news item to the effect that the American writer, Don DeLillo, was working on a novel about the Kennedy assassination. My heart, as they say, sank. I had been reading DeLillo's novels with growing admiration and excitement – but how could even he, for all his wonderfully strange ways of getting at what he generically calls 'the American mystery' (for which read 'the mystery of America'), avoid being beset and distracted by all the clichés of paranoia and conspiracy theory which swarmed to the event as flies to honey. I need not, of course, have worried. *Libra* is a triumph; all the possible pitfalls, as I see it, brilliantly by-passed or side-stepped. Let me remind you of his concluding 'Author's Note':

> In a case in which rumors, facts, suspicions, official subterfuge, conflicting sets of evidence and a dozen labyrinthine theories all mingle, sometimes indistinguishably, it may seem to some that a work of fiction is one more gloom in a chronicle of unknowing.
>
> But because this book makes no claim to literal truth, because it is only itself, apart and complete, readers may find refuge here – a way of thinking about assassination without being constrained by half-facts or overwhelmed by possibilities, by the tide of speculation that widens with the years.

You may remember the concluding meditation of Nicholas Branch, the retired CIA analyst, hired to write a secret history of the assassination (and thus, in part, a DeLillo stand-in):

> If we are on the outside, we assume a conspiracy is the perfect working of a scheme. Silent nameless men with unadorned hearts. A conspiracy is everything that ordinary life is not. It's the inside game, cold, sure, undistracted, forever closed off to us . . . All conspiracies are the same taut story of men who find coherence in some criminal act.
>
> But maybe not. Nicholas Branch thinks he knows better. He has learned enough about the days and months preceding November 22, and enough about the twenty-second itself, to reach a determination that the conspiracy against the President was a rambling affair that succeeded in the short term due mainly to chance. Deft men and fools, ambivalence and fixed will and what the weather was like.

Amidst swamps of temptations, and against pretty high odds, DeLillo keeps his poise, not to say his sanity, and does not succumb to the darkly glamorous seductiveness of the murderously appealing material he is handling. But by the time of his next novel, *Mao II*, something has gone wrong.

From a recent *New Yorker* profile by David Remnick, we learn that DeLillo has for a long time been interested in a passage in John Cheever's journals where he wrote, after a ballgame at Shea Stadium: 'The task of the American writer is not to describe the misgivings of a woman taken in adultery as she looks out of the window at the rain but to describe 400 people under the lights reaching for a foul ball . . . The faint thunder as 10,000 people, at the bottom of the eighth, head for the exits. The sense of moral judgments embodied in a migratory vastness.'[1] So – no more pottering about with old Flaubert, groping for his miserable *mot juste*; but off to the ballgame with Whitman, and 'the city's ceaseless crowd' in which Whitman rejoiced (as he rejoiced in baseball: 'It's our game: that's the chief fact in connection with it: America's game: has the snap, go, fling, of the American atmosphere'). DeLillo has long been fascinated by crowds (and Elias Canetti's *Crowds and Power*) – at least since *Great Jones Street* ('The people. The crowd. The audience. The fans. The followers.') – so perhaps it is not surprising that he starts *Mao II*, very arrestingly, with a powerful description of the vast undifferentiated horde of a Moonie mass wedding at Yankee Stadium. (Also not surprising that he starts *Underworld* with a swirling, hundred-eyed account of a famous baseball game.) The crowd motif is taken up with references to the Hillsborough football disaster and Khomeini's funeral, with Mao's Chinese millions milling in the background. 'The future belongs to crowds' – so the introductory section blankly, bleakly concludes.

So much might be prophecy, or warning, or simply downhearted sociology; but, of itself, it does not generate narrative. Accordingly we have some (concluding, as it turns out) episodes from the life of an intensely reclusive writer named Bill Gray – who incorporates, I imagine, a glance at J. D. Salinger, a nod to Thomas Pynchon, and perhaps a wink from DeLillo himself ('When I read Bill I think of photographs of tract houses at the edge of the desert. There's an incidental menace.' That 'incidental menace' fits; and the desert features in nearly all of DeLillo's novels as a sort of 'end zone' of meaning – silent, non-human, absolute, ultimate). Bill Gray tells us things that DeLillo's fiction has been telling us from the start: 'There's the life and there's the consumer event. Everything around us tends to channel our lives toward some final reality in print or film.' When David Bell sets out on his questing journey in *Americana* looking for origins, he isn't sure if he is discovering his real, unmediated family and country, or just so much print and film. America – or Americana? What kind of 'real' life people can shape for themselves in a mediated, consumer culture swamped in images and information, is an abiding concern. But Bill Gray also has some things to say about the novel and the novelist which bear thinking about.

The novel used to feed our search for meaning. Quoting Bill. It was the great secular transcendence. The Latin mass of language, character, occasional new truth. But our desperation has led us toward something larger and darker. *So we turn to the news*, which provides an unremitting mood of catastrophe.

This is where we find emotional experience not available elsewhere. We don't need the novel. Quoting Bill. (my italics)

Quoting Bill, not Don. Certainly. But here is David Remnick quoting Don:

I think there's something in people that, perhaps, has shifted. People seem to need news, any kind – bad news, sensationalistic news, overwhelming news. It seems to be that news is a narrative of our time. It has almost replaced the novel, replaced discourse between people. It replaced families. It replaced a slower, more carefully assembled way of communicating, a more personal way of communicating.[2]

When Bill Gray is on a ship bound for Lebanon, he appreciates the families crowded on deck, together making 'the melodious traffic of a culture'. In *The Names*, James Axton relishes the gregarious, sociable street life in Athens.

People everywhere are absorbed in conversation. Seated under trees, under striped canopies in squares, they bend together over food and drink . . . Conversation is life, language is the deepest thing . . . Every conversation is a shared narrative, a thing that surges forward, too dense to allow space for the unspoken, the sterile. The talk is unconditional, the participants drawn in completely.

   This is a way of speaking that takes such pure joy in its own openness and ardor that we begin to feel these people are discussing language itself.

So to the concluding paragraph of the novel (prior to the Epilogue), at the Parthenon:

People come through the gateway, people in streams and clusters, in mass assemblies. No one seems to be alone. This is a place to enter in crowds, seek company and talk. Everyone is talking. I move past the scaffolding and walk down the steps, hearing one language after another, rich, harsh, mysterious, strong. This is what we bring to the temple, not prayer or chant or slaugh-tered rams. Our offering is language.

Clearly this kind of crowd, and this way of conversing are, alike, admir-able and much to be desired. But it is not entirely churlish to point out that the American onlookers cannot be assumed to have under-stood a word that was spoken. This is communicating community as exotic (and idealised) spectacle. Or perhaps we might say that it is like a Catholic mass, where it doesn't matter to the experience if the com-municants do not understand the Latin words. The point here is that back in DeLillo's America where people *do* understand the words, there is precious little communicating – or communing. 'Discourse between people' has gone; 'families' have gone; as a result, following DeLillo's line of thinking, the novel has become, effectively, redundant. 'So we turn to the news' – which is just what DeLillo has done in *Underworld*.

I'll come back to this, but I want to call on some more of Bill's pronouncements about the novelist.

There's a curious knot that binds novelists and terrorists . . . Years ago I used to think it was possible for a novelist to alter the inner life of the culture. Now bomb-makers and gunmen have taken that territory. They make raids on human consciousness. What writers used to do before we were all incorporated . . . What terrorists gain, novelists lose. The degree to which they influence mass consciousness is the extent of our decline as shapers of sensibility and thought. The danger they represent equals our own failure to be dangerous . . . Beckett is the last writer to shape the way we think and see. After him, the major work involves midair explosions and crumbled buildings. This is the new tragic narrative.

Quoting Bill – I know. But I feel that DeLillo is standing dangerously close to him. *Libra* was only the culmination of a long-standing – and perfectly legitimate – fascination with terrorism and terrorists (just such an interest gave us *The Secret Agent* and *Under Western Eyes*); but Bill's proposition that the novelist once was a fully operative terrorist who now, in his neutered state, has ceded his ground to real terrorists, is, when thought about, ridiculous. Henry James may be said, I would suppose, to have 'altered the inner life of the culture', yet it would be absurd to make of him even a metaphorical terrorist. In *Americana* the (failed) writer, Brand, wants to write a novel that will 'detonate in the gut of America like a fiery bacterial bombshell'. But he didn't; and anyway, it wouldn't. This is all metaphor. With much 'Blasting' and fulminating gnashing of teeth, Wyndham Lewis tried to demolish the difference between literary and literal terrorism; and, rebarbatively enough, failed. Perhaps DeLillo might consider giving him a careful, pensive read. And to suggest that midair explosions and crumbling walls are the novels *de nos jours* is, really, mad if meant seriously (silly if not). Owen Brademas, seemingly privileged as wise in *The Names*, aphoristically muses: 'In this century the writer has carried on a conversation with madness. We might almost say of the twentieth-century writer that he aspires to madness.' To the real, loony, Moonie, Khomeini, Red Guard thing? Aspire to that? Come now.

Bill Gray betakes himself to the Middle East, now engaged in some of that clandestine activity so important in DeLillo's fiction. (In a *Rolling*

Stone article of 1983 DeLillo suggested that the great leaps in science and technology had helped to create a kind of 'clandestine mentality. We all go underground to some extent. In an era of the massive codification and storage of data, we are all keepers and yielders of secrets.'[3] It is the mentality of many of his characters.) But he succumbs to a 'helpless sense that he was fading into thinness and distance'. So he does – and so does the novel. It isn't going anywhere, so it just peters out – as they used to say when a vein of ore came to an end. The best of novelists can produce a disappointing book (Pynchon gave us *Vineland*), and it would be gross to go on belaboring *Mao II*. But I do think the book opens up certain problems which become rather important in *Underworld*, and in this connection I fear I must make a final negative comment.

An ancillary character named Karen (an ex-Moonie) figures in the book. Drifting around New York, she comes upon a 'tent city' in a park. It is a shantytown abode of the down-and-outs, the thrownaways, the insulted and the injured, the despised and rejected – the human junk of the modern city. We get it itemised. 'There was a bandshell with bedding on the stage, a few bodies stirring, a lump of inert bedding suddenly wriggling upward and there's a man on his knees coughing blood . . . Stringy blood looping from his mouth.' And so on. Karen goes into a nearby tenement. 'In the loft she went through many books of photographs, amazed at the suffering she found. Famine, fire, riot, war. These were the never ceasing subjects . . . It was suffering through and through.' A voice says 'It's just like Beirut.' At the end, a photographer is driving through the real Beirut. 'The streets run with images . . . The placards get bigger as the car moves into deeply cramped spaces, into many offending smells, open sewers, rubber burning, a dog all ribs and tongue and lying still and gleaming with green flies.' No one doubts the reality of unspeakable suffering and squalor; but just heaping it up in a novel in this way seems a bit easy, even opportunistic, and, by the same token, slightly distasteful. It begins to read like a form of atrocity tourism. I suppose that if you think that people 'need bad news' and 'don't need the novel', then you may as well give them lists of horrors to sup on. But, even then, it doesn't work like 'news'. A direct report from Beirut by Robert Fisk of the London *Independent* has far more impact than anything in DeLillo's novel. But 'news' is what we get in *Underworld*.

News is, of course, 'bad news, sensationalistic news, overwhelming news'; and, in the relative absence of significant characters or narrative plot (matters to which I will return), the book presents us with a string of more or less sensationalist news items or crises from 1951 to, presumably, the present day – as another way of getting at 'the American mystery'. The shock of Sputnik, the Cuban missile crisis, the Kennedy assassination, the Madison anti-Vietnam riot, civil rights marches and police brutality, the midair explosion of the Challenger space shuttle, the Texas Highway murders, the great New York blackout, J. Edgar Hoover, AIDS, and so on – and over everything the shadow of 'the bomb' ('they had brought something into the world that out-imagined the mind' – again, it seems as if the novelist is ceding his imaginative rights to a superior power). There is also a certain amount of atrocity tourism – 'They saw a prostitute whose silicone breast had leaked, ruptured and finally exploded one day, sending a polymer whiplash across the face of the man on top of her . . . They saw a man who'd cut his eyeball out of its socket because it contained a satanic symbol.' Near the end, a visit to a 'Museum of Misshapens' in Russia, which houses damaged fetuses and victims of radiation from near the early test sites, allows DeLillo to present us with a gallery of grotesques ('there is the cyclops. The eye centered, the ears below the chin, the mouth completely missing. Brain is also missing'), and a clinic full of 'disfigurations, leukemias, thyroid cancers, immune systems that do not function'. I don't know if such a place exists, but in DeLillo's dark world it seems plausible. And that's the agenda. Bad news, and 'suffering through and through'.

As I am sure readers know, DeLillo presents his 'news' items in a roughly reverse order. After the opening ballgame in 1951, there are six sections which run – Spring 1992; Mid 1980s to early 1990s; Spring 1978; Summer 1974; Selected Fragments Public and Private in 1950s and 1960s (twenty-one of these, discontinuous and unrelated); Fall 1951 to Summer 1952; and an Epilogue with a more or less present-day – or timeless – feel to it. Two things to say about this. Of course novelists can and often should disrupt and rearrange unilinear chronology – think only of the scrambled narrative of Conrad's *Nostromo*. And of course, something is bound to happen if you juxtapose apparently unrelated fragments – you might sense an uncanny similarity, or register an ironic parallelism (Henry in his court; Falstaff in his tavern); or you might experience a shock of cognitive dissonance, or a disorienting sense of incongruity. But in a work of art, unless it is avowedly or manifestly aleatory, you usually feel that the scramblings and wrenched juxtapositionings have some point. Conrad was certainly getting at late Victorian attitudes to history and progress in a very corrosive way. But – it may of course be my obtuseness – I just did not see the point of DeLillo's randomisings. He has admitted to being strongly influenced by the cinematic techniques of Jean-Luc Godard, and in an interview with Tom LeClair, DeLillo said that the cinematic qualities which influenced his writing were 'the strong image, the short ambiguous scene . . . the artificiality, the arbitrary choices of some directors, the cutting and editing'.[4] These qualities are all evident in *Underworld*, and the phrase I would hold on to in particular is 'arbitrary choices'. At the end of the opening account of the ballgame, a drunk is running the bases and leaps into a slide. 'All the fragments of the afternoon collect around his airborne form. Shouts, bat-cracks, full bladders and stray yawns, the sand-grain manyness of things that can't be counted.' In an over eight hundred-page book, you may be sure that DeLillo has quite a go at 'the sand-grain manyness of things', and the sheer voracious energy of his appetitive attention is genuinely impressive. But the fragments do not collect around anything – unless you think that 'Cold War America' will do the gathering-in work of the airborne drunk.

DeLillo must feel, I suppose, that he is assembling some of what he calls 'those distracted events that seemed to mark the inner nature of the age'. Where the novelist can go crucially one better than the news reporter is, presumably, in imaginatively illuminating the 'underground network' of society, intimating the unofficial history of the period, tracing out some of those power flows, 'under the surface, far beneath the level you and I live on'. Surface events may seem random and discrete enough – a ballgame here, an atom-bomb test there – but, ah! what if they are in some way connected? DeLillo's fiction has long concerned itself with what Axton, in *The Names*, calls 'Complex systems, endless connections', and that last word is used to exhaustion in *Underworld*. Indeed it would not be entirely facetious to say that if anything does connect the fragments of American 'manyness' that pack the book, it is the word *connection*. Far-flung listeners to the ballgame commentary are 'connected by the pulsing voice on the radio'; 'The Jesuits taught me to examine things for second meanings and connections'; 'technology . . . connects you in your well-pressed suit to the things that slip through the world otherwise unperceived'; 'I . . . wrote down all the occult connections that seemed to lead to thirteen'; 'the feel of a baseball in your hand, going back a while, connecting many things'; 'They sensed there was a connection between this game and some staggering event that might take place on the other side of the world' (There you are!); 'she drew News and Rumors and Catastrophes into the spotless cotton pores of her habit and veil. All the connections intact' (this is a nun); ' "Knowing what we know." "What do we know?" Simms said . . . "That everything's connected," Jesse said.' The baseball which, as I am sure you know, 'passes through' the novel from owner to owner, is said to make 'connections'. 'He was surrounded by enemies. Not enemies but connections, a network of things and people'; 'He felt he'd glimpsed some horrific system of connections in which you can't tell the difference between one thing and another'; 'Because everything connects in the end, or only seems to, or seems to only because it does.' 'Find the links. It's all linked' (that's J. Edgar Hoover). Then, finally, on the world wide web: 'There is no space or time out there, or in here, or wherever she is. There are only connections. Everything is connected . . . Everything is connected in the end.' There is lots more about 'undivinable patterns'; 'something . . . saying terrible things about forces beyond your control'; 'underground plots', not to mention a Conspiracy Theory Cafe; and – of course – paranoia. 'There's genuine paranoia. That's the only genuine anything I can see here.' 'He thought of the photograph of Nixon and wondered if the state had taken on the paranoia of the individual or was it the other way around?'; 'Paranoid. Now he knew what it meant, this word that was bandied and bruited so easily, and he sensed the connections being made around him, all the objects and shaped silhouettes and levels of knowledge – not knowledge exactly but insidious intent. But not that either – some deeper meaning that existed solely to keep him from knowing what it was.' There are so many forms and manifestations of paranoid consciousness (or paranoid voices) in this novel that I abandoned my list of examples since it promised to be not much shorter than the book itself. It may be claimed that paranoia is as American as violence and apple pie (as I believe they used to say), but in the case of *Underworld* it gives the book a rather wearingly uniform paranoid texture. Even figures who say they aren't paranoid, pretend to be. This is the significance of my third epigraph. Matt and Eric do secret underground work at a missile site, and Eric enjoys spreading 'astounding rumours' about terrible things happening to workers at the Nevada Test Site who lived 'downwind' of the aboveground shots and were exposed to fallout: 'here and there a kid with a missing limb or whatnot. And a healthy woman that goes to wash her hair and it all comes out in her hands . . . Old Testament outbreaks of great red boils . . . And coughing up handfuls of blood. You look in your cupped hands and you see a pint of radded blood.'

'You think the stories are true?'
'No,' Eric said.
'Then why do you spread them?'
'For the tone, of course.'
'For the edge.'
'For the edge. The bite. The existential burn.'

This sounds like playing at dread, thereby devaluing it; and you may feel that it would be better kept for the real thing. Now it may be reprehensible on my part, but in Eric's answers I hear DeLillo. It certainly gives his work its 'tone', ever alert to hints of 'insidious intent'; but finally the paranoia comes to seem factitious and manufactured, we weary at the iterated insistence on never-explained 'connections', and the 'existential burn' fades.

At the risk of repeating what may have been already endlessly pointed out, in all this DeLillo is engaged in a prolonged and repetitious quoting, or reworking, of Pynchon (for whose work he has stated his admiration). Just to remind you – in *Gravity's Rainbow* Pynchon diagnosed two dominant states of mind – paranoia and anti-paranoia. Paranoia is, in terms of the book, 'nothing less than the onset, the leading edge of the discovery that everything is connected, everything in the Creation, a secondary illumination – not yet blindingly one, but connected'. Of course, everything depends on the nature of the connection, the intention revealed in the pattern; and just what it is that may connect everything in Pynchon's world is what worries his main characters, like Slothrop. Paranoia is also related to the Puritan obsession with seeing signs in everything, particularly signs of an angry God. Pynchon makes the connection clear by referring to 'a Puritan reflex of seeking other orders behind the visible, also known as paranoia'. The opposite state of mind is anti-paranoia, 'where nothing is connected to anything, a condition not many of us can bear for long'. As figures move between the System and the Zone, they oscillate between paranoia and anti-paranoia, shifting from a seething blank of unmeaning to the sinister apparent legibility of an unconsoling labyrinthine pattern or plot. In *V.* these two dispositions of mind are embodied in Stencil and Benny Profane, respectively (and behind them are those crucially generative figures for the western novel – Don Quixote and Sancho Panza). And there is the poignant figure of Oedipa Maas at the end of *The Crying of Lot 49*: 'Either Oedipa in the orbiting ecstasy of a true paranoia, or a real Tristero. For there either was some Tristero beyond the appearance of the legacy of America, or there was just America and if there was just America then it seemed the only way she could continue, and manage to be at all relevant, was as an alien, unfurrowed, assumed full circle into some paranoia.'[5] Pynchon is a truly brilliant and richly imaginative historian and diagnostic analyst of binary, either-or thinking, and its attendant dangers. DeLillo, by contrast, rather bluntly disseminates a vaguely fraught atmosphere of defensive voices, sidelong looks, and intimations of impending eeriness. And, crucially, *Underworld* has no Tristero.

There is one character in *Underworld* who stoutly insists that he is free of all paranoid delusions. 'I lived responsibly in the real. I didn't accept this business of life as a fiction . . . I hewed to the texture of collective knowledge, took faith from the solid and availing stuff of our experience . . . I believed we could know what was happening to us . . . I lived in the real. The only ghosts I let in were local ones.' This is Nick Shay, intermittently a first-person narrator, and effectively the main figure in the book (the last section recreates his Bronx childhood – which must overlap with DeLillo's – and culminates with his shooting a man). But Nick is not your sane, well-rounded, genial empiricist. For a start, the local ghosts loom large, as his brother Matt explains, telling 'how Nick believed their father was taken out to the marshes and shot, and how this became the one plot, the only conspiracy that big brother could believe in. Nick could not afford to succumb to a general distrust . . . Let the culture indulge in cheap conspiracy theories. Nick had the enduring stuff of narrative, the thing that doesn't have to be filled in with speculation and hearsay.' But this 'narrative' is no more securely grounded than the conviction of the man who sees Gorbachev's birthmark as being a map of Latvia and thus a sign of the imminent collapse of the Soviet Union. Nick has simply put all his superstitions into one basket. Welcome to the club, Nick.

But as a character, Nick is just not there at all; and, more to the point, nor does he want to be. Like nearly all DeLillo's characters – call them voices – he seems to aspire to the condition of anonymity. 'He was not completely connected to what he said and this put an odd and dicey calm in his remarks.' This is said of a character in *Mao II*, but it applies to Nick, indeed across the board. Another figure in *Mao II* says: 'If you've got the language of being smart, you'll never catch a cold or get a parking ticket or die', and defensive 'smart language' is what Nick talks. It is a form of cultivated self-alienation, and is common in DeLillo's world. Lyle is one of the players in *Players*, and there is 'a formality about his movements, a tiller-distinct precision' which preserves a 'distance he's perfected'. To keep himself at arm's length he engages in tough-guy routines at work. As does Nick. 'I made breathy gutter threats from the side of my mouth . . . Or I picked up the phone in the middle of a meeting and pretended to arrange the maiming of a colleague.' Even, perhaps especially, when he has to convey something important – such as the fact that he has killed a man. 'I had a rash inspiration then, unthinking, and did my mobster voice. "In udder words I took him off da calendar."' Invent-and-spread-the-bad-news Eric 'affected a side of the mouth murmur', but that's the way to talk round here. A woman artist has 'a tough mouth, a smart mouth' – pity anyone who hasn't.

'He gave me a flat-eyed look with a nice tightness to it' – compare the supremely 'indifferent' work of Andy Warhol which 'looks off to heaven in a marvelous flat-eyed gaze'. Nice. Marvellous. Rub out the affect. Be 'laconic'; go for 'a honed nonchalance'. Nick reads approvingly in a woman's eyes an 'unwillingness to allow the possibility of surprise'. Henry James spoke of 'our blessed capacity for bewilderment', recognising it as the essential precondition for true learning. Well forget that, all ye who enter DeLillo's world. The thing here is never to be caught off-guard or risk being wrong-footed. Seal yourself off. 'We talked on the phone. In monosyllables. We sounded like spies passing coded messages.' It's as if it is too risky, no – impossible – to speak in a natural, unself-consciously communicating voice, such as Axton imagines he is hearing at the Parthenon. Intimacy seems not a possibility, perhaps not a desirability. Nick's father 'always kept a distance . . . Like he's somewhere else even when he's standing next to you.' Nick is felt by his younger brother to have 'the stature of danger and rage', but this hardly constitutes an identity. He admits 'I've always been a country of one', maintaining 'a measured separation'. He uses an Italian word to explain his temperament to his wife: 'lontananza. Distance or remoteness, sure. But as I use the word, as I interpret it, hard-edged and fine-grained, it's the perfected distance of the gangster, the syndicate mobster – the made man. Once you're a made man, you don't need the constant living influence of sources outside yourself. You're all there. You're made. You're a sturdy Roman wall.' It's not clear that anything in the book would disapprove of, or regret, this aspiration to cultivate just such a hard, self-dehumanising remoteness. Indeed, at the very end Nick says: 'I long for the days of disorder . . . when I was alive on the earth . . . heedless . . . dumb-muscled and angry and real . . . when I walked real streets and did things slap-bang and felt angry and ready all the time, a danger to others and a distant mystery to myself.' Nothing wrong with this, if that's how you feel – but you cannot expect such a limited and self-restrictive presence – or voice – to maintain a thread of human interest as the book trawls through the news archives. (DeLillo has owned to having some of this 'lontananza' himself, intimating that it might have some-thing to do with his having been brought up an Italian Catholic. 'I suppose what I felt for much of this period was a sense of unbelonging, of not being part of any official system. Not as a form of protest but as a kind of separateness. It was an alienation, but not a political alienation, predominantly. It was more spiritual.' By coincidence, I read this in the *Guardian* in a piece by Hugo Young, also brought up a Catholic. 'I also absorbed and relished the sidelong stance, the somewhat distanced obliqueness as regards the established state, which the Catholic inherit-ance conferred.' You feel DeLillo would agree.)

In bringing us voices rather than more traditionally delineated characters, DeLillo is working in an honorable line – *Ulysses* is, after all, a novel of voices. And DeLillo catches and transcribes American voices as no other writer can. You feel that, as with Bill Gray, it makes 'his heart shake to hear these things in the street or bus or dime store, the uninventable poetry, inside the pain, of what people say'. His ear is, indeed, marvellously attuned to the poetry inside the pain – or, as I sometimes feel, the panic inside the plastic – 'of what people say'. For some of the exchanges between voices in his book – flat, deadpan, comic, menacing, weird, cryptic, gnomic, enigmatic, absurd, disturb-ing, moving – you can think of Beckett (or Ionesco, or Pinter) in America. But there is a risk. Speaking specifically of the characters in his *End Zone*, but by implication more generally, DeLillo said they 'have a made-up nature. They are pieces of jargon. They engage in wars of jargon with each other. There is a mechanical element, a kind of fragmented self-consciousness.' Tom LeClair, who conducted the interview, comments: 'without stable identities as sources of actual communication, the characters often seem, like one character's favorite cliché, "commissioned, as it were, by language itself" '.[6] *End Zone* was a seventies novel – the time we were hearing a lot about our being '*serfs du langage*' and 'being spoken' rather than 'speaking'. But DeLillo some-times takes this very far, and a robotic feeling starts to creep in. And in *Underworld*, the many voices start to seem just part of one, tonally invariant, American Voice. There are hundreds of names in the book, but I would be prepared to bet that – apart from the real figures such as Sinatra, Hoover, Lenny Bruce, Mick Jagger – none will be remembered six months after reading the novel. As I find, for instance, are Pynchon's Stencil and Benny Profane; Oedipa Mass (!); Tyrone Slothrop and Roger Mexico; and – I predict – Mason & Dixon. It is not a question of anything so old-fashioned as 'well-rounded characters'; rather I'm thinking of memorably differentiated consciousnesses.

The real protagonist of this novel is 'waste'. I don't know when garbage moved to centre stage in art (as opposed to occasional litter). In a recent exhibition I came across 'Household Trashcan' by Arman dated 1960, and it was, indeed, trash in a Plexiglas box. A book called *Rubbish Theory* by Michael Thompson came out in 1979, and I made use of it in a small book on Pynchon I wrote shortly thereafter. For Pynchon is the real lyricist of rubbish. No one can write as poignantly or elegiacally about, for example, a second-hand car lot, or an old mattress. And what other writer, in the course of a long and moving passage about Advent in wartime, would consider embarking on a curiously moving meditation triggered off by the thought of 'thousands of old used toothpaste tubes' (in *Gravity's Rainbow*)? Many actual rubbish heaps or tips appear in his work – not as symbolic wastelands (though those are there too), but exactly as 'rubbish'. One of Tristero's enigmatic acronyms is W.A.S.T.E., and by extension Pynchon's work is populated by many of the categories (or noncategories) of people whom society regards as 'rubbish', socially useless junk: bums, hoboes, drifters, transients, itinerants, vagrants; the disaffected, the disinherited, the discarded; derelicts, losers, victims – collectively 'the preterite', all those whom, for the Puritans, God in His infinite wisdom has passed over, overlooked. Pynchon forces us to reassess, if not revalue, all those things – and people – we throw away. And DeLillo follows in the master's footsteps.

There is a memorable trash bag in *White Noise*:

An oozing cube of semi-mangled cans, clothes hangers, animal bones and other refuse. The bottles were broken, the cartons flat. Product colors were undiminished in brightness and intensity. Fats, juices and heavy sludges seeped through layers of pressed vegetable matter. I felt like an archaeologist about to sift through a finding of tool fragments and assorted cave trash . . . I unfolded the bag cuffs, released the latch and lifted out the bag. The full stench hit me with shocking force. Was this ours? Did it belong to us? Had we created it? I took the bag out to the garage and emptied it. The compressed bulk sat there like an ironic modern sculpture, massive, squat, mocking . . . I picked through it item by item . . . why did I feel like a household spy? Is garbage so private? Does it glow at the core with personal heat, with signs of one's deepest nature, clues to secret yearnings, humiliating flaws? What habits, fetishes, addictions, inclinations? What solitary acts, behavioral ruts? I found crayon drawings of a figure with full breasts and male genitals . . . I found a banana skin with a tampon inside. Was this the dark underside of consumer consciousness?

Terrific! DeLillo absolutely cresting. But in *Underworld* it all gets rather labored and repetitive.

Nick Shay is professionally involved with waste, which, perhaps not very subtly, allows for heaps of the stuff in the novel. 'My firm was involved in waste. We were waste handlers, waste traders, cosmologists of waste . . . Waste is a religious thing.' He lives it; he thinks it. He and his wife 'saw products as garbage even when they sat gleaming on store shelves, yet unbought'. His workmate Brain goes to a landfill site on Staten Island: 'He looked at all that soaring garbage and knew for the first time what his job was all about . . . To understand all this. To penetrate this secret . . . He saw himself for the first time as a member of an esoteric order.' Another workmate, Big Sims, complains that, now, 'Everything I see is garbage.'

'You see it everywhere because it is everywhere.'
'But I didn't see it before.'
'You're enlightened now. Be grateful.'

Nick's hard-hat humour never lets him down. Perhaps inevitably, there is a former 'garbage guerrilla', now 'garbage hustler', with his theories:

Detwiler said that cities rose on garbage, inch by inch, gaining elevation through the decades as buried debris increased. Garbage always got layered over or pushed to the edges, in a room or in a landscape. But it had its own momentum. It pushed back. It pushed into every space available, dictating construction patterns and altering systems of ritual. And it produced rats and paranoia.

Everywhere, there are abandoned structures and artifacts – 'the kind of human junk that deepens the landscape, makes it sadder and lonelier'; along with any number of Pynchon's 'preterite' – 'wastelings of the lost world, the lost country that exists right here in America'. Perhaps unsurprisingly, there is the contention that 'waste is the secret history, the underhistory' of our society. And Nick maintains that 'what we excrete comes back to consume us'. An unattributed, oracular voice (DeLillo's?) announces at one point: 'All waste defers to shit. All waste aspires to the condition of shit.' Nick's final appearance in the novel is – of course – at a 'waste facility', where he and his grand-daughter have brought 'the unsorted slop, the gut squalor of our lives' for recycling. The light streaming into the shed gives the machines 'a numinous glow', and the moment prompts a final meditation. 'Maybe we feel a reverence for waste, for the redemptive qualities of the things we use and discard. Look how they come back to us, alight with a kind of brave aging.' Clearly there is waste and waste, since we hardly think of 'shit' as coming back to us 'with a kind of brave aging'.

What there is is waste turned into art – 'We took junk and saved it for art', says one artist in the book. And of course, there are the Watts Towers – 'a rambling art that has no category' – visited once by Nick, and once by the artist, Klara. 'She didn't know a thing so rucked in the vernacular could have such an epic quality.'

She didn't know what this was exactly. It was an amusement park, a temple complex and she didn't know what else. A Delhi bazaar and Italian street feast maybe. A place riddled with epiphanies, that's what it was.

And that is what waste primarily is for DeLillo – epiphanic. That, presumably, is why 'waste is a religious thing'.

For a Catholic the Epiphany is the manifestation of Christ to the Magi – by extension any manifestation of a god or demigod. Joyce defined an epiphany as 'a sudden spiritual manifestation', but without a specifically religious implication. It occurs when a configuration of ordinary things suddenly takes on an extra glow of meaning; when, in Emerson's terms, a 'day of facts' suddenly becomes a 'day of diamonds', leaving you with, perhaps, a nonarticulable sense of 'something understood' (George Herbert). A writer can create secular epiphanic moments – Jack Gladney's exploration of his garbage is an epiphany of a rather dark kind. But simply asserting that something is 'riddled with epiphanies' does not, of itself, bring the precious glow. Epiphanies have to be caused rather than insisted on, and *Underworld* suffers somewhat from this failing.

Whether DeLillo still is, or no longer is, a Catholic is none of my business; but he is clearly disinclined to abandon what seems like a proto-religious response to the world. *Mystery* is a much-cherished word in his fiction. 'Mysteries of time and space' is how he begins his essay on the Kennedy assassination, later saying 'Establish your right to the mystery; document it; protect it.'[7] In his statement of admiration for some of the great modernist works – *Ulysses, The Death of Virgil, The Sound and the Fury, Under the Volcano* – he says: 'These books open out onto some larger mystery. I don't know what to call it. Maybe Broch would call it "the world beyond speech."'[8] His fiction is eager to sense out moments in which existence begins to turn mysterious. Pynchon also does this of course – economically, but to quite dazzling effect in *The Crying of Lot 49*, for example. No one can better catch that slowly rising sense of the 'je ne sais quoi de la sinistre' which can creep into a seemingly ordinary scene. DeLillo seems keener on an almost overtly religious dimension. For instance, in *White Noise*, Gladney hears his young daughter murmuring in her sleep – 'words that seemed to have a ritual meaning, part of a verbal spell or ecstatic chant'.

Toyota Celica.
A long moment passed before I realized this was the name of an automobile. The truth only amazed me more. The utterance was beautiful and mysterious, gold-shot with looming wonder. It was like the name of an ancient power in the sky, tablet-carved in cuneiform. It made me feel that something hovered. But how could this be? A simple brand name, an ordinary car. How could these near-nonsense words, murmured in a child's sleep, make me sense a meaning, a presence? She was only repeating some TV voice . . . Whatever its source, the utterance struck me with the impact of a moment of splendid transcendence.

That's another word favoured by DeLillo: 'he liked the voices, loud, crude, funny, often powerfully opinionated, all speechmakers these men, actors, declaimers, masters of insult, reaching for some moment of transcendence'. In some ways, DeLillo is, indeed, some kind of latter-day American urban Transcendentalist. The closing pages of *White Noise* touch on matters of religion, or religious-type feelings, in three ways. First, Gladney says to a nun in hospital: 'Here you still wear the old uniform. The habit, the veil, the clunky shoes. You must believe in tradition. The old heaven and hell, the Latin mass. The Pope is infallible, God created the world in six days. The great old beliefs.' The nun gives him a dusty answer, and explains:

'It is our task in the world to believe things no one else takes seriously. To abandon such beliefs completely, the human race would die. That is why we are here. A tiny minority. To embody old things, old beliefs. The devil, the angels, heaven, hell. If we did not pretend to believe these things, the world would collapse.'
'Pretend?'
'Of course pretend. Do you think we are stupid? Get out from here.'

She adds that 'Hell is when no one believes. There must always be believers.' It is an interesting position; and one rather wonders where DeLillo himself stands on this. Shortly after, in the last chapter, there is what may or may not be a miracle when Gladney's young son rides his tricycle mindlessly across a busy highway, and survives unhurt. After this the Gladneys start going to the overpass, joining other people watching the sunsets in seemingly patient expectation.

This waiting is introverted, uneven, almost backward and shy, tending toward silence. What else do we feel? Certainly there is awe, it is all awe, it transcends previous categories of awe, but we don't know whether we are watching in wonder or dread, we don't know what we are watching or what it means, we don't know whether it is permanent, a level of experience to which we will gradually adjust, into which our uncertainty will eventually be absorbed, or just some atmospheric weirdness.

Immediately after this, the novel concludes in a supermarket, where there is 'agitation and panic in the aisles' because all the items have been rearranged. 'There is a sense of wandering now, an aimless and haunted mood, sweet-tempered people taken to the edge.' There is of course an element of comic exaggeration in all this; but I wonder how comic the very last lines of the book are, as the shoppers approach the cash point.

A slowly moving line, satisfying, giving us time to glance at the tabloids in the racks. Everything we need that is not food or love is here in the tabloid racks. The tales of the supernatural and the extraterrestial. The miracle vitamins, the cures for obesity. The cults of the famous and the dead.

Ironic? Or perhaps not. One character, Murray Siskind, goes to the supermarket as to a church. 'This place recharges us spiritually, it prepares us, it's a gateway or pathway. Look how bright. It's full of psychic data.' It is here that he seeks to fulfil his ambition – 'I want to immerse myself in American magic and dread.' Siskind is the most eloquent spokesman for 'the American mystery'. As a lecture in popular culture he is an amusing character. He is also a sinister one, as when he persuades Gladney to attempt a murder. Yet, according to LeClair in *In the Loop*: 'It's in Siskind's realm, the supermarket, that the tabloids, which DeLillo states are "closest to the spirit of the book," are found. These tabloids, DeLillo says, "ask profoundly important questions about death, the afterlife, God, worlds and space, yet they exist in an almost Pop Art atmosphere," an atmosphere that Siskind helps decode.'[9] DeLillo writes of 'the revenge of popular culture on those who take it too seriously', and I wonder what he really thinks of the low lunacies of the tabloids. Has the 'religious sense' come to this?

In *Underworld*, the lights from night-flying B-52s give Klara 'a sense of awe, a child's sleepy feeling of mystery'. The fireball from a missile – 'like some nameless faceless whatever' – so impresses a boy that 'It made him want to be a Catholic.' Matt believes in 'the supernatural underside of the arms race. Miracles and visions.' Old post-beats are 'still alert to signs of marvels astir in the universe'. In his Jesuit school, Nick studies 'thaumatology, or the study of wonders'. No doubt drawing on his Jesuit education, Nick discusses *The Cloud of Unknowing* with an unsuspecting pick-up. 'I read this book and began to think of God as a secret, a long unlighted tunnel, on and on. This was my wretched attempt to understand our blankness in the face of God's enormity . . . I tried to approach God through his secret, his unknowability . . . We approach God through his unmadeness . . . we cherish his negation.' (In theology, I believe this approach to God is called *apophasis* – it feels a little out of place here.) The need or hunger for some kind of 'religious' experience seems ubiquitous. 'Sometimes faith needs a sign. There are times when you want to stop working at faith and just be washed in a blowing wind that tells you everything.'

But in DeLillo's world there is more than one kind of faith or belief. At the end, when Sister Edgar learns that a young vagrant girl, Esmeralda, has been brutally raped, murdered, and thrown from a roof, she 'believes she is falling into crisis, beginning to think it is possible that all creation is a spurt of blank matter that chances to make an emerald planet here, a dead star there, with random waste in between. The serenity of immense design is missing from her life, authorship and moral form . . . *It is not a question of disbelief.* There is another kind of belief, a second force, insecure, untrusting, a faith that is springfed by the things we fear in the night, and she thinks she is succumbing' (my italics). In DeLillo's world, where there is always 'some unshaped anxiety' hovering, where things are as often 'ominous' as they are 'shining', it is this other kind of belief which seems to have the stronger purchase on people. Yet the novel ends – again – with a sort of miracle which both is-and-isn't-but-might-be an epiphany. The beatified face of the dead Esmeralda appears on a billboard whenever a passing commuter train's lights fall on it. Watching crowds gasp and moan – 'the holler of unstoppered belief'. The sceptical Sister Grace explains it as 'a trick of light', but Sister Edgar feels 'an angelus of joy'. And so the key question is posed – the last of many in a long book:

And what do you remember, finally, when everyone has gone home and the streets are empty of devotion and hope, swept by river wind? Is the memory thin and bitter and does it shame you with its fundamental untruth – all nuance and silhouette? Or does the power of transcendence linger, the sense of an event that violates natural forces, something holy that throbs on the hot horizon, the vision you crave because you need a sign to stand against your doubt?

Sister Edgar dies 'peacefully', and we assume happy in her recovered faith. And the book ends there (apart from a short, visionary coda). For me, the novel deliquesces into something close to sentimental piety; and here, perhaps, is the source of my reservations about DeLillo's writing in this book. It can either be very hard – all those 'marvellous' flat-eyed looks and that smart, brittle talk; or it goes rather soft, inserting easy intimations of transcendence. In a little essay called 'The Power of History', which appeared in the *New York Times Magazine*, DeLillo wrote: 'The novel is the dream release, the suspension of reality that history needs to escape its own brutal confinements . . . At its root level, fiction is a kind of religious fanaticism, with elements of obsession, superstition and awe. Such qualities will sooner or later state their adversarial relationship with history.'[10] But, having pretty much given up on people and plots (conventional ones, anyway), DeLillo in *Underworld* is totally reliant on history from the opening events of 1951, onwards (he has 'turned to the news'). By all means be adversarial to the so-called official versions of the times – as Melville said in *Billy Budd*, such histories have a way of 'considerately' 'shading off' any discreditable events into 'the historical background'. But it seems odd to write of 'the brutal confinements of history' per se, particularly when your subject is, manifestly, Cold War America. And I cannot see it as the novelist's task to substitute 'religious fanaticism' for the cold prose of the real. There is – God knows – enough of it around already.

NOTES

1 David Remnick, 'Exile on Main Street: Don DeLillo's Undisclosed Underworld', *The New Yorker*, 15 September 1997, p. 44.

2 Ibid., p. 48.

3 Don DeLillo, 'American Blood: A Journey Through the Labyrinth of Dollars and JFK', *Rolling Stone*, 8 December 1983, p. 27.

4 Tom LeClair and Larry McCaffery (eds.), *Anything Can Happen: Interviews with Contemporary American Novelists* (Urbana: University of Illinois Press, 1983), pp. 84–5.

5 Thomas Pynchon, *The Crying of Lot 49* (London: Picador, 1979), p. 126.

6 Tom LeClair, *In the Loop: Don DeLillo and the Systems Novel* (Urbana: University of Illinois Press, 1987), pp. 63–4.

7 DeLillo, 'American Blood', pp. 21, 27.

8 Quoted in LeClair, *In the Loop*, p. 20.

9 Ibid., p. 228.

10 Don DeLillo, 'The Power of History', *New York Times Magazine*, 7 September 1997, p. 61.

CHAPTER 12

'The Rubbish-Tip for subjunctive Hopes': Thomas Pynchon's Mason & Dixon

he didn't even know there was a country all divided and fixed and neat with a people living on it all divided and fixed and neat because of what color their skins happened to be and what they happened to own . . .

> (Faulkner, *Absalom, Absalom!*)

of course Empire took its way westward, what other way was there but into those virgin sunsets to penetrate and foul?

> (Pynchon, *Gravity's Rainbow*)

'Good Christ. Dixon. What are we about?'
> (Pynchon, *Mason & Dixon*)

Here is a representative piece of American landscape in the 1960s, as seen by Pynchon:

But there was nothing about the little, low-rambling, more or less identical homes of Northumberland Estates to interest or haunt . . . no small immunities, no possibilities for hidden life or otherworldly presence: no trees, secret routes, shortcuts, culverts, thickets that could be made hollow in the middle – everything in the place was out in the open, everything could be seen at a glance; and behind it, under it, around the corners of its houses and down the safe, gentle curves of its streets, you came back and kept coming back, to nothing: nothing but the cheerless earth. ('The Secret Integration')

This is hygenic, sanitised, plastic America – depthless, dimensionless, all mystery erased or bleached and blanded out. Now here is another bit of American terrain, this time from the 1760s. This is 'the Delaware Triangle', also known as 'The Wedge'. 'To be born and rear'd in the Wedge is to occupy a singular location in an emerging moral Geometry.' I don't understand surveying, but clearly the appropriate lines haven't quite met, leaving a piece of territory which is, as it were, off the map.

the notorious Wedge, – resulting from the failure of the Tangent Point to be exactly at this corner of Maryland, but rather some five miles south, creating a semi-cusp or Thorn of that Length, and doubtful ownership, – not so much claim'd by any one Province, as priz'd for its Ambiguity, – occupied by all whose Wish, hardly uncommon in this Era of fluid Identity, is not to reside anywhere.

This is the sort of area which has been well and truly tidied up in 1960s America, with – so the implication goes – a concomitant loss of ambiguity and fluidity, uncertainty and mystery. But there is more to the Wedge:

Yet there remains to the Wedge an Unseen World, beyond Resolution, of transactions nere recorded, – upon Creeksides and beneath Hedges, in Barns, Lofts, and Spring-houses, in the long Summer Maize fields, where one may be lost within minutes of entering the vast unforgiving Thickets of Stalks, – indeed, all manner of secret paths and clearings and alcoves are defin'd, – push'd over or stamp'd into being, roofless as Ruins, but for a few fugitive weeks of lull before autumnal responsibilities come again looming . . . 'Tis no one's, for the moment. A small geographick Anomaly, a-bustle with Appetites high and low, their offerings and acceptances.

This is clearly the kind of area favoured by Pynchon, and recreated in the generous, inclusive, permissive, endlessly suprising, secret-packed topography of his own prose. But Pynchon imagines more yet as obtaining to that 'slither' of land that, as it were, somehow didn't get on to the map. Could it be, perhaps, 'a sort of Repository'?

anything may be hiding in there, more than your Herodotus, aye nor immortal Munchausen, might ever have dreamt. The Fountain of Youth, the Seven Cities of Gold, the Other Eden, the Canyons of black Obsidion, the eight Immortals, the Victory over Death, the Defeat of the Wrathful Deities? Histories ever Secret. Lands whose Surveys will never be tied into any made here . . .

This is the 'demented' voice of Captain Zhang, and Mason and Dixon duly exchange a rational, eighteenth-century, English 'Grimmace'. But Pynchon likes demented imaginings, and he certainly hopes, if he is not sure, that there are more things in heaven and earth than were dreamed of in the Age of Reason, or pinned down on its maps. What he likes, and looking back the evidence is everywhere in his work, are times and places, or mentalities and moods, in which things have not been 'reduc'd to certainty . . . all Islands possible'. And America in the 1760s was very exactly *the* place where all the old certainties – religious, political, territorial – were breaking up, and anything began to seem possible as the country was preparing to shake itself free of England, and to expand into the then seemingly infinite and boundless west. The Rev Cherrycoke, who comes across as an amiable, eighteenth-century proto-Pynchon, notes: 'I was back in America once more, finding, despite all, that I could not stay away from it, this object of hope that Miracles might yet occur, that God might yet return to Human affairs, that all the wistful Fictions necessary to the childhood of a species might yet come true, . . . a third Testament.'

In this connection, I want to look at a word which plays an important role in this book – I don't remember, and haven't had time to check, whether it figures in his earlier work, though you can see that, all along, it was a word made for Pynchon. The word is 'subjunctive', glossed in the dictionary as '(of a mood) denoting what is imagined or wished or possible'. I will run together some quotations. Concerning Mason's unhappy relationship with his father, with whom he never properly communicated, Pynchon has a long paragraph starting 'Had he gone to his father . . .', but concludes: 'All subjunctive, of course, – *had* young Mason gone to his father, this *might have been* the conversation likely to result.' The great subjunctive premiss underlying Pynchon's work is – *had* America taken a different path . . .

Mrs Edgewise is a sort of frontier Magician – 'trouping on, cheerfully rendering subjunctive, or contrary to fact, familiar laws of nature and of common sense'. In an 'Undeliver'd Sermon' Cherrycoke writes: 'Doubt is of the essence of Christ. Of the twelve Apostles, most true to him was ever Thomas . . . The final pure Christ is pure uncertainty. He is become the central subjunctive fact of a Faith, that risks everything upon one bodily Resurrection.' Chinaman does *Feng-Shui* jobs for Americans – they don't hire him out of respect for the Dragon – rather, 'when 'twas not innocently to indulge a fascination with the exotic, 'twas to permit themselves yet one more hope in the realm of the Subjunctive, one more grasp at the last radiant whispers of the last bights of Robe-hem, billowing Æther-driven at the back of an ever-departing Deity'. Mason and Dixon under threat on the Indian Warrior Path: 'With Indians all 'round them, the Warpath a-tremble with mur'drous Hopes, its emptiness feeling more and more unnatural as the hours tick on, into the End of Day, as the latent Blades of Warriors press more closely upon the Membrane that divides their Subjunctive World from our number'd and dreamless Indicative.' And when they turn back and prepare to return over the Allegheny Crest Pynchon says – 'once over the Summit, they will belong again to the East, to Chesapeake, – to Lords for whom Interests less subjunctive must ever enjoy Priority'.

But the most important use of the word occurs in a marvellous paragraph which, in effect, is a distillation of all Pynchon's work. I must quote at length:

Does Britannia, when she sleeps, dream? Is America her dream? – in which all that cannot pass in the metropolitan Wakefulness is allow'd Expression away in the restless Slumber of these Provinces, and on West-ward, wherever 'tis not yet mapp'd, nor written down, nor ever, by the majority of Mankind, seen, – serving as a very Rubbish-Tip for subjunctive Hopes, for all that *may yet be true,* – Earthly Paradise, Fountain of Youth, Realms of Prester John, Christ's Kingdom, ever behind the sunset, safe till the next Territory to the West be seen and recorded, measur'd and tied in, back into the Net-Work of Points already known, that slowly triangulates its Way into the Continent, changing all from subjunctive to declarative, reducing Possibilities to Simplicities that serve the ends of Governments, – winning away from the realm of the Sacred, its Borderlands one by one, and assuming them into the bare mortal World that is our home, and our Despair.

You will recall that Thoreau, who, by a happy, indeed significant, irony was, like Mason and Dixon, a surveyor, informs us that some people thought Waldon Pond was 'bottomless', then goes on to say:

But I can assure my readers that Walden has a reasonably tight bottom at a not unreasonable, though at an unusual, depth. I fathomed it easily with a codline and a stone weighing about a pound and a half . . . The greatest depth was exactly one hundred and two feet . . . This is a remarkable depth for so small an area; yet not an inch of it can be spared by the imagination. What if all ponds were shallow? Would it not react on the minds of men? I am thankful that this pond was made deep and pure for a symbol. While men believe in the infinite some ponds will be thought to be bottomless.[1]

Walden Pond – believed to be bottomless; actually fathomed. America – a symbol for boundlessness; historically boundaried. The new country, the United States of America, depended for its existence both as entity and concept on two things – appropriated, surveyed, legally apportioned land; and a sense of an unchartered, inexhaustibly bounteous west, a plenitude of possibilities. Measurement and dream – in Pynchon's terms, the indicative and the subjunctive. Among many other things, this novel is a celebration of America as a last realm of the Subjunctive, and an elegiac lament for the accelerating erosion of that subjunctivity. 'Rubbish-Tip for subjunctive Hopes' sounds dismissive. But so-called 'rubbish' is very important to Pynchon, as are those human beings he designates as the preterite, those regarded by the System as human junk, to be overlooked, discarded. Pynchon imagines the legends, myths,

beliefs that the Age of Reason in Europe threw out as 'rubbish', emig-
rating and finding refuge in the great, generous spaces of America –
spaces into which, however, the surveyors were already, at the very
time of the birth and inception of this new country, making lethal but
unstoppable inroads.

I'll come to surveying, but first I want to look at the context in
which that amazing paragraph appears in the book. Once they are out
surveying, a lot of Mason's and Dixon's time is spent in taverns among
frontier folk. In a way, this is the America that Pynchon delights in –
you remember William Slothrop in *Gravity's Rainbow* (author of *On
Preterition*, advocate of Judas against Christ, who represents the road
not taken – 'Could he have been the fork in the road America never
took, the singular point she jumped the wrong way from?') who headed
west in 1634 or 1635: 'He enjoyed the road, the mobility, the chance
encounters of the day – Indians, trappers, wenches, hill people', 'Everything good is on the highway', said Emerson.[2] From that point of view
Mason & Dixon is Pynchon's American Road-novel. And in those
frontier taverns, the very English Mason and Dixon encounter some,
well, rather un-English types.

Every day the room, for hours together, sways at the verge of riot. May
unchecked consumption of all these modern substances [tobacco, alcohol,
coffee] at the same time, a habit without historical precedent, upon these
shores be creating a new sort of European? less respectful of the forms that
have previously held Society together, more apt to speak his mind, or hers,
upon any topic he chooses, and to defend his position as violently as need be?

Throughout the book, we are reminded that we are on the eve of the
War of Independence; riot is in the air, and there are frequent references
to such contentious contemporary issues as the Stamp Act and Virtual
Representation. At least since Mark Twain there has been some sense
that the really *American* American emerged from the frontier conditions,
not the European-derived east – Andrew Jackson rather than John
Adams. Mark Twain rather heroised the illiterate, vernacular frontier
tough as a figure to set against genteel New England; though when he
actually went west, in *Roughing It*, he found people living a savage, barbarous life. As early as 1782, Crèvecoeur noted the degenerate state
and 'lawless profligacy' of what he called the 'back settlers' – the men
'appear to be no better than carnivorous animals of a superior rank';
they are 'the most hideous parts of our society'. 'Thus are our first steps
trodden, thus are our first trees felled, in general, by the most vicious
of our people.' In particular, he noted their abominable treatment of

the Indians – they get them drunk, they defraud them, and they massacre them. 'Hence those shocking violations, those sudden devastations which have so often stained our frontiers, when hundreds of innocent people have been sacrificed for the crimes of a few.'[3] Mason and Dixon arrive to hear news of just such massacres – at Conestoga and Lancaster. 'They saw white Brutality enough, at the Cape of Good Hope. They can no better understand it now, than then. Something is eluding them. Whites in both places are become the very Savages of their own worst Dreams, far out of Measure to any Provocation.' Out of curiosity, they go to Lancaster to see the 'Massacre Site'. In the inevitable tavern, they encounter hostility – 'you can't just come minuetting in from London and expect to understand what's going on here' – and the atmosphere turns distinctly threatening when Dixon questions their motives for the massacre. They finally get safely to bed, and there follows the paragraph I quote – 'Does Britannia, when she sleeps, dream?' Next morning, Mason creeps out early to visit the site of the massacre. 'He is not as a rule sensitive to the metaphysickal Remnants of Evil . . . yet here in the soil'd and strewn Courtyard where it happen'd, roofless to His Surveillance – and to His Judgment, prays Mason, – he feels "like a Nun before a Shrine," as he later relates it to Dixon'. Dixon himself goes after Mason.

He sees where blows with Rifle-Butts miss'd their Marks, and chipp'd the Walls. He sees blood in Corners never cleans'd. Thankful he is no longer a Child, else might he curse and weep, scattering his Anger to no Effect, Dixon now must be his own stern Uncle, and smack himself upon the Pate at any sign of unfocusing. What in the Holy Names are these people about? Not even the Dutchman at the Cape behav'd this way. Is it something in this Wilderness, something ancient, that waited for them, and infected their Souls when they came?

I note that the idea of an evil being already waiting there in the land, before men came, is very William Burroughs, and I don't think it lies near the heart of Pynchon's vision of things. But the bewildering inexplicability of what we might call immeasurable, unfathomable human vileness certainly is, and there must be some point in his placing his paeon to, lament for, American subjunctivity squarely in the middle of this chapter recording the worst atrocity in the book. I suppose if you see America as the Land of Possibilities, then that must include the possibility of the engendering of a whole new kind and dimension of Evil. Or put it this way. If America is what Britannia dreams, those dreams must include nightmares.

Let me turn to surveying, and Pynchon's version of how Mason and Dixon drew their Line, and what that Line signified and portended. In Fenimore Cooper's *The Deerslayer*, when Deerslayer (later Natty Bummpo of course) first sees Lake Glimmerglass he is arrested in wonder, and asks: 'Have the governor's or the King's people given this lake a name? . . . If they've not begun to blaze their trees, and set up their compasses, and line off their maps, it's likely that they've not bethought them to disturb natur' with a name.'[4] Setting up their compasses and lining off their maps is just exactly what Mason and Dixon were doing. As Cherrycoke puts it: ''Twas not too many years before the War, – what we were doing out in that Country together was brave, scientifick beyond my understanding, and ultimately meaningless, – we were putting a line straight through the heart of the Wilderness, eight yards wide and due west, in order to separate two Proprietorships, granted when the World was yet feudal and but eight years later to be nullified by the War for Independence.' His is, necessarily, a restricted, contemporary perspective. That, indeed, was literally what they were doing, but the Line continued to accumulate meaning until the Civil War, never to be nullified. And Pynchon takes it all the way back. To Mr Edgewise, he gives a possible speech. ' "It goes back," he might have begun [more subjunctive], "to the second Day of Creation, when 'G-d made the Firmament, and divided the Waters which were under the Firmament, from the Waters which were above the Firmament', – thus the first Boundary Line. All else after that, in all History, is but Sub-Division"', which, to me, sounds like Genesis continued by Pynchon. Zhang later offers what we might call an elaboration: 'Nothing will produce Bad History more directly nor brutally, than drawing a Line, in particular a Right Line, the very Shape of Contempt, through the midst of a People – to create thus a Distinction betwixt 'em, – 'tis the first stroke. – All else will follow as if predestin'd, unto War and Devastation.' Given hindsight, this is perhaps an easy prophecy to implant at this point. As a Virginian says to Mason and Dixon – 'the West Line must contribute North and South Boundaries'. So America becomes divided into Slave States and Free States, though as is made clear, there are plenty of modes of enslavement north of the line, never mind back in England, with, for example, the wretched condition and brutal putting down of the Weavers, as recalled by Dixon. 'North and South' is just one more example of the pernicious binary habit of thought which Pynchon sees as having been so disastrous for America. He traces it back to the Puritan division – or line of demarcation –

between the Elect and the Preterite, the Saved and the Damned, Us and Them. It afflicts Oedipa Mass in *The Crying of Lot 49* in her final meditation as she wanders, distraught, along the rail tracks – 'waiting for a symmetry of choices to break down . . . and how had it ever happened here, with the chances once so good for diversity? For now it was like walking among matrices of a great digital computer, the zeroes and ones twinned above, hanging like balanced mobiles right and left, ahead, thick, maybe endless. Behind the hieroglyphic streets there would be either a transcendent meaning, or only the earth . . . Ones and zeroes.' Either one great explanation of every-thing, or no meaning at all – Revelation, or nihilism. That is the danger of a line. Dixon, working as a surveyor in England on Enclos-ures (which caused so much brutal disruption and misery) recalls – 'He had drawn Lines of Ink that became Fences of Stone.' Surveying, like Cartography, is a far from innocent activity. Lines become walls; differences become oppositions. Shelby, another surveyor, realises the 'Power' of the surveyor, particularly in America at this time – 'pure Space waits the Surveyor – no previous Lines, no fences, no streets to constrain polygony however extravagant'. And there is something par-ticularly brutal and insensitive about drawing, or carving, a dead *straight* line across an immensely variegated terrain. Mason says that what they are drawing is simply 'a Boundary, nothing more', which drives the Chinaman Zhang to exasperated fury. 'Boundary! . . . Ev'rywhere else on earth, Boundaries follow Nature – coast-lines, ridge-tops, river-banks, – so honoring the Dragon of *Shan* within, from which Land-Scape ever takes its form. To mark a right Line upon the Earth is to inflict upon the Dragon's very Flesh, a sword-slash, a long, perfect scar, impossible for any who live out here the year 'round to see as other than hateful Assault. How can it pass unanswer'd?' He goes on: 'Tho' Degrees of Longitude and Latitude in Name, yet in Earthly reality are they Channels mark'd for the transport of some unseen Influence . . . Who'd benefit most? None, it would seem, but the con-sciously criminal in Publick Life as in Private, who know how to tap into the unremitting torrent of *Sha* roaring all night and day, and convert it to their own uses.' *Sha* is bad energy, and we might feel that some counter-culture dottiness is here being allowed play. But there is a revealing exchange between the two Englishmen, with reference to the Indians' hostility to their work (which, of course, in actual fact halted it). Dixon, his Pynchonite empathy with the under-dog ever at the ready, sympathises with the Indians.

'They want to know how to stop this great invisible Thing that comes Straight on over their Lands, devouring all in its Path.'

'Well! of course it's a living creature, 'tis all of us, temporarily collected into an Entity, whose Labors none could do alone.'

'A tree-slaughtering Animal, with no purpose but to continue creating forever a perfect Corridor over the Land. Its teeth of Steel, – its Jaws, Axmen, – its Life's Blood, Disbursement. And what of its intentions, beyond killing everything due west of it? do you know? I don't either.'

'Then – just tidying up these thoughts a bit, – you're saying this Line has a Will to proceed Westward, – '

'What else are these people suppos'd to believe? Haven't we been saying, with an hundred Blades all day long, – This is how far into your land we may strike, this is what we claim to westward. As you see what we may do to Trees, and how little we care, – imagine how little we care for Indians, and what we are prepar'd to do to you. That Influence you have felt, along our Line, that Current strong as a River's, – we command it. . . . We might make thro' your Nations an Avenue of Ruin, terrible as the Path of a Whirl-Wind.'

'But those are Threats we do not make.'

'But might as well make. As the Indians wish, we must go no further.'

'No. We must go on.'

Finally, though, both Mason and Dixon 'understand that the Line is exactly what Cpt. Zhang and a number of others have been styling it all along – a conduit for Evil'.

The whole book serves as a meditation on all kinds of lines and boundaries – boundaries of innocence, of marriage; boundaries between 'the Settl'd and the Unpossess'd'; the boundaries between reality and representation; boundaries of style – 'to cross Schuylkill were to transgress some Rubicon of style, to fall from Quaker simplicity into the Perplexity . . . of the World after Eden' – this, concerning hats!; not to mention the barriers between people – 'I believe now . . . that Mason and Dixon could not cross the perilous Boundaries between themselves', says Cherrycoke, and though some mute affection clearly passes between them, it is evident that all too often boundaries become barriers. Everywhere, and increasingly, there is manifest 'the Power of the Line'. Mason and Dixon finally reach a point 224 miles west of the Delaware River, where their work was indeed stopped by the Indians. As they turn back to return east, Dixon makes a last gesture to the west – ' "Yet all those, – " ', and 'Mason nods back, impatiently. "They will have to live their lives without any Line amongst 'em, unseparated, daily doing Business together, World's Business and Heart's alike, repriev'd from the Tyranny of residing either North or South of it. Nothing worse than that, whatwhat?" ' It is impossible to estimate how

much irony there is in his words; but needless to say, he is outlining
a condition of life which for Pynchon is devoutly to be desired. But
of course, the Line lived on long after the departure and demise of
Mason and Dixon – until, effectively, it was everywhere.

Towards the end of *The Great Gatsby*, Nick Carraway says 'I see
now that this has been a story of the West, after all.' Perhaps all
American literature is a 'story of the West' in one way or another –
certainly *Mason & Dixon* is. 'Yet, supposing Progress Westward were a
Journey, returning unto Innocence, – approaching, as a Limit, the
innocence of the Animals', speculates Mason – as he holds up a bath
containing a giant eel, and I'll come to that aspect of the book later.
But their journey west turns out to be a rather more complicated
experience than a return to innocence. 'To stand at the Post Mark'd
West, and turn to face West, can be a trial for those sentimentally
inclin'd, as well as for ev'ryone nearby. It is possible to feel the combin'd
force, in perfect Enfilade, of ev'ry future second unelaps'd, ev'ry Chain
yet to be stretch'd, every unknown Event to be undergone, – the
unmodified Terror of keeping one's Latitude.' Throughout the book,
while there is recurrent 'rapture' at the incredible beauty and abundance of this as-yet unsurveyed America, there is – this is very Pynchon
– often a growing feeling of incipient terror, a scalp-prickling sense of
something waiting or gathering at what he calls 'the fringes of readability'. This phrase occurs very late, describing Mason – 'desperate to
pretend all was well, face kept as clear as the bottom of a stream in
August, nothing visible at the fringes of readability – who knew him,
truly? What might wait, at the margins of the pool, mottled, still, river-
silt slowly gathering upon its dorsal side?' Anyway, as they are warned,
'across [the Susquehanna] things are not so civiliz'd', and so, of course,
it turns out – 'West being for Americans what North is for Geordies,
an increasing Likelihood of local Power lying in the Hands of Eccentrics, more independence'. Pynchon likes independent eccentrics, and
there are plenty of them in this book. But also Mason begins to sense
'the illimitable possibilities of Evil in this Forest'. Mason again:
'observe you not, as we move West, more and more of those Forces,
which Cities upon Coasts have learn'd to push away, and leave to
Back Inhabitants . . . We trespass, each day ever more deeply, into a
world of less restraint in ev'rything, – no law, no convergence upon
any idea of how life is to be, – an Interior that grows meanwhile ever
more forested, more savage and perilous, until . . . we must reach at
last an Anti-City, – some concentration of Fate, – some final condition

of Abandonment, – wherein all are unredeemably alone and at Hazard as deep as their souls may bear.' We know that 'Mason is Gothickally depressive as Dixon is Westeringly manic', but something in Pynchon surely speaks through each of them. And 'Jointly . . . they have continu'd to find regions of Panick fear all along the Line', and they have a sense that *something* indefinable and unsurveyable is there in the land they are penetrating – 'This is none of the lesser Agents, the White Women or Black Dogs, but the Presence itself, unbounded, whose Visitations increase in number as the Party, for the last time, moves West.' Dixon, with his different disposition, succumbs to what a song calls '*Rap-ture de West*'. And such can be the spell, 'who might not come to believe in an Eternal West? In a Momentum that bears all away? "Men are remov'd by it, and women, from where they were, – as if surrender'd to a great current of Westering."' But as they move deeper into 'the savage Vacancy ever before them', there is more terror than rapture – 'Apprehension rising, Axmen deserting, the ghosts of '55 growing, hourly, more sensible and sovereign, – as unaveng'd Fires foul the Dusk, unanswer'd mortal Cries travel the Forests at the speed of Wind. Ah Christ, – besides West, where else are they heading, those few with the Clarity to remain?'

Of course, in addition to the west, there is the south, and a fierce sense of the iniquities of slavery runs right through – in the Cape, whatever else is going on, 'behind all gazes the great Worm of Slavery', and that applies to the whole book. As Dixon realises near the end of their American work, 'Ev'rywhere they've sent us, – the Cape, St Helena, America, – what's the Element common to all? . . . Slaves. Ev'ry day at the Cape, we lived with Slavery in our faces, – more of it at St Helena, – and now here we are again, in another Colony, this time having drawn them a Line between their Slave–Keepers, and their Wage–Payers, as if doom'd to re-encounter thro' the World this public Secret, this shameful Core . . . Christ Mason . . . Where does it end? No matter where in it we go, shall we find all the World Tyrants and Slaves? America was the one place we should *not* have found them.' No one doubts that Pynchon's heart, like Dixon's, is in absolutely the right place, and his outrage is impeccable. But I've been doing him something of a disservice, perhaps, by making it sound as if the book is a sort of politically correct disguised tract concerning the treatment of Indians and Blacks by white settlers. This makes it sound rather homiletic and pofaced which is exactly what it is not. Consider this account by Cherrycoke: 'their tangle of geometrick hopes, – that somehow the

Arc, the Tangent, the Meridian, and the West Line should all come together at the same Point, – where, in fact, all is Failure'; and Pynchon adds, 'Indeed, a spirit of whimsy pervades the entire history of these Delaware Boundaries, as if in playful refusal to admit that America, in any way, may be serious.' In the present of the book, 1786, Cherrycoke discusses the writing of history with various members of the family he is staying with. He – I think – is defending the idea that an historian should both 'seek the Truth and not tell'. He elaborates. 'Just so. Who claims Truth, Truth abandons. History is hir'd, or coerc'd, only in Interests that must ever prove base. She is too innocent, to be left within the reach of anyone in Power, – who need but touch her, and all her Credit is in the instant vanish'd, as if it had never been. She needs rather to be tended lovingly and honorably by fabulists and counterfeiters, Ballad-Mongers and Cranks of ev'ry Radius, Masters of Disguise to provide her the Costume, Toilette, and Bearing, and Speech nimble enough to keep her beyond the Desires, or even the Curiosity, of Government.' Someone else speaks up for Facts, and 'a single Version, proceeding from a single Authority', while another mockingly says 'Then, let us have only Jolly Theatrickals about the Past, and be done with it.' Pynchon does not care for single authorised official versions; so that, although his novel is seeded with 'facts' from the period – we meet Franklin and Washington, not to mention Dr Johnson and Boswell; we have Whitefield and the Great Awakening, the growing discontents and riots aginst the Stamp Act and Virtual Representation, various discoveries of the time, including the Sandwich, and doubtless much more – the 'history' is presented in cartoonstrip form, and there are lots of 'jolly theatricals'. Mason and Dixon, memorable and endearing as they are, are not 'characters' in any Jamesian sense; rather, they are drawn like favourite figures in an ongoing comic-strip – rather like, say, Desperate Dan, or Lord Snooty (speaking personally). Just so, all the fantastic characters, events, and phenomena – talking dogs, flying boys and coaches, Jenkin's pickled ear which *listens* and demands to be spoken to, the Asian pygmies inhabiting forever the eleven days lost when the calendar was changed, the weird goings-on in Castle Lipton, the magic eel in the bath-tub, the giant beetroot, the truly bizarre pornographic story from the magazine *The Ghastly Fop*, the St George-and-the-Dragonish medieval story of the fight with the great Lambton Worm, the mad Jesuit and the Jesuits' incredible secret communications system (cf. the Tristero in *The Crying of Lot 49*), the demented Chinaman, a host of figures with cartoon names like Captain Volcano – all these, and much, much more, are readily acceptable, and very amusing and enjoyable, if we submit, for the moment, to a cartoon version of history. At the same time, very serious and momentous events are in fact being looked at and engaged with, but through a ludic and distinctly unofficial medium – 'indeed', if I might quote Pynchon on Mason and Dixon's labours and apply it to his own work, 'a spirit of whimsy pervades the entire history of these . . . Boundaries, as if in playful refusal to admit that America, in any way, may be serious.' This enables Pynchon to give his weirdly funny imagination full rein, and at the same time to handle his material with a very light, indulgent touch; and it goes some way to accounting for the immense good-nature of the book. What Pynchon realises, beyond any other contemporary writer, is that the best way to be deadly serious is to be whimsically unserious. The serious unseriousness of Pynchon's writing is a very wonderful thing.

I have omitted from the above short list of the marvels in the book the mechanical duck, with its magical, very unduckish gifts. This looks like the most fantastic of fictions; yet – as you might expect in Pynchon – it is rooted in eighteenth-century fact, since '*le canard de Vaucanson*' actually existed. Vaucanson was a doctor and later a factory owner, as well as an engineer. He applied his talents to textile machinery and set up factories at Aubenas and Romans, but these were not successful. But he was very successful with his mechanised animals, the most famous and outstanding of which was his duck (attracting admiring praise from no less a person than Voltaire). It even included a schematic digestive system. The irony of Vaucanson's career – an irony certainly not lost on Pynchon – was that, drawing on his mechanical and technological skills, he invented a loom for brocaded material and tried to introduce automation into a small number of factories. Had he succeeded, the Industrial Revolution would have been under way that much sooner. His mechanical duck, therefore, may be taken as a weird adumbration or harbinger of those technological inventions and innovations which were so dramatically to change the world – above all, America.

Some of the most amusing passages in the book centre on this magic duck, but even here, one can see how, imaginatively, Pynchon has one eye on history. The mechanical duck, you will remember, has been so cleverly made that it can eat and excrete. 'A mechanical Duck that shits? To whom can it matter' says a certain Mr Whitpot, and you might feel he has a point. But Armand, the French chef to whom the duck has become attached, bristles at this unappreciative irreverence.

'Some . . . might point rather to a Commitment of Ingenuity unprecedented, toward making All authentic, – perhaps, it could be argued by minds more scientifick, 'twas this very Attention to Detail, whose Fineness, passing some Critickal Value, enabl'd in the Duck that strange Metamorphosis, which has sent it out of the Gates of the Inanimate, and off upon its present Journey into the given World.' . . .

Vaucanson's vainglorious Intent had been to repeat for Sex and Reproduction, the Miracles he'd already achiev'd for Digestion and Excretion. 'Who knows? that final superaddition of erotick Machinery may have somehow nudg'd the Duck across some Threshold of self-Intricacy, setting off this Explosion of Change, from Inertia toward *Independence, and Power*.'

As the duck, so America in the 1760s, where various events had indeed set off an 'explosion of change' and the people were moving 'from Inertia toward *Independence*' – a 'strange Metamorphosis' indeed. You may recall that in the assembled history of the Tristero in *The Crying of Lot 49*, the important moments in that history were all periods marked by 'explosion of change' – England and New England in the 1630s and 1640s, the disintegration of the Holy Roman Empire, the French Revolution and the end of the Ancien Regime, the European revolutions of 1848, the open American west in the 1840s and 1850s, culminating in the Gold Rush of 1849. These were times when the 'chances of diversity' were at their greatest. To these we can add the German Zone in 1945, in *Gravity's Rainbow*.

Decentralizing, back toward anarchism, needs extraordinary times . . . this war – this incredible War – just for a moment has wiped out the proliferation of little states that's prevailed in Germany. Wiped it clean. *Opened it*.

and

maybe for a little while all the fences are down, one road as good as another, the whole space of the Zone cleared, depolarized, and somewhere inside the waste of it a single set of coordinates from which to proceed, without elect, without preterite, without even nationality to fuck it up . . .

The America of the 1760s was another anarchic moment, simmering with the accumulating passions and aspirations, forces and drives which will come to a head with the Declaration of Independence, and explode into a war from which will evolve an entirely new, and new kind of, country – the USA. A metamorphosis indeed – you might say that, as in the case of the duck, a category boundary has been crossed. Pynchon is at his happiest in these anarchic periods and territories, and the tavern life along the moving frontier offers him endless opportunities to let his imagination go. But there is an underlying irony.

This is the moment when the fences were going *up*, and the straight road to the west gradually obliterating the 'chances of diversity' has begun. That was Mason's and Dixon's job.

I have emphasised the word 'metamorphosis' in connection with the emergence of the USA, and indeed it is a crucial word which runs right through American literature. Above all, it is central in Emerson's writing. 'Men have really got a new sense, and found within their world, another world, or nest of worlds; for, the metamorphosis once seen, we divine that it does not stop.' Of course, for Emerson, the end of nature is '*ascension*, or, the passage of the soul into higher forms' – he does not even consider the Kafka man-into-cockroach possibility. And the poet 'stands one step nearer to things, and sees the flowing or metamorphosis' ('The Poet').[5] There is, of course, a figure named William Emerson in Pynchon's novel, a sort of wizard or thaumaturge in eighteenth-century Durham who, among other things, teaches boys to fly along the Ley-Lines. It is this Emerson who gives Dixon the unstoppable watch which shows distinctly ascensual metamorphosing tendencies. In Dixon's dreams, it talks to him. ' "When you accept me into your life," whispering as it assumes a Shape that slowly grows indisputably Vegetable . . . yes, a sinister Vegetable he cannot name . . . " – you will accept me . . . into your Stomach." ' Dixon takes the vegetable-looking watch to the camp naturalist for confirmation of his impression.

'Vegetables don't tick,' the Professor gently reminds Dixon.
'Why aye, those that be *only Vegetables* don't. We speak now of a *higher form of life*, – a Vegetable with a Pulse-beat!'

This watch belongs with the mechanical duck (and America) – both are escaping category constraints and moving upwards. William Emerson is, among other things, an early English version of Ralph Waldo, and I have no doubt that Pynchon is having his usual allusive fun here. But the similarities are also serious – whimsically serious if you like – and in a way are central to the book. In one of his lessons or lectures William Emerson says: 'mystickal Stuff, Coal . . . Pretending it solid, when like light and Heat, it indeed flows.' Compare Ralph Waldo, on Nature: 'the mind loves its old home: as water to our thirst, so is the rock, the ground, to our eyes, and hands, and feet. It is firm water: it is cold flame: what health, what affinity!' ('Nature' Second Series).[6] Emerson puts an optimistic slant on this, absent from the darker-minded

William. But 'firm water' is exactly a solid flowing, and both apparent oxymorons indicate a sense that nature seems to contain stable identities, and yet is constantly changing. Once seen, the metamorphosis never stops. Pynchon pushes the similarity. Of William Emerson – 'Flow is his passion . . . The first book he publish'd was upon Fluxions.' Compare Ralph Waldo: 'all symbols are fluxional; all language is vehicular and transitive, and is good, as ferries and horses are, for conveyance, not as farms and houses are, for homestead' ('The Poet').[7] I'll come back to ferries. All of Emerson's negative terms are to do with 'fixity', the 'stationary', arrest: all evil, he says, has to do with 'limit' ('the only sin is limitation' – 'Circles').[8] Throughout his essays, the image of the 'wall' serves to indicate the least-desired thing or state. 'Suffice it for the joy of the universe, that we have not arrived at a wall, but at interminable oceans' ('Experience').[9] Whatever makes for fluidity is seen as a positive force – 'Flow is his passion' too. He even makes 'flux' into an active transitive verb. 'Every solid in the universe is ready to become fluid on the approach of the mind . . . If the wall remain adamant, it accuses the want of thought. To a subtler force, it will stream into new forms' ('Fate').[10] Life, for Emerson was indeed 'a flux of moods', and for him it was a sign of health to go with the 'flux' and, indeed, keep on and on 'fluxing'. Which, by the end of their time in America, is what Mason and Dixon feel they are doing. Here are the last two sentences of the American section of the book. 'Betwixt themselves, neither feels British enough anymore, nor quite American, for either Side of the Ocean. They are content to reside like Ferrymen or Bridge-keepers, ever in a Ubiquity of Flow, before a ceaseless Spectacle of Transition.' There are the ferries again; and here is Ralph Waldo: 'Power ceases in the instant of repose; it resides in the moment of transition from a past to a new state, in the shooting of the gulf, in the darting to an aim' ('Self-Reliance').[11] 'Nothing is secure but life, transition, the energizing spirit' ('Circles').[12] Mason and Dixon are at their work exactly when America was 'in the moment of transition from a past to a new state', and living 'ever in a Ubiquity of Flow, before a ceaseless Spectacle of Transition'; they are, willy-nilly, quintessential Emersonians – as, indeed, I think is Pynchon (remember the wise old man who reads out Emerson's essays in the woods, in *Vineland*), but he is an Emersonian with shadows. He has a dark, Mason side, which the more resolutely Dixonite Emerson mainly lacks, or suppresses. Here is a tavern scene:

As torch- or taper-light takes over from the light of the sunset, what are those Faces, gath'rd before some Window, raising Toasts, preparing for the Evening ahead, if not assur'd of life forever? as travelers come in by ones and twos, to smells of Tobacco and Chops, as Fiddle Players tune their strings and starv'd horses eat from the trough in the Courtyard, as young women flee to and fro dumb with fatigue, and small boys down in strata of their own go swarming upon ceaseless errands, skidding upon the Straw, as smoke begins to fill the smoking-room . . . how may Death come here?

But, in Pynchon, in all the bustling, seething life, Death, or forms and reminders of it, is everywhere – 'Death or its ev'ry day Coercions – Wages too low to live upon, Laws written by Owners, Infantry, Bailiffs, Prison, Death's thousand Metaphors in the World.' This is *à propos* of Mason's eighteenth-century England. By *Gravity's Rainbow* Pynchon will see America as having created a 'culture of death'. When William Emerson shows them his 'Dark-Age Maps' and explains the traces of long-gone Roman Britain, he concludes, 'The moral lesson in this being, – Don't Die.' But, of course, they do.

NOTES

1 Henry David Thoreau, *Walden* (New York: Library of America, 1985), p. 551.
2 Ralph Waldo Emerson, *Essays and Lectures* (New York: Library of America, 1983), p. 481.
3 J. Hector St John de Crèvecoeur, *Letters from an American Farmer* (New York: Penguin Books, 1986), pp. 72, 79.
4 James Fenimore Cooper, *The Deerslayer* (New York: Penguin Books, 1987), pp. 44–5.
5 Emerson, *Essays and Lecture*, pp. 461, 458, 456.
6 Ibid., p. 542.
7 Ibid., p. 463.
8 Ibid., p. 406.
9 Ibid., p. 486.
10 Ibid., p. 964.
11 Ibid., p. 271.
12 Ibid., p. 413.

Index

239